Marshalling
BEATS of YOUR Heart

Marshalling Beats of Your Heart

BEATS of YOUR

HOW TO LEAD FROM YOUR HEART

and

REDISCOVER THE RHYTHM OF JOY AND MEANING

AMANDA JOYCE

FOREWORD BY HAL ELROD

Marshalling Beats of Your Heart © Copyright 2022 Amanda Joyce

For more information, email aj@wildlyhealthy.com.

ISBN:

979-8-88759-141-4 - paperback
979-8-88759-142-1 - ebook
979-8-88759-773-7 - hardcover
979-8-88759-774-4 - audiobook

Joy Journal and Music:

Throughout this book, you will find heart jolts to complete to help you live your life with a fuller heart. Complete those in the accompanying free joy journal created especially for these jolts or straight from the text while reading this book today. AJ is a health and life coach, so you can discover more of what she has to offer on her website **amandajoyce.com** for further heart-centered learning. You can also hear more of Marshall's music and heart on You-Tube, Spotify, Itunes, and on his website, **marshalljmusic.com**.

GET YOUR FREE GIFT!

To get the best experience with this book, readers can download or have the joy journal emailed to them and use the free PDF pages.

You can get a copy by visiting:

amandajoyce.com/joyjournal

For Kezman, Jubilee & Jonathan

May you lead lives you love with your hearts

I feel grateful to share this timeless story with you, but Marshall wrote many of his experiences down. This book would not exist without the help of many people who aren't even mentioned along the way. Special Thanks to Leslie Stitt who I wouldn't have known without the amazing Elizabeth Stitt, Megan Febuary and For Women Who Roar, Barbara Hartzler, John McKay, Teri Durfee, Luke Palmer, Jill Hyde Wright Family, Cyndi Simmons, Lucile & Keith Jensen, Landon Gallant, Alejandro Martin, The Edwards for allowing me to share how their hearts intertwined with ours, Abby Jean Jensen and Jason Fingers Brown for their artistic skills, the amazing Colleluori family (who I call the good mafia of the east) and the Headstrong Foundation, Hal Elrod and the Miracle Morning community, Elizabeth Weiler, Brett Hilker, my loving and supportive parents Dave and Margaret and siblings, for my Grandma Joyce (who is pictured in this book) who I take after in many ways, and the many other friends and families who supported me as I busted my heart open to create this book for you.

And for you dear reader, for wanting to strengthen your heartbeats.

TABLE OF CONTENTS:

BEFORE THERE WERE WORDS   1

PART ALPHA: BEAT, BEAT, BEAT   5
THE BASIC UNIT OF TIME, THE PULSE,
REGULARLY REPEATING EVENT

FOREWORD HAL ELROD   9

INTRODUCTION   11

BEAT 1   13
BEATS OF ATTITUDE

BEAT 2   45
BEATS OF GRATITUDE

PART MU: RIFF, RIFF, RIFF   87
A REPEATED CHORD PROGRESSION, PATTERN, OR MELODY.
THE BASE OF THE MUSICAL COMPOSITION;
A SHORT REPEATED PHRASE IN POPULAR MUSIC
AND JAZZ. A MELODIC PHRASE,
OFTEN CONSTANTLY REPEATED

BEAT 3   89
BEATS OF SONG

BEAT 4   121
BEATS OF LAUGHTER

BEAT 5   147
BEATS OF GOLD

PART OMEGA: FRET, FRET, FRET   169
WORRY, AGONIZE, GRIEVE ON GUITAR- PRESS DOWN

BEAT 6   171
BEATS OF NUMBERS

BEAT 7   199
BEATS OF SOUL

CODA   239
A CONCLUDING EVENT, REMARK, OR SECTION.
THE CONCLUDING PASSAGE OF A PIECE OR MOVEMENT
IN MUSIC, TYPICALLY FORMING AN ADDITION TO THE
BASIC STRUCTURE

CODING   241
REMIND MYSELF TO BREATHE

ACKNOWLEDGMENT   287

COACHING REVIEWS   289

AUTHOR BIO   291

AUTHOR'S NOTE   292

NOTES   293

NEXT STEPS   298 α

Before There Were Words

Pulsing drums

Raise thunder from the ground

Calling the stars down

Sparkling vast expanse

Moonlight spider web

Fire is the center

Light reveals

Shining smiles

Men bounce and shout

Thundering rhythm

Pause

Stamp Stomp Stamp

Women whirl and shake

Loose jewelry clatters

Wild gyrations

Exaggerating their breasts

I turn to my interpreter, "What is this song about?"

The heavy heart, he replies. The next is about the harvest.

I inquire again, "What do the words say?"

There are no words, he replies.

We've been singing since before there were words.

BEAT, BEAT, BEAT:

THE BASIC UNIT OF TIME,

THE PULSE,

REGULARLY REPEATING EVENT

There's a time for space

And a space for time

I'm stuck somewhere

In the middle

And I can't make up my mind

I try to want

And I want to try

But I'm stuck somewhere

In the middle

And I just keep wondering why

So I push away from everything

I thought I could see

Because it's all just numbers

Who's counting anyway

I can't help but feel I'm wasting my time

Thinking of ways to spend it in my life

What I have bought when the day is through

What's the point in this pointless point of view

All we are doing is splitting up the pieces

There is a reason for the law of time

The Beat of my drum like the sweat of my skin

Reflecting the stars of the universe

The universe is written upon a camel skin

I use for my drum

It resonates through the sky

And pushes the sound

Manna from heaven

In the form of hum

That shakes human kind

The universe repeats itself

In an atomic way

An infinite solution to a question never asked

I'm getting tired of the mindless speculation

The destiny of man is far too sacred for a guess

(by Marshall Jensen)

FOREWORD FROM HAL ELROD
AUTHOR OF MIRACLE MORNING

This book will help you transcend the limitations of the mind and tap into the wisdom of your heart.

In Marshalling Beats of Your Heart, you'll explore sources of love to commit to, why leading with your heart is a must, and why other people deserve a better version of you.

If we don't enjoy life now, we will likely look back one day and realize we worried about things that were out of our control, instead of enjoying each moment.

Every moment can be your best moment simply because you are alive. Even when you're depressed, the quality of the moment is based on your perspective, not what's happening to you.

The ultimate freedom is to be at peace with life exactly as it is. Affirm that by saying: I already have everything I need to be the happiest I could ever be. It's called "life." Find the place inside you that allows you to lead from a place of love.

And from that place of total peace and "unconditional" happiness, you can create whatever you choose. Whatever will bring you added joy. But not because you need it. Not because your happiness is dependent on it.

You are liberated when you realize that nothing outside of you can make you happier than you can choose to be. You can choose joy or suffering, especially in the midst of diversity when you allow your heart to drive your life instead of your head. You can't control life, but don't allow life to control you. Choose for the inside of your heart to be one of peace, love, and joy. You realize this when you consciously choose to find that place inside of you that is an infinite source of love.

And from that place, you are free to enjoy every moment of your life—exactly as it is.

You can consciously choose how you feel and how you show up. You can consciously choose to have a life with stronger beats of your heart and this book can teach you how to make each beat more powerful through routine and being present.

No matter how difficult your life has been, it is now or may be in the future, this book shows you how you can enjoy this one life you've been given.

Marshalling Beats
of Your Heart

This is a memoir teaching you to live each heartbeat to the fullest. It inspires you to enjoy life more by providing insights into a fuller life by understanding the beats of your heart and how to be open in love instead of closed to fear in Marshall's story. This book will help you:

- Lead the heartbeats of your life in a golden direction and learn to get the greatest worth out of your life. Learn to appreciate every moment, good or bad. If you are having a hard time finding joy in hard times or struggling to find the meaning behind your daily grind, use this book to simplify the meaning enough that it fits in your heart or the palm of your hand when holding this book. You need this book now because it's been hell for years and you want it to end. You want to learn to squeeze the joy out of the sour lemons and limes that have been thrown at you. The canceling of life plans, the depression of the economy, etc. are getting you down. Re-discover the joys in the simple things. Change from the dog-eat-dog

mindset to the light attracts light, and goodness more goodness mindset.

- I am a certified health and life coach with the goal of pioneering wellness and the heart. This book still teaches me every day. I am a very logical person and I see in myself and others the inability to get out of our heads and live life more with hopeful hearts. If you are already living every day as if it were your last and you'd be happy with your life completing now, this book is not for you. Don't wait another day to live the life you dream of every day. It will be too late. Read now to find out how.

- This book will change your perspective to being grateful for every heartbeat, being cheerful through bad times, and being a light for yourself and others when all around you is darkness and gloom. It will teach you how to lead and guide however many minutes you have in the course of your life to make a difference for others; to give more than you take and practice more than you preach; to do more with your value system than just believe; to become a deeper human for the rest of humanity.

Beat 1

BEATS OF ATTITUDE

MARSHALING YOUR HEARTBEATS REQUIRES ATTITUDE.
YOU'RE IN CHARGE OF YOUR CHARGE, BE IT POSITIVE
OR NEGATIVE.

"Just stick the padded part on your eye, not the sticky side," Conrad says as he peels off the small strip of wax paper on one side of a maxi pad from mom's bathroom, unbeknownst to our working mother. Two hours earlier, my brother and I had been squealing with delight as I was pulled on roller skates behind an old truck. The 'accident' happened as the truck took a quick turn that sent me flying into a large stick protruding out of a tree's elongated trunk. Fortunately, the stick missed my strong-willed head, but unfortunately, it parachuted a few inches down right into my soft eyeball. I anxiously and quickly pulled it out. That's when the blood started gushing and I knew we had to be home in a hurry.

When we arrive at our house, the thickest device to catch the oozing blood Conrad can think of is the sanitary pad resting atop a bathroom toilet. Painstakingly, I am getting a premature lesson in what in the world women do with this thick napkin as it is saturating the oozing blood from my own head. The pad is doing a good job at keeping the gushing red blood in check and Conrad is pretty proud of himself for such a mature idea after watching his brother get spearheaded in the eye. I know we should probably call mom, but I am terrified of how she will react to Conrad's genius idea of pulling his little brother on rollerblades with a rope from the back of the truck.

My eyes are feeling heavy and now that I'm home, all I want to do is lie down and sleep forever. Mom will be home soon according to Conrad. When she arrives home from work the first thing she does after hearing of our shenanigans (which aren't uncommon in our home of six boys and one baby girl) is to take me straight to the doctor's office. The doctor looks me over and says, "He seems fine. Go home and get some rest."

I soon notice a clear fluid trickling out of my nose. That doesn't seem right. I mention it to my mother and her eyebrows furrow together. Suddenly, I begin to feel a trembling inside and a seizure sends my body into convulsions, which takes us right back to the hospital. The stick has penetrated all the way to my skull where it has made a slight cut, causing spinal fluid to drip out from my nose. "Cool, I can see my own brain!" Then the lights go out.

My body lies deep in a coma. My brothers even bring the cardboard sign into my hospital room that I had made for the window I'd broken with a baseball earlier that week. The words "Fix Me" were written in my own handwriting in black permanent marker; my smart aleck way of telling my parents of another shenanigan. My brothers punnily display the cardboard sign I made for the window underneath my arm denoting that now I am broken and need fixing. My parents worry over which of my cognitive functions I will lose if I ever wake up from the coma. Will I be a vegetable for the rest of my life? Will they need to take care of me like a child for the rest of their days if my mind was damaged? Exactly how broken am I?

During one visit, my parents pass another couple in the elevator visiting their daughter Jill. Jill is suffering severe heart problems due to allograft coronary artery disease and it's her second month at the children's hospital. Neither of the couples has any idea that one day our families will become one; that one of their six boys will give Jill her very heartbeats.

Jill hears about me—the boy down the hall deep in a coma from a stick perforating his eye after a skating accident. She knows I am in a coma and all I know is what my mind is creating for me to see in the form of deep dreams.

BACK TO THE FUTURE: THE CONTEST

I dreamed a dream. The details of which are now obscure. What I do remember is this.

At the commencement of the dream, I am amidst a contest. In front of me was something very desirable. The other contestants were standing in a line with me, and they also had an object of great desire before them. The object itself is locked somehow—not necessarily by a key, but by some puzzle or riddle. The object and the puzzle seem to be different for each person. More desirable than the prize before me is to be the first one to crack the code—there is glory in it. Over a loudspeaker, a voice is urging everyone to hurry. Hurry and be the first to win the race!

Although I don't know what being the first will bring me, I do know I really want to win! It seems I use all my mental capacities and

physical skill to solve the puzzle box before me. The box requires a series of discoveries. My efforts are fruitless and I begin to despair.

Soon I notice a commotion. One contestant has left their station and has begun walking down the line and opening other people's boxes—I wonder how one person could be so innovative as to know how to solve so many puzzles that nobody else can? I watch in amazement and wonder why this individual hasn't been announced the winner. It is then that I realize that their box, their riddle, their dilemma has not been solved . . .

I see my body lying in the hospital bed as I'm hovering above it. I am floating up, up, up, and down the hall to visit my elderly widow neighbor, and she is not pleased to see me in this state. I have a lot of respect for this woman, so I listen to her cranky words as her wrinkles visibly deepen with a command to "get back in that body where you belong, my boy! You're too young to fly with the eagles!"

I make a full recovery from the coma two weeks later with no issues. I even remember ALL my lines for the sixth-grade school play *Bye Bye Birdie* as the prominent father role.

I would go back and do it again. I'd do the same things, I'd be the same kid. I want to go back and do it all again because I miss the good ol' days when I was just a kid. I see the lemonade stand on the corner of the street. We were making more than lemonade, we were making memories. We'd pick up every penny and save a quarter or two. We'd spend it all on basketball cards or a pack of big league chew.

*****

Two years later, my brother Conrad plunged over an overpass in a moment of destitution and depression from a world full of trauma, sadness, and remorse. A huge semi swerved to miss him, but he drowned in his bodily fluid. Conrad was seventeen years old. As I clung to my guitar at his service, the music was my greatest protector from tears taking over. My guitar became my outlet, and I was able to express my greatest pain, loss, and love through tightly tuned strings. At the tender age of 14, this loss taught me to love every minute of life genuinely. Conrad was a wonderful person who succumbed to a moment of deep sadness and depression.

We all go through dark, dark moments. And in those moments, we tend to forget that so many love us. May this book and all it has to offer be a small guide to remembering how precious every heartbeat is; how precious it is to be alive even when the weight of the world seems too heavy. Messy is also beautiful. Sun is on the other side of the cloud in the rain. We are an ocean, and the tidal waves are a part of us. Don't let the waves engulf you, instead engulf them. Remind yourself that as an ocean, the waves that are crashing down on you in your life don't consume you, you consume them. Don't judge them for good or bad, drink them up and automatically they will contribute to your vastness and give you the power to restore your energy through them. Consider writing about your waves of life to help you overcome them. If you're feeling strong, get out and ride them. Perfection is not what we are aiming for, but rather progress. Surround yourself with bright colors, and light, and help for the darkness. Life isn't just for endurance, but for enjoyment. If I could write down what's on my mind, the words would come from beyond the barriers of time. They might tell you I'm trying to find a reason for the reason the world is so unkind. There's too much evil here. I can feel it like fog in the air.

Conrad David J.

It's a strange feelin' standing on the ceilin'
Looking down on catastrophe and how it has to be
The fence frames the city in a diamond window
Street light shining down yellow mellow glow

Dark night all around everywhere I go
Clever lies tied around everything I know
Look down at the water where the people died below
How will it be when it is my time to go?

Think back to the overpass how I miss you so
Never thought I'd lose you bro
And years and years from this day
I'll remember how I-80 took away Conrad David J.

A fall from a bridge, a bridge in the Fall
Some people drowned on their way to St. Paul
Ya there's a difference or is there at all?
Blood, water, death, pain, who is at fault?

Who is to blame, the wind or the rain?
The sin or the shame of the blood in the stain?
How many lines is enough to write in your name?
How many dimes have I smoked since the day?
Every theory I can't see clearly
I trace your steps so nearly

THE GIRL JILL WHO WAS IN THE HOSPITAL AT THE SAME TIME AS I WAS IS NOW WAITING ON THE TRANSPLANT LIST AND CONRAD'S HEART HITS ALL THE MATCHING REQUIREMENTS. JILL'S CHEST IS CUT OPEN TEN INCHES ALLOWING THE DOCTORS TO ACCESS HER HEART. DOCTORS LITERALLY REMOVE THE STRUGGLING HEART FROM HER CHEST WHILE A MACHINE TAKES OVER HER HEART'S PUMPING ACTIONS, MOVING THE BLOOD AWAY FROM HER ORGANS AND OXYGENATING THE BLOOD FOR HER. HER WEAK HEART IS REPLACED BY CONRAD'S STRONG ONE. HER VERY HEARTBEATS AND JOLTS ARE HEALTHIER AFTER HOURS OF SURGERY. THAT PROCEDURE WAS MUCH MORE INVASIVE AND TOOK LONGER THAN IT WILL TAKE YOU TO READ THIS BOOK. MY HOPE IS IT HAS A SIMILAR EFFECT TO STRENGTHEN YOUR DAILY HEARTBEATS.

CONRAD ALSO DONATES A KIDNEY AND CORNEAS BESIDES HIS PRECIOUS HEART THAT BEATS IN JILL FOR TWENTY-SEVEN YEARS. JILL LOVES SO HARD THAT SHE WEARS OUT THREE HEARTS AND EVEN TRIES FOR A FOURTH. I OFTEN JOKE THAT JILL LITERALLY HAS MY BROTHER'S HEART AND SHE REFERS TO ME AS "HER HEART'S LITTLE BROTHER," THE ULTIMATE GIFT THAT CAME FROM THE ULTIMATE SACRIFICE. WHEN YOU ARE ACUTELY AWARE THAT LIFE IS BASED ON OTHERS UNLOCKING YOUR BOX AS I SAW IN MY DREAM, IT IS EASIER TO REMIND YOURSELF THAT YOUR "INNER AND OUTER LIVES ARE BASED ON THE LABORS OF OTHER PEOPLE, LIVING AND DEAD AND THAT YOU MUST EXERT YOURSELF IN ORDER TO GIVE THE SAME MEASURE AS YOU HAVE RECEIVED AND ARE STILL RECEIVING"[1] AS JILL DID.

The life of Jill planted a seed in my heart. Decide today to soften the hardness of your heart, to procure a fullness of your heart daily, to lift up sorrowful hearts along your journey, to help other hearts, and in return heal your own. This book is written with a heart full of gratitude in hopes to lift one heart, your heart to rise above the hardness and hatred in the world.

*****

If you follow this book, it will carry you beyond a vale of sorrow into a far better life of promise and hope. It will guide you to look up, live, and be happy. My heart is beating in my chest thanks to others, and I am acutely aware of my beats being finite. I have a goal of turning my somedays into yesterdays. There is no time to procrastinate, procrastinate later.

You may feel infatuation
One love expands across the nations
One life is lived in segregation
One love to live in separation

This mighty greedy generation
has two eyes to see our destination
No time- we love procrastination
We get what we want, our hearts are racin'

All around the world
We all can see people in need
But oh we just pass by
Leave them to die, murderous pride

We turn our heads in degradation
They plead, they bleed in desperation
They cannot breathe for suffocation
Will spread to hearts across the nation

Oftentimes we are kept from our goals not by obstacles, but by a clear path to a lesser goal.[2] Fix your mind on your heart region and establish a routine to use every chapter when you come across the heart jolt sections. While reading the beats of this book outlining some of the beats of my heart, dedicate yourself to every chapter with a specific goal to better your own heartbeats with the heart jolt section in each beat. Write down specifically the way you will improve after reading each beat. Envision the cycles of birth and death in this life and establish your version of what to do after reading each beat to live a heart-filled day. I promise if you do this, your heart will be full of love and happiness each day. It won't matter when your life is over because the day before will be the best day you have ever lived. You will have less regret at the end of your life, truly living and loving during your finite beats. Understanding is linked primarily to the heart. For a mighty change of heart, commit to doing the heart jolt exercise in each chapter and even using the journal that accompanies them. They are opportunities to look upward and live in relation to your heart more each day.

How do you improve your heart's condition? Imagine wearing a watch on your wrist, knowing the very second and hour the watch will die. One day you will run out of seconds and beats. Monitor the way you use those beats in time, pulses, or regularly repeating events. How can you improve those beats? You can choose your attitude, live daily in gratitude, know that love is the most powerful force on earth, contin-

uously grow your power, remember that no matter your age you still have the wisdom to gain, dedicate yourself to service, practice patience, endurance, change, and know how lucky you are to have a beating heart. One day you will be ready to go fly with eagles flying to the best beats.

Doctors said if I ever came out of my coma, my brain would be severely damaged and the rest of my life would be a questionable existence. Though my existence is a unique one, I miraculously came out of that coma with my brain fully intact. I performed my sixth-grade play flawlessly just as I intend on performing life, exuberantly and whole. In Hebrew, the word perfect means complete, whole, not perfect like we often read in the English translation. You can be whole and be rough, natural, and uncured. You have it all when you intend to live with a whole purpose of heart.

Charles R. Swindoll opened one secret box about attitude for me, "Life is ten percent *what* happens to us and ninety percent *how* we react to it."

You're in charge of your charge; be it positive or negative. Author of *Miracle Morning*, Hal Elrod fought acute lymphoblastic leukemia. His statement, "The reality is you can go through the most painful, horrible experience of your life and *choose* to be the happiest you have ever been"[3] is another puzzle solved. My personal strategy is to strive for a) a positive attitude b) belief in myself, others, and a higher power, and c) courage.

Thinking like a river my thoughts flow to the ocean
Would you like to sail my secret sea of sorrows?
The ocean where my memories dwell
Storms my pain the waves swell
Discouraged yet I set sail

And ride the storm, my pain it borrows
Attracted to the glistening waves by
The moon's reflection drifting through
My thoughts to undecided indirection
I've tried to want to change
It's my imagination
Drifting through my thoughts
To no predestined destination

(by Marshall Jensen)

Consider all conditions as your allies. If they didn't hurt, you wouldn't try to change or fix anything. You would stay in the same box with no predestined destination doing the same thing day after day. Is your heart experiencing something terrible or a wonderful catalyst? Re-jolt—electrify your perspective throughout every heartbeat. Hardship is both the worst and the best thing that will happen in your life. If you feel that hurt and it hurts to feel, and your dreams feel like they are real, turn the hardship into a heartship. Don't just sit with your feet in the water because sooner or later you're going to take a swim. If you're taking your time you are making it harder.

Sailing through endless circumstances we are curiously submersed in life. There are those who fight the current; facing the wrong direction, struggling with themselves, and dwelling on the past. Growing weary they are swept downstream in a tiresome stupor. Others of us race in life's current. Blindly rushing through time. Failing to find that time is but the distance of our journey. Forgetting the past. Forcing the future. Nevertheless, there are an intuitive few that drift in harmony

with life. Calmly being guided down the landscape. Living in the moment, remembering the past, and pondering the future. Who are you?

Allow your "heartship" to sail you, guide you, to harmonized waters beyond your closed boxes. Every outcome or circumstance can be turned into a gift and opportunity.[4]

You may have forty years, four years, or four months to sail. Look up and command the waters surrounding you. No matter what waters lie around you, your circumstances, what lies inside of you—you have all you need to be to live the life you want to live. You may be sailing in search of happiness, money, fame, or perfection. Re-jolt and redirect your sails to love and kindness, social connection, using your time well and keeping your heartbeats healthy.[5] No heart is broken beyond repair. If you choose to be gentle and kind instead of harsh and hard-hearted[6], you will find a heart-filled life and your heart can heal and be made whole no matter how often it is broken. Remember the box Charles R. Swindoll opened for me that "Life is ten percent what happens to you and ninety percent how you react to it." You'll discover a powerful, purposeful plan for your heartbeats. Your existence and your heartbeats are all you need. The very breaths you are taking right now are the winds sailing to your dreams. The view you are beholding right now—palm trees, red rocks, baby spit, freezing ice, peace, poverty, luxury, dry desert, green forest—beauty, and juxtaposition lie in every view, in it all. You don't need to be in another place, see another sight in order to experience the pure, blissful joy that comes from inside yourself. "We cannot entirely prevent adversities, but we can determine how we react to them."[7] Living life in worry and fear won't stop bad things from happening. Good things still happen in the midst of chaos. During a storm, you need only find the eye of the tornado in order to stand strong and calm while everything is whirling around you. You've got it all inside of you.

Soft like the breeze,
I try not to be
Like the bees
There's too much busy
I'm at ease
I've got all the honey
I need

(by Marshall Jensen)

I'VE GOT IT ALL

I have an adorable family; a beautiful, intelligent wife who speaks Portuguese and a seven-month-old cherub baby boy with a Gerber baby face.

After a lot of pushing from all the moms–my wife, my mother-in-law, and my own mother, I go to the doctor to try to figure out why I look so pale and have headaches. Twilight books and movies are popular and I defend myself by telling them, "Vampires are IN." I do not know how vampire-like I am about to become or I may have used a different defense tactic. The doctor agrees I look exceptionally pale. Numbers look good so he sends me to the lab for a blood draw. I go back to work leading my team to help others better their credit scores.

A call comes in from the doctor at 4:30 p.m. He says my blood counts are severely low. A normal hematocrit level is from 40 to 50 percent and I clock in at an awesome 15 percent. The doctor asks me to check in at the nearest emergency room. He calls ahead to let them

know I am on my way. That isn't scary or anything. I get to wear a glowing blue and white gown complete with an open back and dark blue string to tie in the emergency room.

One of the first tests they make me take is a CAT scan. I tell them there must be some mistake because I clearly noted on my medical paperwork that I am allergic to cats. My nurse and wife giggle while our seven-month-old son plays with the metal railing on my hospital bed as we wait for test results.

Everything looks good the first day, but they commit me to a room upstairs for future testing. I can't watch the basketball game on the hospital TV, so I am forced to watch live coverage of the Iowa caucuses all night!

The next morning I have the privilege of taking part in a bone marrow biopsy, sooo fun. They drill into my hip bone and extract the marrow. They can't get enough out of the left hip so they drill into my right hip too. Then I put my right foot in and spin myself around.

In the afternoon they break the news. . . I've got it A.L.L. Acute Lymphoblastic Leukemia.

In other words, I have cancer.

My cancer cells are Hyper Diploid Chromosome 9—I think that means that they're hyper-reacting like a nine-year-old. Does that mean I'm becoming a child?

*****

I can't leave my room without suiting up in Hazmat gear like I've got some hazardous materials to clean up. It makes for some good practical jokes on the elevator.

I have a new life in the east wing of the hospital. It's more strict than where they originally placed me in the west for suspected viral infection. The outlook is bright, and now that we know the specific type of cancer, I've begun chemotherapy. I have a revolving door of a team of doctors and dietitians, coordinators and social workers, physician assistants, nurses, and certified nurse assistants.

We made the exciting decision to join a clinical trial which means another exciting bone marrow biopsy. And after all the poking, twisting, and grinding is over, we are still unsuccessful in getting a sample of bone marrow. This is not uncommon when you have leukemia because your cancerous cells multiply so quickly that your marrow becomes ultra-dense and difficult to extract...a tidbit of knowledge that I may have liked to know before we started drilling.

The clinical trial regimen is a hybrid developed from the pediatric (I told you I was becoming like a child) approach to fighting leukemia because children have better cure rates than adults. The doctors tell me that I am young and resilient. . . but is it that I am childlike or just childish that makes them feel this treatment is for me?

The daily schedule goes something like this:

An optimistic shot glass full of different colored pills. One of which I believe is called asparaginase and is for all the little kids that got cancer because they wouldn't eat their asparagus. I hate taking pills. I had my mom buy children's chewable Tylenol until I was 12. The phobia originated from a violent gagging incident that took place with a hearty orange slice. I take my pills one by one and go through about two glasses of water just to finish them off.

Some fun steroids hype me up like a pot of coffee.

The main line is sewn into my chest and neck–an uncomfortable contraption that prevents the continuous poking of my inner elbows which are beginning to look suspicious from an addict's point of view. It allows medical staff to extract blood and inject whatever kind of fun medication they would like directly into my heart without any poking around. Other than appearing like I have three gangly nipples, it's not

so bad. I call it my Triple Nipple. My sweet mother is working some special seamstress magic that will allow me to wear an undershirt and then pop out the three ganglies when necessary for maximum comfort. Yes, she is a compassionate genius. She had some practice with this sort of thing while breastfeeding seven children!

I make a new friend and decide to name him Papa Wheely, pronounced Willie. We are pretty much attached at the hip. He's a thin, wiry guy that resembles a hat hanger, and he delivers all the right medicine at the right time. Earlier in the week, Willie and I went for a stroll. Me in my hazmat gear and Willie in his robotic bag of hangers with three white mini-computers on his belt. We are actually attached at the heart through my triple nipple. As you can imagine, he doesn't speak but he is a really good listener.

TO DO LIST:

a. Walking
b. Sitting
c. Using this nasty salty mouthwash
d. Breathing ten breaths in a spirometer four times a day. It's like a slow-motion bong without any of the hallucinogenic side effects.
e. Remind myself of my strategy for a positive attitude, belief in myself, others, a higher power, and courage. Knowledge, action, and love are the three themes of the Bhagavad Gita and I also read that holy work in the mornings to remind myself to stick to the strategy.

This may seem easy, but this is only the beginning. When it comes to attitude, there's that cliche question: do you see the glass half-full or half-empty? I say, *Half-full? Why not filled to the brim?* When my wife and I were dating she gave me a pin that read, "Ballistic Optimistic." She told me that when she saw it she thought, "That's so Marshall." I'm not entirely sure what's optimistic about ballistics, but the little character does appear to have a bald head and I am headed there too.

If you want to live in an inspirational way, I must let you in on a little secret: we often don't have a lot of choices in our calamities. I can't choose to not have cancer, all I can do is choose how I react to the situation. I can wallow in self-pity and spend my days lamenting "why me," or I can choose to find the joy in each day, be grateful, and be faithful. When you think about it like that, the choice is easy. As my often hyperactive, awesomely inspired cousin says, "It's funny how the things you don't want to happen end up teaching you the things you need to know the most." The hard moments are the growth moments and more opportunities for growth are coming for me and for you.

As I make my many laps around the bone marrow transplant unit—you gotta get your exercise—I can't help but notice the titles of the different rooms and offices. One plaque reads, "Mid-Level Providers." This made me wonder if the mid-level providers are on the eighth floor, where do they put the high-level providers? On the roof? Furthermore, what do you tell people if you work for the

low-level providers? "I'm sorry, we only provide the crappy low level of service. If you wanted quality, you should have signed up with the guys on the roof."

Another plaque reads "Consultation Room." People in this room often seem somber and serious. I had thought that maybe if we change the name of the room that will help. Why does it have to be a **con**sultation room ... Why not a **pro**sultation room? That way they can focus on the pros of the situation rather than the cons.

This could be a huge opportunity. Think about it: we often invite colleagues to a "**con**ference." What would happen, though, if we had them attend a "**pro**ference"? Who knows? Instead of conversations, people might have **pro**versations. This would lead them to come up with new **pro**structive ideas. Think—Congress would be changed to **Pro**gress and might actually make some progress! The economy would be transformed into an e**pro**nomy. Unemployment would be obliterated!

Wishful thinking? Probably, but still fun to contemplate; or should I say protemplate?

*****

I have my first clump. I am busy watching a basketball game when the nurse comes in to take my vitals. My blood pressure is a little bit higher than normal. Close game, imagine that. So I'm sitting up nervously in my fancy bed, my hands on my head and there is some ridiculous foul call. I yank my hands forward in protest, arms out, palms up, pleading at the television, "Whaaaaat!" and then I see it. My eyes refocus from the TV to my right hand, and there, pinched between my middle and index finger is a tuft of hair. My horror over the foul is replaced by a new and more personal horror, "Whaaaaa!" I shout again, but there's no need for a referee on this call: I have my first clump ...

It doesn't matter what phase of denial I was floating in prior to that—the clump snaps me out of it. I will soon look like all the others on east eight.

I do my best to hang on to my hair for a few days. My brother shaves his head with me. It's a good thing he keeps his facial hair because you can hardly tell us apart. I am tempted to slip my hospital band on his wrist and go out for a night on the town. So many friends and family—men and women– shave their heads in support that I wouldn't be surprised if beanie sales rise in my city. My family drives long distances to show their support sporting several shaved heads and all decked out in orange leukemia-fighting garb.

My aunt is the first one that walks into my hospital room with no hair. She is a wound care nurse here at the hospital. Aside from stunning everyone with her fabulous shaved head which even our baby likes to touch, she has doted over me and checked in on me every chance she gets.

One day I'm out for my "walk"—gas mask, gown, gloves, you know the drill—and this nursing cart comes flying from around the corner to impede my course. There's my aunt with three bottles of the most magical lotion I've ever used. She said she "heard through the grapevine" that my knuckles are dry and cracking. As per my low microbial diet, I can't even eat grapes!

Hospital routines start off normal most days. Eat breakfast, take pills, call the CNA to change my sheets while I jump in the shower. Some days are a little rough when chemo treatments finally catch up to me. Blood levels get low, and soon I am due for a blood transfusion. Depending on how low, they give me one to two units, then I feel much better. I truly am like a vampire, just as I said in my defense to the women who told me I was pale.

Not feeling well, I haven't shaved for a few days and I am starting

to get some whiskers going. So I'm in the shower and I have the washcloth out and I kid you not——yes, gentlemen, be jealous——I wipe it across my lip and my mustache just washes right off!

Later that day my wife texts me, she is out and about for some girl time, and they have just gotten their nails done. Leukemia's ribbon color is orange. They had their pedicures done with bright orange and 'ALL' written on the big toe. With that and the shaved heads, I'd say I have support from head to toe.

As a child, my wife adored Albert Einstein and the way he dedicated his life to learning and research. One of my wife's dreams as a little girl was to find a cure for cancer and now she's researched more about leukemia than she ever would have without this obstacle in our path. Majoring in biology equipped her to steer toward research. As I lie in hospital beds around the U.S., I find her diligently at my bedside researching what more can be done, what treatments are less abrasive than chemotherapy and radiation, and which trials I qualify for. She is my rocking researcher while I rock my guitar. I am scheduled to start full-body irradiation where I will be blasted from head to toe with powerful energy that Einstein helped harness for the use in treatment of cancers.

*****

FULL BODY IRRADIATION THERAPY: TATTOOS AND A FACIAL

I am scheduled to undergo six days of TBI (Total Body Irradiation), but before we get to the details on that, let's address this whole radiation versus irradiation situation. In physics, the word "radiation" is used to describe energized particles that are traveling through a medium. "Irradiation" is the process in which an object (in this case, me) is exposed to "radiation." The side effects of this treatment are extremely irritating, so irradiation is a fitting title. Enough of that nonsense, what does all this have to do with me getting a tattoo? Well, four tattoos actually.

The TBI takes place in a radiation machine that looks like a giant telephone with an eyeball on one end of the receiver. The eyeball is what shoots out the energized particles. During my treatments I stand in a strange apparatus that kind of looks like one of those home gym infomercial rigs. . . "The bones of a steel home gym come fully equipped with a bike seat, parallel bars, armpit rests, and hand grips. Be one of the first 100 callers and we'll throw in a custom-fit facemask free of charge! So what are you waiting for? Pick up the phone and order your bones of steel today!"

The purpose of this peculiar contraption is to help me stand completely still while they zap me. Apparently, the lungs and heart are particularly sensitive to this kind of treatment. A set of lead plates hang in front of my heart and lungs to minimize the radiation they are exposed to. To ensure that the shield is in just the right place to cover my heart and lungs they tattoo a couple of marks on my chest and back to ensure it is aligned properly each time. During my treatment, I spend about ten minutes facing forward and then ten minutes facing backward. Luckily, I am allowed to bring music and headphones.

After I got my tattoos, it was time to design my face mask. I wear this mask when I have radiation done to my brain. Yep, right to my head. When chemotherapy was first being tested they made great strides with leukemia patients. Using multi-drug regimens they were able to send cancer into remission for nearly a year. Sadly, however, patients who were seemingly cured returned with cancer in their brain and spine, and ultimately died.

This is why lumbar punctures (chemo injected into my spinal fluid) and radiation to my brain are necessary and crucial for treatment. In order to help me hold still during radiation to my head, I am fitted with a custom face mask by stretching a hot, wet piece of netted plastic across my face and then letting it dry and cool. Markers are attached to the mask that lines up with lasers to ensure that the radiation is administered with exact precision.

If all goes well, I will be in the hospital for six to eight weeks. Though it can take up to two years for my immune system to rebuild and recover. This is partially due to immuno-suppressant medications that ensure I do not reject the transplant.

I Nearly Become Spiderman

I nearly become Spiderman on my first round of total-body irradiation. When the tech from radiation comes for me, I put my nifty mask and breastplates to the test. It's quite a trek down to the north end of the first floor so they bring a wheelchair for me. I haven't used it much so far just on days when I have an extreme spell of nausea. I figure as long as I have the strength to walk I could use the exercise.

In the radiation room, I step onto an elevated platform while they secure my bracings and hang the thick, metal plates specifically shaped to cover my lungs and my heart during the treatment. All situated and strapped into place, a couple of preliminary x-rays confirm that everything is set up correctly.

I notice a big, furry spider crawling out of the air vent two feet in front of my face. For the first round of radiation, I face backward and can see the vent with the lingering spider on the ceiling just behind me. To make matters worse, I am told to remove my shirt for the procedure, and I feel quite exposed to my spotted little friend. When the tech comes in and lets me know that we are about to start I tell her, "That's fine, but I'm not holding still if this spider crawls on my face." She comes back with a hospital chart and swats him against the wall. The hairy creature isn't quite finished though and makes an acrobatic descent, plummeting downward on a thin silky cable. She swats again and that is the end of him.

At first, I am relieved and verbally justify the murder of the likely harmless arachnid, "If you think about it, we did him a favor and put him out of his misery. He was about to get nuked by radiation." We have a good chuckle about that. But then I realize my blunder. What if we hadn't killed the spider? It's likely he would have acquired mutant abilities from the radiation, thereupon biting me and transferring his mutant powers. I could have been the next Spiderman! A once-in-a-lifetime opportunity lost to the irrational fear of a helpless invertebrate. CNS irradiation is administered with laser precision to my brain. I see blue lights and smell something similar to bleach, neither of which actually exists. Yep, I am tripping. This is not due to any of the functions of the machinery, but rather how one's brain reacts to pulses of radiation.

I walk into the chamber with a mesh mask fit just right to my scalp and new tattoos on my chest for the metal plates to protect me from the radiating rays meant to take out cancer. The walk leads to a new immune system from an anonymous donor, a second birthday for me, and the potential for other diseases caused by my treatments. All of this also holds the potential for living instead of dying.

We are taking one day and sometimes one minute at a time. My wife is a nerd and does all the research and reading. We make tough life-and-death decisions daily. For example, deciding between the bone marrow transplant and staying on the study. Doctors are not even sure if they should recommend transplant or not. The weight of the num-

ber of life-versus-death decisions, and turn-of-event serious situations have accrued and become heavy. We can carry so much more than we think by searching for guides and teachers through every step.

No matter the outcome, strength and being better equipped to handle the hard stops on the road of life is the journey to my destination. Transplant is the harsher choice of the two options. We are continuously buoyed up on our voyage. I am embracing the opportunities for growth during the rollercoaster ride: reaching my hands high in the air and feeling exhilaration when the times are high, feeling the sinking in the pit of my stomach on the way down, and grasping hospital bed bars tightly on the low days while waiting to slowly go up again. We are living outside our comfort zones. We enjoy the quiet and calm days. Our sweet baby boy starts walking the night before my wife's birthday. Coolest birthday present ever, except that now he doesn't want to sit. He's too independent and excited to try out his new skill. We squeeze out fun when we can, knowing that the majority of our time together will be stuck in small hospital rooms. Oftentimes I'm not allowed to leave the unit and my family is avoiding germs, causing us to essentially become hermits.

We celebrate my wife's twenty-seventh birthday by attending a Utah Jazz basketball game that gets them into the playoffs. My wife and I are a young team too. I am growing back a good amount of hair, but want to shave it into a "J." My wife doesn't even make the connection to the Jazz basketball team until our friend outlines it in purple and green Jazz colors. "Just keep it on—tomorrow at church it can stand for Jesus!" Marshaling beats of your heart is a choice to live and die crying or laughing.

We successfully sneak a whole jar of peanut butter and celery sticks into the game. Celery dipped in peanut butter never tasted so good. The next day my voice is gone from screaming. I don't remember who won, but we had the time of our lives.

I'm not able to travel for a few years and my wife's little brother stopped by on his way to Japan. The day is cold and my wife's red heels keep sinking into the mud. My bald head gives me the opportunity to sport my favorite newsie cap. Just as the *Newsies* is one of my favorite shows, when it comes to traveling, Brazil is one of my wife's favorite places. She lived in Brazil for a couple of years as a missionary when she was twenty-one to twenty-three. We eat s'mores after sending her brother off to Japan and I catch myself thinking, "I wonder if they have s'mores in Japan or Brazil?" In my childhood I learned the ultimate instructions for s'mores from the movie *Sandlot*: "First you take the graham. You put the chocolate on the graham. Then you roast the mallow. When the mallow's good and flamin', you put the mallow on the graham. Then you scarf." I was so chunky when I was my son's age that they called me Marshallmallow.

After six days of radiation treatments, I'm done! I ring the bell of celebration! More adventures to come, but for now, I am going to celebrate good times, come on! Here's another of my secrets: Celebrate ALL the wins, big and small.

*****

TRANSPLANT TRANSFORMATION

The nurse looks at my wife furrowing her brows today and bluntly says, "The transplant is going to happen. Your husband is going to get an infection and be readmitted because he will have no immune system. You can choose whether to worry or not, but it will happen." His perspective comes from years of working with transplant patients and their unknowns. That is what we are embarking on. I have two

complete matches who are willing to donate their bone marrow to me. We cannot know anything about them except that they are male and young. What a precious gift they are willing to give. For the rest of my life, I hope to remember the value of a gift and to give the best. I will be taking fifteen nasty pills a day for a few more days this week on top of all my others then I'll have a few weeks for my blood counts to recover, meaning a level that's not death hanging by a thread, for the last time before transplant.

Is transplant even harder for the donor than the patient? They used to actually drill into the bone marrow of the donor. I know the drill well. I'm drilled into often to check the status of the cancer. The science of bone marrow transplants is better now. A donor is given medication that helps produce excess bone marrow blasts in their blood. I will need to engraft these blasts as soon as my bone marrow is completely killed off. The cells are collected and centrifuged while the rest of the donor's blood is given back to them through the other arm. Picture an exaggerated blood donation. The medication can make the donor achy, and it may take a few days to collect all they need. To save a life, go to bethematch. com. The actual receiving of the stem cells is like a blood transfusion. Except they knock me out with benadryl and other things beforehand to try to counteract an allergic reaction to the materials they use to keep the marrow fresh. It is the transplant preparation that makes it tedious.

Six days of full body radiation. Three days of strong chemotherapy followed by a day of rest. Two days of poisonous cytoxin. In two weeks, they will kill off my entire bone marrow. Without the grafting of a donor's bone marrow, I will never recover. From there, it's a wait to see if the new cells engraft and if there is, graft versus host disease. I expect to be in the hospital for two months if all goes well. Most survivors have stayed anywhere from four to seven months. It's the unknown all over again.

Remission is achieved after six days of irradiation and two days of chemotherapy infusions, two days of ATG (Anti-Thymocyte Globulin) infusions. My cancer is in remission! One of the nurses tapes a picture of a rabbit with a comment bubble above him saying, "What's up Doc?" ATG is an antibody that rabbits produce to fight infection. They take the rabbit's blood, filter out the ATG, and give it to me by infusion. Luckily the side effects have been minimal, I don't mind the floppy ears so much, but the white whiskers that sprout out under my nose are a little distracting.

After letting the rabbit globulins flow through my bloodstream and destroy my T-cells, it's time for my transplant. At this point, the radiation, cytoxin, and ATG wipe out my bone marrow and immune system completely.

*****

TRANSPLANT TIME

The cells arrive in a white and red American Red Cross box and we are ecstatic! Peripheral bone marrow cells flow through my central line—the line that is surgically directed to the main valve in my heart.

A range of emotions overwhelms me on this special second birthday. My donor gave me so much hope from his selfless sacrifice. The good news is my donor, who will remain anonymous from us for at least another year, produced 24 million cells. That is a lot! In one bone marrow transplant, the receiver can only have 10 million cells transplanted. I am pretty drowsy through the infusion because they pre-medicate me with Ativan for nausea, Benadryl, and Tylenol to prevent an allergic reaction. The transplant itself isn't very exciting, but the little dance my wife puts on to Michael Buble's "Feelin' Good" is

quite entertaining. Buble is one of my favorite musicians and it cheers me up. For several days after the transplant, I receive blood and platelet transfusions because the donor cells take time to engraft so my blood counts remain dangerously low. While waiting, I develop sores in my mouth and throat making it difficult to eat.

Mouth sores are nothing new to me, but the overwhelming nausea that accompanies the transplant is a battle. For a while, I'm on a pain pump. I push a nifty button when my pain starts rising and I don't have to call my nurse. If the light is green I can give it a pump. This is most helpful at night when my throat becomes dry and the sores are most painful. It is rough, but I am uplifted through emails and visits from neighbors and my wife being at my side.

Trials, emotions, and physical challenges can be a blessing with the right attitude. I admire those who step forward for us right now even when their lives aren't going perfectly as planned. Clear says, "It is un-likely that your actual path through life will match the exact journey you had in mind when you set out. It makes no sense to restrict your satisfaction to one scenario."[7]

*****

I'M A CHIMERA!

In mythology, a chimera is a fire-breathing lion with a goat head com-ing out of its back and a serpent for a tail. Unfortunately, in genetics, a chimera is just a living organism with two different sets of DNA. Still kind of cool, but I won't be able to breath fire or grow a tail.

Going through with the bone marrow transplant is a gamble. The trouble is that chemotherapy isn't working as fast or effectively as the doc-tors had planned. Due to a far worse chance of survival, I take the risk.

What are the risks of a bone marrow transplant?

Graft versus host disease is one. In a nutshell, this means that the donor marrow doesn't recognize me and decides to attack me. With a peripheral blood stem cell transplant, counts may recover faster, but there is an increased incidence of graft versus host disease.

Graft versus host disease has two phases: acute, which occurs within 100 days of the transplant, and chronic, which is recognized after 100 days following the transplant. Acute GVHD can affect the GI tract, and liver, and can cause stomach issues as a result. Chronic GVHD can affect nearly every organ in the body. There is a 50 percent chance I will be affected by chronic GVHD; to what extreme is indeterminable.

Since we reviewed the scary stuff, I think it's only fair to mention some of the positive benefits of the transplant. For example, I won't have to pump any more toxic chemotherapy drugs through my body, whereas my initial treatment protocol required years of chemo. Another plus is that the donor cells are prone to fight off any residual cancer that may be hiding out.

They test the ratio of my chimerism—how much of my bone marrow is me and how much is the donor—as well as if the cancer is still in remission. The graft is good, and I am so happy that I am still in remission! Getting that news has me reflecting on what my life was like when I was not in remission.

ONE YEAR AGO I . . .

- woke up and got ready just like any other day
- knew nothing about leukemia or bone marrow transplants
- met with a doctor about persistent headaches
- submitted a comprehensive training portfolio at work
- received a phone call from the doctor requesting I go to the emergency room
- spent nearly an hour in the bathroom because I refused to let the doctor "obtain" the fecal sample
- had a dangerously low blood count
- ate a baconator that my brother brought me from Wendy's
- did not know that over 90 percent of my bone marrow was packed with cancerous cells
- received my first blood transfusion
- did not know I would be diagnosed with cancer the next day

Today I do not wish to repeat any of those things except the waking up part . . . and maybe the baconator.

Fortunately, I have a fairly secluded workspace to avoid germs. I ace all three online classes I took this semester. I have my central line removed and no longer have to do three-hour infusions every day. I finished physical therapy, and I am approved to skip town for the holidays.

Heart Jolt 1:

RESPOND AS IF IT'S THE FIRST DAY OF YOUR LIFE AND THE LAST DAY OF YOUR LIFE.

-LOOK AT THE SKY AND AVOID JUDGING THE WEATHER FOR GOOD OR BAD. INSTEAD, THINK OF IT AS UNIQUE WEATHER.

-LOOK AT THE FACES, ESPECIALLY THE EYES OF PEOPLE. EVEN TAKE THE TIME TO NOTICE THE DETAILS LIKE THEIR EYE-LASHES. EACH HAS AN INCREDIBLE STORY.

-GIVE TO SOMEONE ELSE. IF THERE IS WATER, DRINK IT AND LET THE BLESSINGS FLOW THROUGH YOU TO OTHERS.

-BLESS OTHERS WITH YOUR EYES, YOUR SMILE, YOUR PRESENCE. THESE ARE THE SECRETS TO MAKING EVERY DAY THE BEST DAY.

YOU CHOOSE YOUR 'TUDE

Victor Frankl in *Man's Search for Meaning*, said "Everything can be taken from a man but one thing: the last of the human freedoms—to choose one's attitude in any given set of circumstances, to choose one's own way."[8]

You choose your 'tude. This is my challenge each day—to remember that I may not be able to control many of my present circumstances but I can choose how I react to them.

At times I find inspiration from reading to my son. His book preference displays his optimistic attitude. His self-proclaimed favorite

book right now is **Rain Brings Frogs,** which tells a story of a little boy who is happy with what he has and can see the good in even the darkest moments. Nate says, "Behind the Clouds I SEE SUN!"[9]

There are many more clouds I need to surpass before I fly high above them toward the sun, but the sun is there and my ultimate goal is to shine through the darkness. To see which clouds I must look behind in order to see the sun next and which oceans to cross to steer my heart ship toward the light.

Our son got a puppy for Christmas and that dog has kept me up more at night than he ever did as a baby! It's not that the dog is terrible either—our son has just always been a good sleeper. It is so fun to watch the two of them giggle-bark and run around the house. They like to pick on each other too. Half the time I'm hollering at my son to play gently with the puppy and the other half the time I'm reprimanding Booker, the puppy, to stop playing rough with my son. As I stare at the white snow covering my lawn, I am reminded there are two different ways to see the snow.

Snow (good): Soft white flakes are delicately drifting through the air. A flurry of powder whirls in the wind. I stick out my tongue and catch a minuscule flake. I taste the moment. I taste the excitement of the February storm.

-or-

Snow (bad): It's freezing. I inhale the frigid air and my fingers are numb from scraping ice. It's so dark and I watch as my breath escapes my lips like an arctic wind. A puff of frozen smoke. I wish it were summer as the snow blinds my view.

Choose to see the bright side of something today. You can have a good attitude in any circumstance; in the exact same scenario as someone else who chooses to see the darkness and has a bad attitude. A.L.L. is about to play rough with me, but it doesn't stop me from choosing positivity and being grateful.

Beat 2

BEATS OF GRATITUDE

MARSHALING HEARTBEATS REQUIRES GRATITUDE.

Fatigue, pain, avoiding people because of germs, being away from my little boy, and relying on others may sound familiar to some of you who have lived through a pandemic. Those things get easier. Or, at least, my strength from them grows. During these times, gratitude grows for those who voluntarily help as front-line workers even under stress. This is hard on everyone.

A lamenting change of pace and lifestyle happens with our baby. His smile is my smile. He learns something new at least once a day. Gratitude has also accrued—for all the tears, the prayers, the service rendered, those who continuously give, and each life moment. My leukemia diagnosis demands yet another change when our son is seven months old. This new perspective brings immediate gratitude when we are able to stay home, watch him, teach him,

learn from him, and smile at his smile. We are glad to be home; for a time, I am free from the hospital. Free to be with family. Free to celebrate. Most of all free from cancer for now. I am still weak, tired, and nauseous. Doctors are impressed and even the hospital administrator stops us in the hospital hall to talk about good attitudes for an upcoming article in the paper. He agrees when my wife tells him that she calls me her "Ballistic Optimistic." Words don't express how grateful I am for the opportunity this newspaper article gives for goodness to be given some space in the media. The article features varying points on how an attitude of gratitude is a huge percentage of any battle.

My wife and mother discuss the gruesome days of transplant recovery while I watch my son in his bright yellow swimming suit play in a small pool of bright, colorful pool balls. I choose not to dwell on those hard moments. The good outweighs the bad if you choose to have that perspective. A second shot at life and realizing what really matters helps me forget the days of never stopping to go to the bathroom, trying to sleep for hours in hopes of escaping the pain, spitting in a cup to be rid of the seemingly eternal mucous coming from my mouth and throat, and not being able to eat or drink for many days. I prefer to block it out of my memory.

It is said in the Bhagavad Gita, "Yadrccha-labha-santusto Dvandvatito Vimatsarah." Whatever is coming to you, have some level of contentment, and with contentment comes gratitude. If you are discontent, how can you be grateful?[10] Our lives are not perfect or free from worry. There are frequent checkups; I am careful to drink a lot, eat enough, which proves difficult with nausea and pill intake, and avoid any illness while on immunosuppressants. We have been so fortunate and blessed by loving family and friends, and hope that the ride will be better from here on out.

Freedom from hospital walls gives us a new vantage point and a new perspective for all who are oppressed in any way. Oppression comes in diverse forms. There are beacons and continuous shining lights through hardships if we look for them. Good moments are not taken for granted now.

*****

At first I don't even notice it is happening; once I return home from the hospital I slowly continue to lose my appetite. Within a few weeks I am hardly eating at all and I have lost more than twenty pounds. My amazing wife is more than a good caretaker; she goes above and beyond just to get me to snack. I am bedridden due to weakness, and I don't realize how scary that is.

The good news is that my brother, who looks a lot like me, is getting married. Weak and sick, I still can't miss that. Doctors are ready to admit me to the hospital, but I beg them to let me go to my brother's nuptials. They oblige, but not without giving me a high-dose shot of steroids, which was the solution to my appetite loss. Steroids are helping, but I am going to taper off of them as soon as possible because they cause a number of undesirable side effects: bone degeneration, muscle degeneration, chubby cheeks, and tummy. It's a bittersweet victory for my bowels. I am happy to announce that I am starting to gain back some of the weight I lost.

It is good to be home and my son is a joy! He makes me laugh until I cry. There are good days and bad days, but my strength and my hair are back. My hair is doing some funny things. Up top, it's growing quite dark, but it is soft like a baby chick. Last week I shaved a black mustache and this week it grew blond. Next time, it might come in gray or something, and I'm not ready for that!

GRATEFUL EVERY DAY ONE HUNDRED PERCENT

My 100-day-post transplant checkup shows my cancer is still in 100 percent remission and my bone marrow is 100 percent donor. Wow, that's a lot of hundreds! What does it mean?

It means that the chemotherapy and radiation in preparation for my transplant did a good job of completely eradicating my bone marrow. My donor's marrow has now engrafted and taken over the job of making blood cells, and it's doing an upstanding job too! I am not expected to reach normal blood levels ever again, although they will improve over the next few months.

My MRI looks good—no traces of cancer or tumors in my brain. This is important because when chemotherapy was first being developed for leukemia patients they would reach remission, but then die of brain tumors within about a year.

The reason this would happen is because of how connected the blood is to the brain. The heart really is connected to the mind. However, there is a barrier between the two. Your body has a barrier in your cardiovascular system. The barriers lie between your heart and blood vessels, your central nervous system, your brain, and your spine. Although cancer in the bloodstream is destroyed by injections of chemotherapy drugs it is still able to hide out in the brain. This is why I had to undergo so many lumbar punctures where they inserted chemo directly into my spinal fluid and shot radiation directly at my brain. When we overthink with our minds, we may be hiding or masking the true desires of our hearts. Just as the brain masks leukemia cells, our minds stop us from showing love sometimes.

One interesting detail discovered is that I have an Arteriovenous Malformation, meaning that the blood vessels in my brain are not formed in the usual pattern. This is not likely to cause any problems, but it is quite rare. Not nearly as rare as my cancer. I told you my life is unique. I heard Einstein had it too . . . okay I made that up, but that would be cool. According to the National Library of Medicine, Einstein's brain has an extraordinary prefrontal cortex and other unique brain characteristics that could have connected neurons in math and spatial work.

My lungs are just a tad weaker than they were prior to the transplant. This is expected, and is likely due to being confined to a bed or a side effect from the radiation. My vision checks out just fine, and my chest x-ray and most of my other tests appear normal. My testosterone level is slightly low, however, so for the next six weeks I get to juice up like a major-league baseball player! One player got busted recently for using testosterone. Unfortunately, I don't anticipate I'll be hitting any home runs soon. I am trying to get back to normal levels. There go my dreams of getting Mark McGwire biceps . . .

Honestly, I am just grateful to be alive every day. Things look good right now, but that doesn't mean that I'm "out of the woods." In fact, I'll be in the woods for the rest of my life. The good news is I like nature and hiking.

I've had people tell me I'm brave or that they admire what I'm doing. I have to admit, however, that I don't feel like a "fighter" or anything like that. I didn't ask for this to happen, it just happened. All I can do is take it one day at a time. No misfortune is so bad that whining about it won't make it worse. I'll have to file that one away for my son when he's older. Why worry or complain about things you can't change? Even when the "glass is half empty" it's really one hundred percent full—just half air and half water. At least, that's the way I like to see it. "Anyone who is grateful does so to the profit of his own soul."[11] In the Bhagavad Gita, I learn to do everything with the utmost devotion and involvement, and yet not expect anything

in return. That is why I try my best to sit in the front row of every class, activity, or conference I participate in. We have control over our actions, but not their outcomes. Focus on actions and not the results, don't succumb to inaction!

*****

Heart Jolt 2:

TAKE AN INVENTORY OF THINGS YOU ARE GRATEFUL FOR LARGE AND SMALL.
WRITE DOWN AND FOCUS ON THE GOOD THINGS YOU'VE BEEN GIVEN THIS PAST YEAR INCLUDING PEOPLE.

INVENTORY OF GRATITUDE

Think of as many people and things as you can to be grateful for and write them all down:

1. The people you know who fought off viruses and other ailments and are still alive. A couple of decades ago, we didn't have the means for cures and vaccinations in the timely manner they are achieved now.

2. The people in your life who set the standard and example of the life you want to live. Some receive national awards for things like beating the odds or books that you can read and be

mentored by—lucky you. Some people are putting their city on the map. Even tireless family members who help you on top of their own heavy load.

3. Spouses, optimistic people, tough people who inspire you in your difficult moments.

4. Donors who sign up with no pay for blood draws, bone marrow transplants, and organ life donors. Sign up on bethematch.com to become a donor if you can! International organizations that help our brothers and sisters all over the world.

5. Your Children. Be they laid back, social, easy, or hard. They are awesome for navigating the world at this time in history.

6. Your Home. Through the impossible expenses of cancer and bone marrow transplant treatments, we don't lose our home.

7. Your Parents. They can be your heroes or great examples of what not to do and ignite the light to burn brighter than before. They can be understanding and uplifting through your trips through Gethsemane.

8. In-laws. Their culture is completely their own, but if you can rely on and lean on them through trial, it is a dream.

9. Work! Whether your work is full-time, little jobs here and there (like tutoring and tending that helped our ends meet with stacks of medical bills). Celebrate work.

10. Wonderful friends and neighbors that pool resources together to overcome trials. Friends and family that graciously watch and care for your children. Neighbors and friends who share food and time with you. Families who adopt you if you are distanced from your own family.

11. Your Knowledge and Education. My wife was a bioethics teacher's assistant for a few years and extensively learned about medical prerogatives, social and physical situations surrounding death, bringing new life into the world, and ethical issues and choices that surround us as people in a modern era. She did not think she would be using what she learned in college so extensively early in life, but heaven knew exactly what would happen.

12. People who have gone before you have given you everything. Life, skills, everything that surrounds you, success stories that keep you going amid the setbacks and failures.

13. Divine source—be that higher power, prayer, scripture, church, nature, or whatever is divine to you. Some actions give you the power to tap into a spiritual side that is otherwise impossible to attain. Spirituality helps to provide an eternal perspective, a broader understanding during a catastrophe, and knowledge of what is really important which does not include "stuff" that will rot away when you die. It also helps you to forgive quickly.

14. Health and your body.

15. An active mind eager to learn and grow. Knowledge is eternal. Stillness begets study. Researching cancer and transplants create gratitude for our journey along the way.

16. Contentment. Being content in knowing whatever is to come is the best for you is pushing you to grow and become stronger.

17. Music. The ability to pick up an instrument or use your voice to sing. Many musical moments in the hospital bless the life of the nurse, the volunteer, and other patients through song. Music gets us through the waiting games, the mundane procedures, and even the repetitive procedures.

18. Wellness houses around the world are tailored to your dire needs. Make friends that are going through similar hard times as you are.

19. Sweet texts that make you smile, a warm bed, letters of hugs and kind words, messages of admiration, heroes, learning new things every day, being able to read, those asking how you are, hair that grows back, help with bills and groceries, being able to run and exercise, volunteers helping to tie ribbons, and the mundane tasks. Life is short and it is up to you to make it sweet or bitter.

BACK IN THE SADDLE AGAIN

The transplant is a success and the leukemia is gone for almost a year! "If anyone desires a reward in this life, We shall give it to him; and if anyone desires a reward in the Hereafter, We shall give it to him. And swiftly shall we reward those that (serve us with) gratitude."[12]

I begin suffering from severe back pain at night and reach for heating pads and heavy medications that still leave me sleepless. One visit to the hospital, stronger pain meds, and one blood test later, a phone call reveals the sobering news that my leukemia has returned, causing discomfort in my spine. I go back to the cancer world.

The evening before re-entering the Eastern long hospital corridors on the eighth floor, I entered my mother's magical kitchen complete with two ovens and her marvelous creations. Sitting around her oval oak table, I find comfort in singing and eating with family as I prepare to once again face cancer that nearly took my life last year. We laugh until we cry. We stuff ourselves with mom's massive strawberries piled

high atop a perfectly browned pie crust. Social support through visits, online, phone calls, musical jam nights, and texts are great strengths for me.

My time this time on East 8 begins as follows:

Day 1 in February: Why are there two r's in February, can't we just change it to Febuary and move on? Who's with me?

I check into the bone marrow transplant clinic. After some lab work, they move me to another room and ask that I refrain from food and drink as I will be undergoing minor surgery in the afternoon.

I am connected to a pain pump for my back pain. My initial blood work indicates that my white blood cells consist of 81 percent leukemia blasts. Early in the afternoon, I roll down to "Angio" (what the cool kids call the place where they specialize in blood flow through your veins and arteries) for a spinal tap while I lie on my stomach. Spinal fluid is withdrawn for testing, and chemotherapy is inserted in my spinal cord to fight cancer. That's why they are the experts in all things blood vessels.

I roll over on my back to surgically insert a new central line (the "triple nipple" is back, baby) into my heart for easy blood and medication transfusions. I am pretty groggy for the rest of the night, but they still run an echocardiograph, an ultra-sound of my heart, and a chest x-ray.

After all the exciting preliminary tests, my chemotherapy regimen starts again. I am taking the steroid Dexamethasone twice a day, an infusion of Vincristine, and what I like to call the "smurf sauce" because it is bright blue, and it's more fun to say smurf sauce than Mitoxantrone.

Mitoxantrone

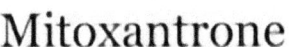

Mitoxantrone

Rather than continue with the day-to-day, and believe me it just keeps going—more chemo, more pain meds, more smurf pee, you name it—I will give you a quick rundown on the general plan for my second fight.

I have a custom chemotherapy schedule. It is based on other treatments that are being tested in a couple of cancer centers across America. The goal is to get the cancer back into remission as soon as possible. We are already looking for another bone marrow donor. If I can reach remission again, the goal is to try a second transplant. In all honesty, it is difficult to achieve remission a second time, particularly if you relapse within a year, but we are hopeful.

An anecdote my father shared with me from my nephew:

Alex: "Grampa, I went roller skating today."

Grampa: "How was it? Did you fall down?"

Alex: "Yes, but I know how to get back up."

And that's just it. I may have fallen down again, but I want all of you to know that I will not shrink from this challenge—I know how to get back up.

I was encouraged by Lawrence Corbridge's words. He visited me in the hospital.

"Don't think you can't. We might think we can't really follow Him because the standard of His life is so astonishingly high as to seem unreachable. We might think it is too hard, too high, too much, beyond our capacity, at least for now. Don't ever believe that. While the standard is the highest, don't ever think it is only reachable by a select few who are most able.

In this singular instance, life's experience misleads us. In life, we learn that the highest achievements in any human endeavor are always the most difficult and, therefore, achievable only by a select few who are most able. The higher the standard, the fewer can reach it.

But that is not the case here because, unlike every other experience in this life, this is not a human endeavor. It is, rather, the work of God. . . . Therefore, while the Lord's invitation to follow Him is the highest of all, it is also achievable by everyone, not because we are able, but because He is, and because He can make us able too . . .

Life is hard, but life is simple. Get on the path and never, ever give up. You never give up. You just keep on going. You don't quit, and you will make it."

*****

BITTER OR BETTER?

Birth is a lottery. Where and when and to whom you are born determines a lot about you. When you stop questioning why things are the way they are and why your life is the way it is, you stop progressing.

There is a question that has been a constant in my life, especially during this cancer battle. **Am I bitter or better?** Bitter moments thrash at me in the form of poison, and radiation, leaving our son, wondering if I will survive or succumb to leukemia. I step back from the bitter taste to get a bigger perspective. That's when the severe sweetness of it all hits my tongue. I realize overall I am **better** for the experiences afforded to me.

"Yesterday is gone. Tomorrow has not yet come. We have only today. Now let us begin," Mother Teresa.

Fair warning: devils and angels fight to make moments bitter or better.

This is the little devil on my shoulder—being **bitter**. The treatments we have paid tons of money for have made me completely sterile. If we want more children of our own we have to pay tens of thousands of more dollars to try and be successful. If we are successful, will daddy even be around for his children?

My wife rarely hears, "How are you?," just "How is Marshall?" She is working part-time to help pay off medical bills. I lost my full tuition scholarship and half a semester of work due to a leukemia relapse. I'm bitter that the plans we made when we got married are on hold to fight a deadly disease, but, hey, whose plans actually do stay the same after they get married, right? Of course, life happens. Plans get overturned, unexpected and bad things do happen, and difficulties have to be dealt with. The world is flawed, no doubt about it. But the world also contains beauty. No one is perfect, but many people are regularly

kind and generous. Some societal trends are bad, but others show improvement and hope for the future. There is sorrow, but there is also joy.[13] I can't be outside a certain mile radius of the treatment center; I've lost the freedom to travel where I want, to have kids when I want, and to study when I want. The struggle is bitterness to make future plans without the constant nagging that another relapse may occur where we will have to drop our entire lives again.

On my other shoulder, there is the angel. I'll let her account for every aspect above and tell you now why they have made me **better.** Shirzad Chamine researched our saboteurs versus our sage perspectives. The angel teaching me to be better is my sage perspective and the devil on my shoulder is my saboteur.[14]

I appreciate the one child I have now more than ever and can relate a little more to people who struggle with infertility. We have the opportunity to adopt different ethnicities if in vitro doesn't work later. My son's birth was super rough. After three days of labor, and three hours of pushing, he was sunny side up and finally pulled out with forceps leaving nerve damage on my wife's right leg. It took nine months for her to be able to walk again.

My cancer battle is fought on display through our clear, transparent windows. My wife is my help and she is always making sure not only the windows are clear, but the whole house is disinfected. We have spent so much time at home and in hospitals around the US together. Dear Retirement, we are ready for ya!

We are learning that some of the events, trips, and things that used to consume most of our minutes and hours are not important. Time spent with those you love and in inspiring books carries less remorse and forms better molds. Our son is molded by people who have so graciously taken him under their wings. They are the credit invested in his strength and the air that buoys his flight path.

Flight paths fly smoother when the pilot can focus more on the present, and less on the future. Live the present moment you have now flying high over your world's terrain. Whatever point you are in your flight, enjoy the best that you can! "You spend your whole life stuck in the labyrinth, thinking about how you'll escape one day, and how awesome it will be, and imagining that future keeps you going, but you never do it. You just use the future to escape the present."[15]

Instead of focusing on what you will be doing, focus on what you are doing. Don't think about the next trip or the next flight when you're in the middle of this one. You can make a difference in your situation, your community, and your local surroundings. You won't notice the vultures circling or the storm lingering right in front of you if you only focus on your destination. Life *is* the journey, not where you arrive at the end. Everywhere you go is the home of someone. Invest in making your little space on earth a better space for the weary travelers who just landed from their flights.

I had the opportunity to talk to the President of the Headstrong Foundation Cheryl Colleluori. She makes a huge difference in her community and situation. She is the mother of Nick, a cancer warrior who devoted his final days to something bigger than himself. It is because of his desire to serve and his wonderful family bringing about his dying wish to create Headstrong, that we have a place to stay while I'm being treated in Philadelphia.

As I spoke with her last week I shared my gratitude, and let her know that I had been thinking about the sacrifice their family has made. It must be challenging to be reminded of her son's death every day. I think of the brother I lost to suicide, and even though the circumstances are not comparable, the heartache from the loss of a loved one never goes away.

I admit that I feel guilty that I have days in which I become so distracted with my day-to-day activities that I don't think about my brother. The Colleluori family doesn't have that luxury; they are surrounded by their son's legacy every day, and I'm sure that there are times when it is difficult. I admire them.

As I reflect back upon our conversation, I am reminded of another parent who lost a dearly beloved child in my favorite verse of scripture.

"For God so loved the world that he gave his only begotten Son, that whosoever believeth in him should not perish, but have everlasting life" John 3:16.

I have a painting depicting a man carrying the world on his back. It reminds me that I lost another brother, who died on the cross and overcame death by the power of the resurrection that we too may share in this wonderful gift. It reminds me of promises I make to always remember Him.

In a poignant parallel, the Colleluori family remembers their son and brother Nick every day, even when it's hard, even when it hurts— they remember and turn it into something beautiful. They paint a beautiful painting every day from the very ashes of death. Strive to remember every day to turn sin into sanctification, suffering into serenity, and great worry into good works. On another marvelous Friday the 13th, I receive the honorable Nicholas E. Colleluori award for being relentless. The award gives me the determination to battle.

To truly paint the ashes of our lives into beautiful portraits, gratitude is the main paint color. I write a letter of gratitude to Nick.

Dear Nick,

I've heard it said that "life isn't fair" but I disagree. Life is beautiful, painful, joyful, and sorrowful, but life is a blessing. Death, it's death that's not fair. It's not fair that cancer took you from us. It's not fair that someone so young and active can be afflicted with this disease. You were at the prime of life, a student planning a future with your sweetheart, a division one college athlete, a teammate, a friend, a brother, and a son.

I wish I never knew about you because that would mean that you may still be here. I wish that I didn't know your story because maybe that would mean that I wouldn't have mine. I wish that cancer considered the circumstances of those it afflicts before it overtook them.

I don't know if I would have been cool enough to hang with you and your brother, but I think we would have gotten along. Growing up, several of my close friends played lacrosse and I always enjoyed going to their games. I played basketball in high school and I was a good defender, a "scrapper"—I had to be at my size. My coach used to put me in the game just to shut some players down on the other team. You might even say I was "relentless."

I want to thank you for letting my family stay at your house. I feel privileged to stay here and get to know your family. As you know they are doing an amazing job with HEADstrong. I don't know if you realized how many lives you would change, but your drive and vision have affected countless individuals and their families. The ripples of your influence continue to extend.

I wouldn't be surprised if you're teaching and inspiring others in the world of spirits. I've had the impression that you are allowed to check in on my family from time to time. It's good to know we have a special guardian angel with a lacrosse stick :)

With love,

Marshall

LIMES TO LIMEADE

I never miss a lemonade stand. My wife doesn't make a whole lot of lemonade, but she does make this Brazilian drink called limeade. In Portuguese, it's limonada, so it sounds like lemonade. Except you use limes, not lemons. Lemons or limes, the point is that it is possible to take something sour and turn it into something sweet. Brazilians actually include the most bitter part of the lime in their recipe—the rind. All of us in our lives have bitter parts or rinds. It all depends on how good we are at sweetening things up to make our lives happy. Some ingredients and tools are essential to make this limeade delicious: creme de leite or sweet and condensed milk, sugar, and a strainer. Parallelly, to make our bitter lives sweet, throw in optimism, positivism, humor, and an eternal perspective.

Rind after rind after rind has been thrown at me during this fight. Maybe you can relate to this feeling. One day those rinds thrown at you will strain out after going through the chaotic blender of life. You are realizing not to wait for all the bad things to go away to do the good. Bad things don't just go away. The bad things are placed in the world to teach you that those lime rinds are a necessity to your recipe and your job as the chef of your recipe, the leader of your heartbeats, is to learn how to sweeten them up. When things go wrong, instead of becoming bitter and resentful, become better by sweetening things up. Here is a recipe for Brazilian limeade if you'd like to try it:

BRAZILIAN LIMEADE
(Limonada Brasileira)
About 4 servings

Ingredients:
3 limes, washed and quartered
8 cups of cold water
1/2 cup sweetened condensed milk
1/2 cup of sugar, or to your taste
1 cup ice cubes, plus more for serving

Directions
Place the quartered limes in the blender with the water, ice, and sugar. Blend on high speed until smooth, 3 to 4 minutes.
Strain the limeade through the sieve and press on the solids until only a dry pulp remains. Pour the liquid into a pitcher, and add the sweetened condensed milk.

Mix well, add more ice and serve immediately or serve with frozen strawberries! Enjoy!

Note: if you try this recipe and it's just too bitter for you, try removing the rinds first.

Every day is a blessing; every problem is an opportunity. The following maxim has always impressed me, I had the blues because I had no shoes, until upon the street I met a man that had no feet.

Sometimes simple or even silly things are overlooked: shoes, crisp mountain air after a rainstorm, a smile from a stranger, quality toilet paper. There is always something to be grateful for!

I could be bitter that my cancer returned, or I could be grateful that I'm still alive! When I'm feeling particularly unappreciative I think of my amazing wife and son, how can I not be grateful for them?

*****

I'm in isolation because I contracted rhinovirus. This is the third time I've picked it up in the last six months—darn my weak-sauce immune system! Don't worry though, it's not as bad as it sounds. "Rhino" is Greek for "nose" and the rhinovirus is actually the common cold. The problem is that my chemotherapy has wiped out my defenses, so I don't have any neutrophils or white blood cells to fight it. Therefore, I'm stuck with a cold that is stuck on me. Let's just say, I've gone through a lot of tissues.

Ironically, I am in the same isolation room I had when I was treated for RSV. The familiarity has been comfortable for me. The view is much better than my last room as I can see the mountains in the east and across the valley, to the neighborhood I grew up in. The morning sun welcomes me with a bright cheery atmosphere. I much prefer its natural radiance to the synthetic glow of hospital lighting or phones.

I finished my last dose of chemotherapy for this round and it causes neuropathy (nerve damage). When our son was born, my wife's right leg had damaged nerves from my son's head pressing against the nerve tissue for too long. In my case, my fingers are numb and my hand cramps up in weird shapes. I have to massage it out to move it again. This happened a little bit with chemo vincristine last year, so I'm not too freaked out, but it does make playing my guitar a little more challenging when I can't feel my fingertips. Interestingly, vincristine is derived from a lovely flower, the periwinkle. Periwinkle is often bright pink or purple and is deemed unsafe for human consumption. It causes side effects such as nausea, vomiting, and other stomach and intestinal symptoms and I experience them all! It can also cause nerve, kidney, and liver damage. Large amounts can cause very low blood pressure. Despite all these symptoms, it does kill some fast-growing cancer cells. My big bone marrow biopsy where we will find out whether the chemo was successful in eliminating my cancer or not again is coming up. Again, I await the fate of numbers and tests.

Good news: for the last two weeks there has been no trace of cancer cells in my blood! The plan now is to give my blood and bone marrow time to recover and then do another bone marrow biopsy. The biopsy will tell us whether or not we were successful in eliminating cancer from my bones. If we are successful the next step will be to prepare for a second bone marrow transplant. Finding a donor will take three to five weeks, during which time I will undergo a "maintenance" protocol—weeks of chemo to ensure cancer stays in remission leading to the transplant.

There are a number of "but what ifs" hanging in the balance right now, but we are hoping a second bone marrow transplant will do the trick.

I've been doing my best to stay in shape, although I must admit, I weigh less at present than I ever have in my adult life. On my good days, I walk a mile and I'm eating plenty, but the reality is that chemo depletes my bone and muscle tissue.

Gratefully, I received a letter from the university informing me that I had been awarded the scholarship I applied for—full tuition for two semesters! I don't know if I'll be able to accept it, but the social workers here at the hospital are contacting the university to see if we can postpone it until my treatments are complete.

It may sound strange, but I view every day from a balcony of gratitude.

Everyone has been so generous and kind, and I am humbled daily by examples of goodness and charity, caring, and service.

It takes a team when you're a cancer patient, and an uneventful week is a good thing. My chemotherapy treatments depleted one of my blood clotting agents, so yesterday I received an infusion of Antithrombin III. It sounds like the third episode of a bad sci-fi series, but it is a protein produced by the liver composed of 432 amino acids that assist in blood coagulation—not complicated at all. It would be cheaper if your blood was clotted using tiny yellow sticks of dynamite stuck together with different colors of old chewing gum like all the pictures of protein in biology books.

I've been drinking protein shakes and I recently got a stationary bike in my room that I've been riding while I watch March Madness. One benefit of being hospitalized in March is that you have plenty of time to watch college basketball. The tournament has a tragic moment this year when Louisville guard Kevin Ware breaks his leg against Duke. I am surprised to see many of his teammates and even his coach in tears. To **coach** yourself through anything, get **c**lose to it, **o**rganize yourself, and have a plan of **a**ction, then you can **h**eal.[16] It is clear, they don't want to see their friend in so much pain. Despite the setback they go on to victory, holding up their fallen teammate's jersey and dedicating their victory to him. It is clear to me that my team doesn't like to see their friend in so much pain, and I am confident that this biopsy will be victorious.

In the hall hangs a corkboard race track to help chart our daily walks. My wife brings me some colored pencils and I vibrantly draw a little guitar and beanie for my paper figurine. I will also be victorious in my daily walks around the halls. I love it when my wife joins me and sometimes we even walk for a cause like the Children's Cancer walk. We may not be able to join them at the event, but that doesn't stop my wife and me from joining the team inside these sterile hospital halls and walls.

GRATITUDE AS AN ATTITUDE

I received a nice compliment from the cleaning lady. She's been working on this floor for four years and says she has never seen anyone exercise as I have been. I figure I can't lay in bed all day trying to beat this disease. I've got to get up and fight! I'm doing my best to stick to a schedule to stay active. I told AJ I want to eat vegetables, not become one.

My amazing mother has kept me company in the hospital when my wife is busy with our son. It is a joy to be in her presence. She is a great example of compassion and charity. I also have my amazing mother-in-law to thank for her sacrifice. She has uprooted from her down-home ranch to help take care of our son so that he can be with his mom and dad during this time.

I'd go on to thank my wife now, however, it would take several more pages to describe the smallest fraction of the love and gratitude I

have for her and the amazing strength she is to me.

What am I trying to say . . . I'm grateful.

Yes, it looks pretty grim right now. I can't even close my mouth to swallow without using my finger to help push it shut, but I am grateful.

I am reminded every day that it is easy to be grateful for things when life seems to be going our way. There are days when what I wish for seems to be far out of reach. I see gratitude as a disposition, a way of life that stands independent of my current situation. Instead of being thankful *for* things, I focus on being thankful *in* my circumstances—whatever they may be.

I contemplate a historical experience from a man in jail. Under the most horrific conditions, some of the most amazing revelations were received and recorded.

"You can have sacred, revelatory, profoundly instructive experiences in any situation you are in . . . In the most miserable experiences of your life. In the worst settings, while enduring the most painful injustices, when facing the most insurmountable odds and opposition you have ever faced."[17]

When you show gratitude and humility, you will edify any circumstance. Even my worst experiences have become redemptive experiences.

In this way, your gratitude becomes an act of faith. Faith that we trust in the universe's plan for us. I am grateful because I have faith in an eternal plan of happiness. You can listen to more about happiness musically on my album, *The Plan,* on Spotify and Itunes.

*****

Mr. T-Cell vs Luke Kemia

When my cancer came back, the first thing the doctor asked was if we have any rich relatives to help pay for a potential clinical trial at MD Anderson in Texas since our local institutions said there was nothing more they could do.

"Nothing more they can do." I was not expecting to hear those words for a very long time. I smile at his words, "Ok, what's next?" Through tears, my wife asks a lot of questions, and then gives me some time alone in case I need to cry, but I don't cry. We pack up our bags and start a journey to Texas in hopes of "something more we can do." Here we are beginning a biotherapy trial.

My wife ran a ten miler just before we hit the plane and is limping around the whole hospital looking a whole lot more like the pain-stricken patient than I am. She was nervous about me flying because of blood thinner medications and the possibility of blood clots in cancer patients on airplanes. I have cankles due to water retention and have to balance elevating my feet to avoid more retention and walking around enough to avoid blood clots the entire flight.

The lines here are insanely long. Yet the staff and the doctors are efficient and kind. It's like the In-N-Out of cancer treatments. When we are going through demographics the lady checking us in has never heard of my faith I have checked a little box for on my admission paperwork. When she asks, I share a simple testimony of what I believe in. I accidentally pocket dial my brother while explaining to a person in line my hope that immunotherapy will work . . . hope that Christ overcame death . . . hope that unexpected miracles still happen daily! We meet with staff, nurses, and over twenty doctors in Houston and I receive a cool wristband free of charge.

A couple of the research studies I can try now that I've relapsed include:

T-cells: T-cells are a particular white blood cell that fights off viruses. Think of them as big tough warrior neutrophils. The problem is my T-cells (actually the donor T-cells from my first bone marrow transplant) are not effectively locating and eradicating my cancer.

The drug Blinatumomab helps the T-cells locate and destroy cancer cells. I like to think of it as a fight promoter that is setting up microscopic boxing matches within my bone marrow.

*****

A marvelous couple, John and Sherilyn, pick us up and take us to our home away from home here in hot and humid Texas. Neither of us couples has any idea that one day this act of service will lead to their future children's very heartbeats.

We walk into the library and notice that we have so many of the same books in our library at home. After talking we keep finding more and more similarities. Scrabble, housing foreign students, and a few attempts at fertility treatments are some other things on the long list of connections. John even has the same birthday as my wife! We have some friends who are running across the country to raise money for cancer research. On this day, April 23rd, the running team paints my name, Marshall, on their faces in black to remind them to marshall on through the run.

AJ takes me to lunch at a delicious steakhouse to spoil me a bit before we check into the hospital. It is nice to spend some time with just my sweetheart before being stuck in a tiny hospital room for days on end. I am so lucky to have her here to support me. She is so good about doing research and asking the right questions when we meet with the doctors. I don't know what I'd do without her.

I begin my treatment on the new immunotherapy protocol blinatumomab. The most common side effect is hand tremors (again, not good for a guitar player), but luckily they go away after you discontinue the drug.

Our hope is that this new treatment will bring me back into remission. If we are successful, I will undergo a second bone marrow transplant and hope that my new T-cells are a bit more aggressive than in previous treatments.

KEEP A-GOIN'

I started my high dose Blinatumomab, and so far have no fevers or chills. My face is a bit flushed again, so fevers and chills are on the way.

My face may be flushed also because my heart is touched by some people across the country uniting in love and giving of their time and talents for others. Simultaneously the three warriors I mentioned earlier for AJ's birthday, began a journey running across the entire country to raise money for cancer research and awareness—a nonprofit called Miles To Give. The two forces Miles to Give and Music for Marshall unite in the heart of my city and elevate our lives and our city. I know with this treatment I will reach remission. I realize that I still have miles to give. My heart is so touched that I wrote a song for them the day after the Music for Marshall benefit. Check out the song "Miles 2 Give" on Itunes by Marshall Jensen.

SCAN ME

We celebrate my wife's birthday by watching a musical program that includes John Schmidt, who was taught ukulele by my same fourth-grade teacher. Thanks to some kind-hearted Houstonians we have a decent little evening with cake and presents and all the fun stuff. Earlier in the day, I took her to lunch at the fanciest restaurant in the hospital. She looked so lovely with her hair put up that I had to snap a photo. The next morning I attempted a pencil sketch of it for her. This is what happens when I try to practice "Marshall Art" . . . I call it the *Manda-Lisa*.

I've been reading the best books. A book of poetry was given to me by a surprise visitor in the hospital last week—she is my cousin's husband's sister's neighbor and the dog's previous owner's aunt. Okay maybe just stop after the first three associations, but even then it's a bit complicated. I've enjoyed thumbing through selected works from Emerson, Thoreau, Whitman, Shakespeare, and many others. I particularly enjoy the following down-to-earth verse penned by Frank L. Stanton:

"If you strike a thorn or rose,
Keep a-goin'!
If it hails or if it snows,
Keep a-goin'!
'Taint no use to sit an' whine
When the fish ain't on your line;
Bait your hook an' keep a-tryin—
Keep a-goin'!
When the weather kills your crop,
Keep a-goin'!
Though 'tis work to reach the top,
Keep agoin'!
S'pose you're out o' ev'ry dime,
Gittin broke ain't any crime;
Tell the world you're feelin' prime—
Keep agoin'!
When it looks like all is up
Keep a-goin'!
Drain the sweetness from the cup

Keep a-goin'!
See the wild birds on the wing,
Hear the bells that sweetly ring,
When you feel like surgin, sing—
Keep a-goin'!

I don't know 'bout the rest of ya'll, but I'm-a keep a-goin till then, an' after that I'ma keep a-goin' some more! No time to dwell on "if only's" or "what ifs"—NOW is ALL we have and to keep it we must fight.

*****

Everything is shiny and new in my hospital room in Houston. Every day I provide a handwriting sample to see if I'm experiencing tremors or neuropathy in my hands. My penmanship has never been that great, so good luck to the handwriting analysts.

I go to the hospital exercise class and when I get there everyone is sitting in chairs and stretching while someone plays the harp. I sit down and join them. It is very relaxing. I'm thinking, *if this is exercise then I am in*! Then the instructor tells us it is time for our last stretch and then she is turning the class over to someone else. That's when we have to actually exercise . . . bummer.

Once therapy is successful in bringing me into remission, I will have to undergo some pretty intense chemotherapy in order to completely hollow out my bone marrow again and eliminate my immune system. This will prepare my body for a second bone marrow transplant. This time we can't use radiation. Initially, I am excited about this as radiation was not kind to me last time, but that also means I have to endure chemotherapy with higher toxicity.

If that doesn't kill me (sorry, but that's the truth) then we move for a second bone marrow transplant. Transplants have a 99 percent success rate of grafting, but transplants after relapse only have a 25 percent chance of keeping someone in a long-lasting remission—not odds you want to take to Vegas.

After getting red in the cheeks at first, the fevers and chills start. My fever hits 103 and I soak through two shirts! The good news is that Tylenol seems to be working in bringing the fever down.

For some reason, only my sideburns are growing. If I put on a baseball cap it looks like I have a head of hair underneath. I wish I could grow some huge mutton chops and really pull a gag.

I pull out my guitar and play a couple of songs, that's all I can really give back right now. The kindness of others is truly humbling. I've been thinking a lot about the man in the scriptures afflicted with palsy—a disease that causes night sweats, shaking, and crippling of the limbs, and often proved to be fatal.

There was no way this man could move to be healed on his own. The record states that four people carried him. When they arrived at the house it was too full to get him through the door. Did they give up on their friend? No, they climbed up on the top of the house, pulled the roof apart, and lowered him through!

We often think of the miraculous healing that followed, but I want to focus on these four friends. I've had many friends like these four friends along my journey. I couldn't do this on my own, you have carried me, you have climbed the roof, you have lowered me down at the feet of my Healer.

I've felt so well and blood counts have also been superb lately—my neutrophil number is even the same as my wife's! The doctor here tells

us I can go without medicine and a mask, and fly home for a few weeks during my mandatory break from the blinatumomab.

We take it and run! We fly home without telling any family or friends. My brother says he isn't surprised because that's my nature, to surprise others. My wife wholeheartedly agrees. She tells me she can go the rest of our lives without any more surprises after my initial and second diagnoses.

Our next surprise is to drive to Miracle for Marshall, an event that is put on by my wife's marvelous family. My wife and I sing a duet "Secure Yourself to Heaven" by the Indigo Girls.

We hold a small birthday party for our son, complete with a Thomas the Train cake. Our son loves trains and I can't wait to put up the train banner in the morning. When he sees it the next morning he is ecstatic—shaking and pointing all day saying "choo choo, mommy, choo choo!"

Back in Texas, I contract painful shingles, most likely from my previous donor's chicken pox. It has been one year since my first transplant and I have not yet received the vaccinations I need. I also tested positive for parainfluenza (so many positives). When my son is sick, we have to keep our distance from each other because the slightest cold or fever can send me to the emergency room. Our son is such a happy-go-lucky little guy that he takes it pretty well. But every once in a while he'll pull himself up by where I'm sitting and give me this look, "Dad, why won't you pick me up and hug me?" My wife holds him and cares for him when he's sad he can't be close to daddy.

My shingles spread to my thigh so I am admitted for IV meds instead of just treating it with pills. I sit in the waiting room for three hours. I think they have forgotten about me since no one comes the whole time, so I get up and drive back home with shingles and parainfluenza, despite the hospital calling and telling me to come back and sit in the cold room alone.

Blinatumomawesome

The morning we receive the news, we go to breakfast. I am sitting down to eat my fresh fruit and bread when a sweet stranger comes to our table. She approaches me and declares, "I'm supposed to pray with you!" A little surprised, I stammer, "Okay . . . ya, that'd be great." She explains that she had an impression that she was to pray for someone that morning and when she saw me she knew I was the one. Standing in the cafeteria and holding hands in a circle with my wife and I, she prays that my cancer will be eliminated.

Only minutes later I receive a voicemail from my doctor stating he can meet with me early if I am available. We head straight up to the leukemia floor. The doc comes in beaming; we tell her we haven't heard anything about my biopsy. She happily reports that the test revealed I am in complete remission! I feel much like I did when I first found out that I had cancer—it takes a few days to set in.

I've prayed for the remission of my sins many times in my life. Only recently has it been for my cancer to be in remission. My prayers are answered as they have been previously. My most recent bone marrow aspirate reveals that I have reached complete remission. That means there is no trace of cancer! Pretty remarkable considering that I have only undergone two weeks of Blinatumomab treatments prior to the biopsy—it took me five months of chemotherapy to reach remission last time!

I'm a keep-a-goin' and go through with the second bone marrow transplant. While they are finding a donor I remain in Texas and undergo one more cycle of Blinatumomab to maintain remission until transplant number two.

*****

After the miracle prayer water, remission, and biotherapy treatments in Texas, it's good to be home. While we were in Texas, my brother and his wife moved into our basement and with the help of some generous friends made renovations to the house. I feel like I am on one of those home makeover shows. New carpets, wood floor in the dining room, tile in the kitchen, new paint, and new furniture—they've been busy! They are trying to complete the final touches before my next transplant. I will start preparatory chemo for that soon. This time the drug is Fludarabine which "inhibits DNA synthesis by interfering with ribonucleotide reductase and DNA polymerase." I'm not really sure what that means, but my incredibly intelligent biologist wife can explain it so that it makes sense.

The good news is that my doctor tells me the dose is small enough that I should be able to keep my hair this time! I will also have radiation in very small doses compared to the last transplant.

The reason the chemotherapy and radiation aren't as extreme as last year is that my transplant is going to be a little different. We have a new donor—perfect match again—but this time I will undergo a "non-myeloablative" transplant. This means that we are not counting on the chemo and radiation to kill off any cancer cells that may be lurking. The preparatory regimen is only to weaken my immune system so that the transplant can engraft. We are counting on the donor cells to kill any cancer that's hiding or will try to come back. This is called the graft versus leukemia effect.

After our family transplant consultation, I mean "pro-sulation," my father-in-law asked, "Have you been practicing your tightrope walking?"

It's going to be quite a tightrope walk! I am grateful for the amazing support. I understand how busy life can get; often it almost feels like we are in a race or contest. I appreciate the many who have taken time out of their busy schedules to serve me and my family.

My wife calls me super daddy and it's ALL I need in life! When we were dating she asked me what I wanted to be when I grew up and to her surprise, I answered, "A Dad." So to have her label me as a super daddy is me living my best life and all my dreams coming true. We are potty training our son and my wife is learning a new responsibility at work to help pay off some of these medical bills. He's done really well with potty training so far, even though people tell us he's a little young to be potty training for a boy, but his cognitive skills are getting better and every day he wakes up bigger. We have been discussing more children via in vitro fertilization because we love our son so much and he makes every day better for our family.

Hospital visits are weekly pamidronate infusions for bones as I have osteoporosis caused by my treatments. This infusion is an attempt to avoid breaking bones. Creatinine levels have been high for a while and doctors say it is very typical after being through not only one, but two bone marrow transplants. Paleness and yellowness in my skin and eyes have caused people to ask if I'm ok and although blood levels were low for a while, they weren't low enough to receive a transfusion. How was I not more grateful for the days when my heart and blood were keeping these vital numbers level miraculously on their own daily?

The thirty-day bone marrow aspirate comes out clean with 100 percent chimerism. This means the third set of DNA for me, and we know through a slip of the delivery guy that this time the DNA is foreign as it came from a man outside of the United States. So now not only is my wife married to younger bone marrow, but a foreign bone marrow. Life is never dull with my unique genetic makeup.

After the non-myeloablative transplant, an eye appointment, chest x-ray, bone marrow biopsy, bone density scan, multiple blood draws, and a pulmonary function test, the results are in . . .

The bone density scan reveals my bones are weak for someone my age. This is not surprising considering all the chemotherapy and radiation I've endured. The transplant stifled my thyroid's ability to produce the hormone thyroxine. This is a fairly common ailment known as 'hypothyroidism' and can be treated with medication. Ugh, another pill—two steps forward and one step back. If you fail to plan, you plan to fail.

My tests also determine there is no detectable evidence of residual disease—I'm cancer free! This doesn't mean that leukemia won't return. In fact, we received this same news last year after my transplant. However, I'm in the clear for now and you better believe I'm going to enjoy it!

Humans are like stars, you can *just be* in order to have joy and light. "The brilliance of the stars would be invisible without the vast darkness of space behind them. Do not wish away the difficult portions of life. They provide the contrast needed to appreciate the joyful moments."[18]

No need to prove or do more to have more joy. You don't have to make a certain amount of money, grades, or have a certain amount of things to be happy. God's plan is a plan of happiness. I have been blessed with so many deeds of love and service, moments of elation and delight that never would have been if I hadn't been diagnosed with cancer—roses among my thorns. Sometimes my gratitude wanes when I focus on the thorns. All I need to do is look up to the roses and live happily with the thorns. Roses wouldn't be as beautiful and joyful without the juxtaposition of the sharp ugly thorns growing right next to them. The trick is what you focus on when you are in the thick of the rose bush.

I wish I could thank everyone individually who has helped me through this trial, but here is a synopsis of my gratitude for everyone in dedication to one friend Joy who visited me by bringing me delicious treats one Saturday. Joy has sparkling blue eyes and shining positivity. A true rose among thorns.

Joy dropped by my door with sunshine in her hand. The smile of summer streamed steadily into my heart. A kind smile, a cool treat, a moment of joy. A visit from a parting friend brought a message of good tidings; something wonderful lies in my path—tears in my eyes—melancholy mixed with mirth.

And I still need to thank Joy . . .

We celebrate that sunny Saturday with birthday twins—the earth has circled once since their arrival. Porch swings and swimming pools, umbrellas in the shade. The backyard is beautiful and as I admire the fruit trees I think out loud, "Grandma would be in Heaven with all these fancy fruit trees." Then it occurs to me that Grandma is in Heaven. . . . Tears again, the thought of Grandma's fruit leather plants a seed of delight in my soul.

And I still need to thank Joy . . .

The next day brings several young boys to my home carrying the emblems of the Lord's supper. We bless and break, and I am renewed. A taste of redemption fills my breast, my eyes grow wet once more— solemn felicity.

And I still need to thank Joy . . .

STARTING OVER AGAIN . . .

Occasionally, life gives us a redo, a chance to start over. Last year I did just that; I nearly died fighting off cancer, and then I started over. I began physical therapy to regain my strength and stamina, I took the pills and supplements, I got back to work, I got back in school, I got back into my routine. Things were looking good then . . . Relapse . . .

So here I am again, three months post the second transplant, waiting on the results of my recent biopsy, and starting over again!

We learn by repetition, like listening to our favorite song, we anticipate the next movement, music echoes the refrain, and something beautiful transpires. Fighting through this cancer experience has etched the following lessons about marshaling my heartbeats:

Be Grateful

Every day is a blessing; every problem is an opportunity.

Be Positive

Positivity doesn't demonstrate naivety, nor does it mean things are not difficult; the key is to find happiness in hardness.

I'm not just talking about a mindset. Positive thoughts flow from positive actions; if you're having a bad day, go do some good! Even if it doesn't cheer you up, it may brighten someone else's day.

And don't forget that what you send out will return to you again like a boomerang. It's the law of karma, friends. Spreading some positive vibes scatters seeds to grow more positivity! You are capable of helping the world more than you think. Expel your fears and limitations and the uncertainty that's holding you back. Make your homes, workplaces, communities, and countries better and brighter by thinking positive thoughts that echo outward. Donate time or money, smile at everyone you meet, and lend help to those in need of your assistance that only you can help.

Be Yourself

It is not often that life gives you a chance to start over. Although it may be difficult, it is a great opportunity! Ask yourself if what you're doing today is getting you closer to where you want to be tomorrow, *to **who** you want to be tomorrow.* If it's not, why are you doing it? From the fifth verse of chapter 6 in Bhagavad Gita: Try to lift/raise yourself by your own self. Never ever grieve, neglect, criticize, or abuse yourself. You came here alone and you will leave alone. Be your friend. Assert and love yourself. You are your greatest enemy when you curse or degrade yourself. So never underestimate your capacities and capabilities. No one can lift you if you don't want to be lifted, as a sleeping person can be awakened, but not a pretender. You have to exert yourself to be yourself.[19]

Alright, enough quotations, and cliches. Transplant two is similar, but not as harsh as last year. I'm now over 100 days post-transplant with no signs of GVHD (Graft Versus Host Disease). Some would say this is a good thing, others may worry that the transplant hasn't been aggressive enough. I'm not a fan of worrying so I just try to take things one day at a time. If that gets too stressful, an hour at a time, or even a minute—you get the point.

Shortly after my transplant, I was on so many medications that I used a weekly organizer for just one day! All that said, my kidneys were not handling it very well.

In the last three months, I've been able to decrease my consumption from thirty-seven pills to eleven a day! That, along with generous hydration, has helped my kidneys recover. My baseball hat collection nearly doubled this summer but I'm happy to report that my hair is finally growing. It is much darker, and quite thin and soft, but it's there!

Last week I had my umpteenth (I've stopped counting) bone marrow biopsy. Should this one come back clean, I will begin tapering off my immunosuppressant medication. Not only will my immune system become stronger allowing me to participate in social endeavors, but I will also be able to discontinue my daily magnesium infusions and have my central line removed. I cannot tell you how excited I am

to take a shower without a plastic cover over my chest!

For now, I'm just trying to smile through life's rainstorms. At least I have a poncho, right? Oh, and it doesn't hurt that for my twenty-ninth birthday my wife took me to a Dave Matthews Band concert either. Birthdays are extra special around here because if it weren't for a couple of young men willing to donate their bone marrow, I would not still be alive today.

The best part? Having my son and my wife with me every day! With them by my side, life is a walking musical filled with song.

RIFF, RIFF, RIFF

A REPEATED CHORD PROGRESSION,

PATTERN, OR MELODY. THE BASE

OF THE MUSICAL COMPOSITION;

A SHORT REPEATED PHRASE

IN POPULAR MUSIC AND JAZZ.

A MELODIC PHRASE, OFTEN

CONSTANTLY REPEATED.

It's Winter in my mind,
regardless of the season.
Memories burn like footprints
in the softly falling snow.
Through a landscape cold and dreary
Marks the winding path I chose.
Weary from the Journey
I stop to catch my breath,
And ponder where I'm traveling
and why it was I left.

A part of me I've left behind,
A sacred part I cannot find.
So I turn back from whence I came
And shudder in the Arctic frost.
And I retrace my careless steps
In search of where, my way, I lost.
But time has drifted like a snowstorm
And has buried deep in my tracks.

(by Marshall Jensen)

Beat 3

BEATS OF SONG

MARSHALING HEARTBEATS REQUIRES SONG.
MUSIC IS MAGIC.

The waves of the ocean hitting my skin feel like jazz rhythms and naturally, my left fingers follow the placement of my favorite jazz guitar chords on the skin of my leg. If my soul were a music genre it would be Jazz. The techniques and scales are genius. One of my favorite things is teaching children in my neighborhood jazz scales. When you get good enough, you can be as improvisational as you like. It's like cooking without a recipe. I make my infamous Coriantumr soup with no recipe. My mom is my role model for how to cook without a recipe. "When there's no blueprint you rely more heavily on the calibration of your senses. You weigh ingredients with your hands, confirming with your nose. You assess the progress by changes in color and the hisses and burbles coming from the stove. Nothing is measured, and nothing is perfect. You know the *composition* is good because it just looks right. Perhaps one day an intrepid

mathematician will find the patterns [in my mom's cooking]. Harmony lies not just in the perfect but in the perfectly imperfect. Melodies and harmonies take such a direct route to our emotions that when we pull up a playlist, we are effectively DJing our feelings, calling up sentiments we might need to access but can't elicit in any other way."[20] My favorite thing about jazz music is that I find my own rhythm and feel my own flow.

Life has times of low beats and high beats. Your tone will determine the joy you feel during the slower beats or the faster ones. A dome building sits north of Palm Springs, California, called the Integratron. My wife entered the building initially built for time travel. Time travel is something my son researches because he wants it to be real. Is time really real or something man-made up? Travel however is real as my wife traveled to the Integratron. You can travel up or down. You can move your body to change your frequency and your vibration. Traveling up or down in frequency or vibration shifts resonance. Resonance is equal to reality, individual, and collectivism. Awareness. Shift your awareness to lead with your heart. Shift your frequency and vibration from lower beats to higher ones. Travel like my wife did. Timelines sometimes become our realities and our truths. Simultaneously, in the present, ALL is happening NOW. Multiscene all at once. What scene do you wish to live, and experience? Become aware of it. You think it, you feel it; it exists. Live it. You exist. I exist. We exist. Time, as known, does not actually exist. Travel to your present minute instead of thinking of what's happened in the past or what will happen in the future. Presently, my son is watching a video on Youtube about time travel. We live a choose-your-own-reality life. Want a change? Travel.[21]

My wife's travels brought her to a circular room engulfed in the sound waves created by pure quartz crystal bowls and pure peace in the desert. She calls it the Back to the Future dome. The sound bowls emanate and echo on all sides. Ingrid Lee says it feels "like when you see a guitar and just want to curl up inside of it . . . and [be] suspended in sound, between dreams and awakening." As my wife lies bathing in the vibrations, deep joy and relaxation surround her. She is soaking in the pleasure of music, repeating tones and beats, rhythm and sound waves. Her stillness is surrounded by sound bowls bringing awareness to the beats of her heart.

Your first experience with a beat is in utero. Toward the end of pregnancy, my wife walked into a beautiful, small tabernacle building. Music was oscillating from the huge organ and after a while of sitting on the soft bench, my wife felt a kick, kick, kick. She'd felt him kick before, but noticed this time he was kicking in time with the beat of the music. "Am I imagining this?" she thought, "Can he hear the beat?" The beat of the organ played so loudly that it filled my soul and made the hairs on my arms stand up. She shrugged it off. The organ stopped. The kicking stopped. As soon as the keys were pressed hard against their strings, the beat was back and the kick was back right on beat! She grabbed my hand to prove she wasn't crazy and placed it on her huge belly. "Wow," I said, "he's going to have an awesome tempo!" We sat for a moment in awe as our baby in the womb kicked right to the beat of that organ that filled the whole building. Inside the womb, babies are comforted by the sound of their mother's heartbeat. It's a repetitive, consistent sound that provides comfort. Just as steadily rocking comforts a growing baby in or outside of the womb, children perform better when there is an order, routine, a pattern to their day. They know what to expect next and the chaos of the world doesn't have to influence their day-to-day life when there is a consistent, daily beat that allows for steady safety.

Sounds are universally pleasurable when they hold harmonious intervals and sometimes form shapes in our minds. Just as actual shapes in sands are formed from different vibrational sounds, music is essentially the beats of sound. Just as musical beats exist, you create your beats in your life—joyful or otherwise. Essentially, beats can bring us joy no matter what we are facing. When I enter my mother's magical kitchen and sit around her oval oak table, I find comfort in singing. The irony is that growing up, my parents had a rule that there was no singing at that table. I'm sure it was made when their seven children would burst out loudly in song, each one trying to use their voice to overpower the last. When there was more singing than chewing at that table, the no singing at the table rule was pertinent. However, I admit I often broke that rule, especially on special occasions. "And of mankind is he who purchases idle talks (i.e. music, singing) to mislead (men) from the path . . ."[22] of eating. Krishna said, "I am not a genius or a maverick or a rebel without a cause. I am just serious about my music."[23] The Bhagavad Gita is music to my soul. The word "geet" means song. Gita is derived from song.

Heart Jolt 3:

MAKE A SMILE SONG PLAYLIST

WHENEVER YOU HEAR A SONG THAT MAKES YOU SMILE, ADD IT TO THE PLAYLIST.

TURN TO THESE SMILE SONGS WHENEVER YOU NEED A LIFT.

SIMILARLY, YOU CAN CREATE A HAPPY DANCE PLAYLIST.

BONUS: HAVE FAMILY MEMBERS CONTRIBUTE TO A HAPPY HEART PLAYLIST.

BEATS OF JOY

Song is a propulsive force for joy. Audre Lorde in *Uses of the Erotic* says, "*It's a curious feature of autocratic regimes that forms of joy are often banned. Music is a common one. In China under Mao, listening to the music of Beethoven was a crime. Folk or traditional music is typically condemned, such as in Nazi Germany, which targeted Jewish music. But contemporary hits are just as suspect; the Soviet Union, for example, censored songs by artists as varied as AC/DC, Tina Turner, and Julio Iglesias. In communist Albania, the regime of Enver Hoxha famously banned the saxophone. In Trinidad, the British banned drumming. What dictators know is that joy has a propulsive force, and that anything that gathers and channels that energy threatens to upend the rigid control of a population. Music, dance, art, eroticism: all of these fuel an emotional response that creates momentum, one that can be hard to control. Take, for example, The Singing Revolution: a four-year series of protests involving mass singing demonstrations that swept across Latvia, Lithuania, and Estonia between 1987 and 1991, eventually leading to their independence.*" She continues, "*In order to perpetuate itself, every oppression must corrupt or distort those various sources of power within the culture of the oppressed that can provide energy for change.*" She goes on to point out that this has often been marshaled in patriarchal societies for the oppression of women. "*For women, this has meant a suppression of the erotic as a considered source of power and information within our lives.*"[24] The denigration of feminine forms of joy, such as romance novels and films, fashion, and home decor, is another manifestation of this insidious form of repression.

Joy can be considered resistance because it's a form of "energy for change," and counters and contrasts with the rigidity and control of oppressive structures in a non-violent way. In the society I was raised

in, we often think we need to earn joy after we finish the work, but I say make work joyful. A baby or child is happy, singing, and content without working for it.

There is a level of unity only reached through singing together. "There's a deeper effect here. When psychologists study people engaged in communal singing, dance, or other rhythmic forms of entertainment, they find that we become connected on a physical level. Choir singers' heart rates synchronize; musicians playing the same riff have brain waves that line up. These experiences of synchrony create a physiological experience of community, one that can be profoundly unconscious. Studies show that even when strangers move or vocalize together, they become more generous, more altruistic, and more willing to sacrifice their own needs for the good of the group. Celebratory joy creates unity on an emotional and physical level, and a unified populace is harder to dominate.

"Holocaust survivor and author Elie Wiesel described a memory of a fellow prisoner trading a ration of bread for materials with which to piece together a makeshift menorah during Hanukkah. Shocked that the man would trade something so essential to his survival, Wiesel asked him, 'Hanukkah in Auschwitz?' And the man replied, 'Especially in Auschwitz.'

"The more dehumanizing the circumstances, the more we need these markers of our humanity. In World War I, soldiers on both sides were known to cultivate gardens in the trenches. In 1915, a soldier named Gotthold von Rohden described a trench adorned with Howitzer cartridge cases that had been used as pots to hold snowdrops. Other soldiers wrote home requesting flower seeds to plant. Whether it's the transcendent joy of sacred ritual or the simple joy of cultivating a garden, the pursuit of joy amid great struggle is a way to tend our humanity when it is most threatened."[25]

Cancer is dehumanizing. How can I play songs while I am in the hospital? I play them especially while in the hospital!

Sing! Singing is a surefire route to joy but it's even more powerful when done with others. Singing in a group can actually synchronize heart rates and increase the sense of unity. So join a choir, host a sing-along, or just belt out some tunes.

I was listening to Enya's *Shepherd Moons* album, track three, "How Can I Keep From Singing?" I listened to it again and again and the words are now my personal anthem about how my life goes on in endless song and I keep asking myself how can I keep from singing?

HOW CAN I KEEP FROM SINGING?

Ovation guitar in hand, I perform at the American Cancer Society's Relay for Life complete with white Resistance robots. Before I go on stage, a local beauty pageant winner sings, "The sun will come out tomorrow . . . "

Then it is my turn; unpracticed and feeble from a long stay in the hospital, I take the stage and begin to sing. After three songs a huge wind surge blows the microphone stand right off the stage and rain begins coming down in sheets. We pack my guitar and run for the parking lot to take refuge in our car as waves of rain pummel us from the side.

Drenched and shocked from the ordeal, our little family giggles and jokes as we wait for the storm to settle down before we drive home to warm banana bread and hot chocolate.

I am scheduled to play at another event a couple of days later, and I remember the lyrics of the song and the sun does come out "tomorrow."

Do you know that person in your life that has a song for every-

thing? Or an uncanny knowledge of underground music? Mine brings me a stack of music one day in the hospital. One song is based on a true story about a young father who is diagnosed with cancer and his friends and community rallying to support him. I don't know how my uncle found it, but other than a few minor details I think I am hearing my own story in the song "Manuel Garcia" by David Roth. The music is only getting started with the stack of CDs. If you're from a generation that doesn't know what a CD is, look it up. Imagine a playlist of songs catered just for you.

Nights in the hospital are most entertaining. My bestie Teri hires a talented sound healer bringing musical healing sessions. Highlights include blues jams, some funky flute, ain't it good to be alive lyrics, and even receiving a didgeridoo to the dome. Music is my lifeline to many memorable moments and the didgeridoo definitely helps blast some lymphoblasts!

My third-grade teacher also comes to visit with her guitar and a book full of sing-alongs. If you've ever watched *The Magic School Bus,* she is basically the Irish version of Ms. Frizzle. Her class was such an adventure I would have to dedicate a whole chapter to fully explain it.

Aside from making every other subject fun and interesting (like naming a teddy bear "Fifty-Six" so we wouldn't forget what seven times eight equals), she also taught us to play and perform music. I don't remember how she had the patience to sit with twenty hyperactive nine-year-olds and teach them to play the ukulele! What I do remember is sitting in a circle and tuning up . . . "My - Dog - Has - Fleas" was our phrase for the pitches of each string and it still makes me giggle.

Sitting in real life Ms. Frizzle's class is where I got my first taste of what it was like to strum and sing—life would never be the same. I'm not the only musician to come out of her class either—many of you may have heard of John Schmidt from the Piano Guys; he was also a graduate of her third-grade class.

So Ms. Frizzle comes by for a surprise visit at the hospital and we get to talking, and then we get to jamming. After a couple of songs, she's rescheduling her guitar lesson because there is no way she was leaving in five minutes. We're just having too much fun! On YouTube, you are welcome to watch "If I Had a Hammer" and "The Cat Came Back" on my Marshall Jensen channel. I've also taught many guitar students through the years, and I've loved teaching them one by one. One of my most dedicated guitar students gave me a gift. He stopped by the hospital and presented me with a "Leukemia Guitar." Its custom design and fashion are said to have special cancer-fighting powers. According to him, I am to keep it with me always because it will "rock away my leukemia."

*****

MUSIC FOR MARSHALL

Every year we hold a benefit at an Italian restaurant where I used to walk around and sing romantic Italian tunes to new, budding romances and mature couples with years of love under their belts. The first benefit of Music for Marshall is filled with great food, marvelous music, and the best people. Gratitude resonates from my heart for celebrating life and lightening our financial burdens all in one musical night. We give back now by raising funds for another cancer patient, an organization helping cancer families, or raising funds for research. Some benefactors include the Leukemia and Lymphoma Society, the Headstrong Foundation, and the Emily Whitehead foundation. Emily was the first cancer patient to fight fire with fire and is still thriving today!

The wonderful Tucci's restaurant staff holds a special place in my heart and they listen in while my brother belts out great music on his saxophone and I strum my guitar. The brotherly love shines and it is so rad that even my wife cries. I feel so cared for and there is nothing better than showing others that we care, and realizing how many generous and good people exist all around us. When you give, it exudes a wonderful feeling that you can keep when times get rough. The roughest parts are still to come for me, but I am on that stage doing what I love for a while. Music is the best medicine. As I sing and play I can literally feel my heartbeat grow stronger, my color return, my demeanor change to happiness, and ALL the souls in the room lift me up.

As we prepare for more treatments, the new saying at our house is "air bones."

*****

Waiting for long periods of time during visits to the bone marrow clinic causes my wife's blood to be hotter as she anxiously looks up my blood results. It seems the closer we get to the time of relapse, the more anxiety grows. It is difficult to forget the feeling of anguish that came flooding over me that fateful day I relapsed after the second transplant. After the first transplant, I made it eight months before relapsing. I achieved full remission the second year and after the second transplant, I stayed in remission for ten months.

Besides my dizzy spells that happen a few times a day, things are going well. We are readjusting to my wife's four to eight a.m. work schedule for Brazil. I leave for work right as my wife comes home so we don't need a sitter for our son.

We have been trying to become social again instead of spending hours in the hospital, having to socialize via technology to avoid germs, or on the computer researching different therapies or treatments to try to fight cancer. Sound familiar to anyone post-pandemic? Life is closer to normal for most people around us as we are bouncing around hospitals all across the US trying to find the cure and avoid germs. Everyone is so busy with their overscheduled lives that we have not been a part of the last few years while we are sitting in hospitals. The house is always clean and my wife is reading five books right now and I am reading three. We are gradually trying to build our lives back again. I have high hopes! "Most people pursue pleasure with such breathless haste that they hurry right past it," Soren Kierkegaard.

Ideas are sent to us from people with the best intentions telling us the cancer cure. The most outrageous one is a friend telling my wife I should start drinking her urine! Ick. There's also going vegan or vegetarian, questioning our diet, nutrition, and the cause. These spark my wife's interest even more in cancer research. She explores international health studies and works for the Global Service Center.

We don't want to be 'the cancer family' anymore. We want to socialize. Being anti-social for so many years due to a weak immune system is building a craving in me for activities with others. I have a law degree to finish, and I want to improve my surroundings and roots. Is it something in my surroundings or inside myself that caused this cancer? My scientifically-minded wife wonders what the root cause of leukemia is in the first place. Refineries? Pesticides? Bad air? Food? Stress? Genes? Bad water? Chemicals? Chance? The possibilities overwhelm us.

*****

On the Front Lines Again

We are putting off telling our friends and family when leukemia comes back for the third time. "Well, what is going wrong for it to be back again?" The actual problem is that the cancer never left. Leukemia hides out and grows until it is detectable by human testing again. To come back a third time, it must be an extremely strong strain of leukemia because 1) My own immune system didn't fight it off, 2) My first donor's immune system didn't fight it off, and 3) The second donor's immune system also didn't fight it off as I was fully engrafted both times. We are still so very grateful to the donors because they kept cancer at bay so I could be alive for years. Had I not received the transplants, I would not have seen my son turn three.

I start having night sweats again. After hearing the doctor say that it possibly could be an infection causing a high white blood count, we know. Those exact words rang in our ears when I was diagnosed in 2012. Thirty percent of the white blood cells in my blood are cancerous this third time. That does not sound very high, but before the blasts travel to the blood they have to fill up the bone marrow. No bone marrow biopsy is done because it really does not matter what percentage of the blasts are in my bone marrow. It just matters that they're growing rapidly and crowding out any more room for normal, healthy blood cells to thrive in my body.

We read about a study involving T-cells and HIV. We meet with our coordinator expecting to hear the words, "there are no options" after two failed stem cell transplants. Instead, she hands me the exact twenty-seven-page protocol for the study we read about that very morning. She hands me a chance to survive again after two relapses and two transplants.

So here we are with plans to fly to Pennsylvania and undergo days of testing to see if I can do another trial. It's very risky. Permission for autopsy results will be signed if I am accepted into the study.

The warrior spirit in me would rather die trying than just die. This could be the cure or at least give me more time with my son and wife. We are hopping back on the life-and-death roller coaster ride, and are grateful for the hope and a battle plan.

HOPE

We arrive and settle down in the heart of Philadelphia in an old three-story apartment that's just a few miles from the hospital. It's not quite "West Philadelphia," but that hasn't stopped me from singing the *Fresh Prince of Bel-Air* theme song.

When she finds out I am from out of town the nurse that draws my blood work suggests I try a "wooder-ice" (water-ice). I have no idea what that is but am pleasantly surprised to find it's a deliciously fruity beverage. Imagine a snow cone and a Slurpee have a baby and boom, you've got yourself a "wooder ice."

Our visit to the hospital instills in me hope. The more we discuss the protocol, the more I feel that this is the right place to be. Unlike the drug I was treated within Houston, the modified T-cells will multiply into an army of microscopic soldiers. T-cells are part of the immune system, so they will hopefully fight off any cell with a certain marker that they are being programmed to track. My biomedical engineering wife can explain it better, but picture war and the T-cells are my body's soldiers working to fight off all the extra leukemia cells my body is producing.

I understand that this study has many risks and challenges. Although the outcome of my treatment is uncertain, my faith is not contingent upon outcomes and my hope is for a better world.

FIRST WEEK IN PHILLY

Philadelphia welcomes us with open arms! Not only do we have an affordable place to stay, but our Headstrong foundation friends provide gift cards for groceries and toys for our son. Now if we could just get this treatment underway. We meet with the doctor who explains that he is meeting with the FDA and they are hopeful to get things started. He also listens to my lungs and uses the adjectives "wheezy" and "mucky." In hopes to avoid repeat pneumonia, he prescribes some serious antibiotics.

I still have neuropathy in my fingertips. It doesn't completely disable me from playing guitar, but any song that requires a high level of dexterity presents a formidable challenge. It's akin to trying to play guitar with gloves on. I can scarcely feel and I have to trust my fingers to know what they are doing, but I fiercely prevail. While I'm playing the guitar, I notice our little man is definitely a "threenager" now. I'm curious to know how much of his acting out and crabbiness is due to the constant changes in our living circumstances and how much is typical behavior for a child his age.

It sounds a little scary to participate in treatment after three people have died trying. Some people have undergone this therapy successfully. The harsh reality is that if I don't do something then cancer will win. Although this protocol has its risks, as did my first two transplants, it is the best shot I have at a long-term remission.

Then, the study closes and I am sent home without signing a consent form because a man has died during the trial. I can feel the tension from the head research coordinator as we sit down in apheresis for the vein consultation. The room is freezing, and the nurses double-check my arms to determine if they will be able to collect what they need.

Discouragement surfaces. The last time they tried to collect my blood I was poked six times. I've had two stem cell transplants, and two central lines into my heart (inserted and removed twice), so pokes and prods become harder with every blood collection.

Miraculously, it takes one poke in one arm and one poke in one hand. The T-cells are collected from my right arm and the blood particles not needed after centrifugation are transfused back through my left hand. Three hours later, the T-cell collection is complete!

A super nurse in apheresis prays out loud with us. Now we are home for three to four weeks while the T-cells are being re-engineered.

NOW IS THE TIME TO BE HEADSTRONG

Just when I think my cancer journey is complete, I am shocked to find that I have only reached an apex; my cancer coaster comes crashing down another cliff. My leukemia finds its way into my brain. Irony . . . no . . . this is destiny! As strong as I need my head to be in order to overcome this most recent challenge, I am unable to ignore my heart.

"Trust in the Lord with all thine heart; and lean not unto thine own understanding" - Proverbs 3:5.

I'm amidst my third year battling cancer and there is much that I find difficult to understand with my head. What I do know in my heart is that I have seen more kindness, goodness, and selflessness; more pure love, tender mercies each day, and souls who touch others with their love. These mercies remind me to live each day more with my heart and less with my brain. My brain tends to block my body from acting sometimes.

I blast my brain until one cancer blast is left in my spinal fluid sample. I initially had one hundred blasts, so injections of chemotherapy into my spine twice a week are killing my cells. At blast-free point, I take a break from lumbar punctures to do long-lasting bodily chemotherapy. My spinal fluid needs to be clear of cancer before T-cell treatment. As the re-engineered T-cells begin to destroy, the cancer cells go crazy in a cytokine release syndrome. Cancer cells in my spinal brain fluid could cause significant brain damage and neurological issues.

This risk of neurological damage may be the reason the FDA has yet to approve the protocol for the T-cell treatment. If I'm not the first, I will likely be the second human to undergo this new treatment. I'm not sure when the T-cell study will continue. Most of the kinks with the FDA were worked out and there is a very good chance the study will resume soon and hopefully, before the duct tape and glue that is holding me together falls apart. The scars on my back tell their story of over twenty bone marrow biopsies in the last three years.

It's frustrating waiting for the FDA and for my spinal fluid to come out clean. When I say I am being held together by duct tape and glue what I mean is that I have tumors growing in my arm and shoulder. Also that the chemo that I am taking is causing my hands to cramp painfully and get stuck in strange twisted positions. Waiting is scary because the more time that passes, the more leukemia grows in my bone marrow.

I also go in for a CT scan because I have a persistent cough. It seems I have a viral infection that has developed into bronchitis. I've been prescribed an inhaler for coughing fits. If I can kick this bronchitis I may start the chemo treatments again that prepare me for the T-cell treatment.

*****

I watch my three-year-old son running down the city streets without a care. I really appreciate this time right before I start another debilitating round of chemotherapy or other life-threatening treatment. I decide to throw caution to the wind and take an eighty-minute train ride with wifi and cushy seats. Before I know it, we are standing in line to see *Newsies* on Broadway. Here's a little secret: I've been waiting for a stage version of *Newsies* to show up somewhere since I was in high school. When I caught the news that it came out on Broadway two years ago I was extremely excited but thought I might never get to see it. Well, you can mark that one off my bucket list! It's been a dream of mine for over a decade. I even run into my childhood friends Cookie Monster and Mario on the streets of New York.

As if that isn't enough, my amazing and talented friend takes the train from Brooklyn and meets us for dinner at The London. Her sister works there so the Gordon Ramsay menu prices don't hit our pocketbook like they would have otherwise. We take a walk to Central Park with a ukulele in tow, which I attempt to play with numb fingers.

Imagine this: a game of softball winds down across the walking path as you're seated on a park bench listening to a soulful private musical performance, your dream girl by your side, a backdrop of the sun

sets in shades of orange, purple, and pink behind the silhouette of the city as fireflies begin to sparkle in the grass at your feet.

This is my reality and for a brief moment, I forget all about hospitals and hand sanitizers, tests and treatments, pokes and pills, biopsies and bills, what saves and what kills, and the fine line between them in the nightmare that calls itself cancer. On that green path I am walking, I realize I still have heartbeats and beats of song to give to others even with numb fingers.

*****

Our Hail Mary Pass

When I found out I had relapsed again and sought out the T-cell treatment, I began joking that this is our "Hail Mary" pass. In other words, my cancer and I have been battling back and forth; now it's the fourth quarter and time is running out, it's time for that perfectly placed touchdown pass. The expression began in the 1930s at Notre Dame; the football team referred to a long-range desperation pass with little chance of success as a "Hail Mary" pass.

With my immune system at zero, I fall victim to a nasty, and nearly fatal infection that takes me to the ICU. I am convinced that the faith and prayers of so many carry me through. I am now released from the hospital and I am extremely weak and tired, but I am alive and grateful.

I am so grateful for my amazing wife, friend, and companion AJ. I often feel that her journey is more difficult than my own. I've received such kind and inspiring words from friends and others, but the real hero is my wife. She carries the burden of the unknown, the "how longs" and "what ifs" and of trying to raise a son and care for her husband in several strange cities. She spends sleepless nights on awkward hospital furniture with blinking lights and monitors. She manages medical bills and insurance claims, medication infusions, and aches and pains. She abandons all other plans to be a caretaker, fundraiser, and nurse. Yes, I may have ALL, but she does it ALL.

More lumbar punctures with chemo clean out leukemia in my spinal fluid. We stay busy watching *Seinfeldt* and other comedies since laughter is the best medicine, playing Carcassonne and other board games to keep our minds sharp, cleaning and sanitizing to avoid germs, and, honestly, to also avoid worrying about results. I still work for the law firm and AJ still has her two jobs working with Brazilian finances for the Global Service Center and coding for Uniconnect. When three more tests are clean, we can finally move forward with T-cell treatment. Until then I am focusing on regathering my strength and energy.

Through the whirlwinds of chemotherapy treatments . . . rather than lay back in bed while it infuses, AJ encourages me to walk. Three more clean spinals come, so I start the T-cell study. I will finally receive my re-engineered T-cells in just three days! Prior to the treatment, I'll have another bone marrow biopsy. We've been joking that this week will start with Supplication Sunday, and then continue to Marrow Monday, and T-Cell Tuesday.

After I receive my T-cells it is uncertain what happens next. Some patients have symptoms within the day, while others take over a week. Symptoms and side effects may include high or low blood pressure, tumor lysis from too many dead cells clouding up the bloodstream and other parts of the body, high fevers, kidney damage, liver damage, and neurological problems. I am facing a whirlwind of dangerous possibilities. Ironically, these potential ailments are my path to being healed from this terrible disease. Anderson writes,

"Trees that grow up in a windy environment become stronger.

As winds whip around a young sapling, forces inside the tree do two things. First, they stimulate the roots to grow faster and spread farther. Second, the forces in the tree start creating cell structures that actually make the trunk and branches thicker and more flexible to the pressure of the wind. These stronger roots and branches protect the tree from winds that are sure to return."

There is wisdom in trees. I was walking my dog noticing heavy steel boxes grinding down the cold, metallic train tracks when I decided to turn off the music and just enjoy the quiet of the morning. A bright fingernail of the moon hangs in a cloudy blanket of stars to the west while a vague halo is building over the silhouette of mountains to the east. As I walk through the strange valley that separates night from the day I am taught by the wisdom of trees.

I ponder the absolute strength of a massive tree along my path. The neighbor's oak is a mysterious, dark figure, shifting and swaying easily as if it were an aquatic vegetation submerged and relenting to an invisible current. I marvel at how it stretches in a constant desire to gather light, how anxiously it must anticipate the rising of the sun.

In awe, I contemplate its perpetual resurrection. In spring it toils in steady slow motion, swelling forth, each budding branch expanding into the heat of longer days. Struggling in splendor, reaching its zenith only to whither and burn out in a flash of autumn brilliance, to fall to the ground and decay. An arctic skeleton—is all this effort wasted? No! It has stretched the tree's capacity for grandeur. As the earth swirls back into spring, it strives again to reach a fraction higher. By increments invisible, it climbs into the heavens.

Do you ever wonder how a tree is so much more than what we see?

We know the branches and the leaves, but not what's hiding underneath. The leaves and branches of our lives are the results we see, while our actions are the trunk. The roots are extensive and deep.

When you plant a seed, the roots grow down for a long time before we ever see the fruit they produce. If you concentrate on your roots, on the systems underneath your life, and re-jolting the veins of your heart, your life and your leaves level up. They confidently face toward the light from the sun.

And so it is with you and me and our reality, our minds are blind temporally from our eternity. I wish that you could see that one day you can be one with divinity.

You are infinitely more precious than a tree. Your spirit is strong and capable of being resilient to the whirlwinds of life. Remember the source of your strength. Remember to water your roots and build a solid foundation. A foundation that mighty whirlwinds and storms that inevitably beat upon you have no power over you. Focus on your roots and you won't fall.

My battle with cancer has been a whirlwind. Our family has been whipped by the winds of physical, emotional, and spiritual challenges. One personal challenge has been my inability to worship with my congregation. Notwithstanding, even nearly two thousand miles away from home, we partake of the holy sacrament (also known as communion) with bread and water in my hospital room each week. The importance of communion every week resets my life. Although I am not able to participate socially with the rest of my spiritual tribe, I try to connect with others through this holy act and online.

The internet and social media help me keep in touch with friends and family, but it often paints a picture that is not entirely accurate. When you are going through a rough patch that can be years or a lifetime, remember that online posts are not the whole picture. In the virtual age we live in, it can feel like your life sucks compared to those perfect, very intentional media posts. There was a wise man who could only see the way the world was supposed to be. Talking about it, and

posting about it is one thing, but actually living these moments of perfection all the time is an exhausting life. My wife is a good listener, while I am a good talker. It's important to talk and even post about the hard and real things as well. Aspire to be a good doer, to be real and personable. Einstein invented the equation E=mc2 to try to help the world. If he'd known that it would be used for the atomic bomb he probably wouldn't have lifted a finger. Online, you portray your ideal world through words and pictures, but often it isn't reality. Your joys aren't felt as deeply without your sorrows. You can choose to see yourself as a victim with all that you endure. When the world and friends crumble around you, you can forgive your crucifiers and endure pain for a greater cause of peace and goodwill in life. You can find and finish your personal mission knowing that it won't be an easy feat. At times it means torment and pain, but also joy and love. You can serve each other instead of hurting each other and thus ease each other's sorrows and burdens. Easing your neighbor's burdens equals less pain in the world. Less comparing. Less hurt. More love, goodness, and help. I have my sins, struggles, and follies, and I look forward to that weekly reminder to remember my sins are covered. Sometimes it is difficult to endure the whirlwinds of life.

"Our destiny is not determined by the number of times we stumble but by the number of times we rise up, dust ourselves off, and move forward".[26]

It doesn't matter so much that you fall, in fact, you will fall, what matters is that you dust yourself off and keep on going. Life's whirlwinds will come, it will be hard, but build, rise, and triumph over the storms.

THE CALM BEFORE THE STORM

It has been a week since T-cell Tuesday when I received my re-engineered cells. Over the weekend I had some flu-like muscle aches and a mild fever. Other than that and a few mild headaches, I don't have much to report. I should clarify, they are not exactly "my" cells, they are the cells that were generated by the stem cells I received during my second transplant. I often feel like a walking medical experiment, but hey, at least I'm still walking. And even air-drumming while I ride my stationary bike.

I now have three different forms of DNA in my body—mine plus two donors, and cells that were re-engineered using the Human Immunodeficiency Virus or HIV. Luckily, I am not at risk to contract HIV or AIDS. I may, however, test as a "false positive" for the virus. You heard it right, folks, we are now using HIV to fight cancer! Here's to taking something horrible and using it as a weapon in this cancer war. We are earnestly at the forefront of the war on cancer and finding more ammo to fight the different kinds is a step in the right direction. The potential of a cytokine storm is looming in my near future.

I am most likely to reach the cytokine storm between day ten and day fourteen. So here I find myself at the top of the waterfall—day nine. Either in tragic irony, the cure will kill me, or by some miracle mix of God and science, my raft will survive the plunge and I'll paddle from the mist cancer free. There's no turning back now—the cells are inside me and they are going to do whatever they are going to do.

Dust and Blood

Lab coats and acronyms, making rounds, tapping pens.
Flashing, beeping, lack of sleeping.
Tattooed, tagged, poked, poisoned.
Shaved and radiated, scarred and isolated.
Sustenance suspended, pumps and bags. Germs defended, gloves and masks.
Cellular warfare, remission, relapse. Balding, bleeding, syringes and caps.
Still before the storm, rain before flood. Clash before cure, dust and blood.

(by Marshall Jensen)

*****

I Paddled from the Mist Cancer Free and Cured

It's a wonderful world. The good news needs to be shared just as much as the bad news. There is just as much relief and sunshine as despair and darkness.

In the midst of fighting for my life, I pull off receiving a promotion where I work further away from home and manage more people. Sometimes you choose whether stress is eustress or distress. You can always choose love. With so many weak points, it feels so good to be able to be responsible and have others depend on us once in a while instead of feeling so vulnerable and needing so much help.

What happens in Vegas, usually stays in Vegas; however, I hope that what happens at the Leukemia and Lymphoma Society South-west Regional Conference this year gets spread around the country! We speak to a number of regional representatives that participated in raising money for T-cell research. The work LLS does, the work you do, makes a difference.

AJ speaks first and already has the room applauding before I begin. We share how we met, the shock of being diagnosed with cancer, and the revolutionary T-cell treatment I took part in. I even play a couple of songs on my guitar including "Miles 2 Give":

Last night I witnessed love and charity.
I wondered how I would return the kindness I'd received
I found it's not a debt I'm to repay, but rather how I choose to live each
coming day
In this life we all have miles to go
Some move fast and some move slow
Be grateful to your maker that you live
And find within your soul that you have miles to give
Give your time, give your love
You'll find out you've got enough
Be a friend, be sincere
Perfect love cast out all fear
No one ever left this world regretting their kind deeds
Or wishing they had spent less time serving those in need
In this life we all have troubling times
Don't give up be strong and just keep on trying
Give thanks for every breath that lets you live

And find within yourself that you have miles to give
Give your time, give your love
You'll find out you've got enough
Be a friend, be sincere
Perfect love cast out all fear
When dark clouds fill up your sky and rain begins to fall
Remember there's a glorious light still shining above it all
In this life we all have miles to go
Some move fast and some, they move a little bit more slow
Be grateful to your maker that you live
And find within your soul that you have miles to give

(by Marshall Jensen)

We truly have protecting angels. When we try to run from and ignore sorrow and grief, the only way through it is through it as hard as it may be. Some experiences we may never move on from despite what others tell us. We can encourage each other to move forward. I also write a lullaby for my son. A recording of the song is a simple, soft, and sweet melody.

Goodnight My Treasure

Goodnight my treasure
Goodnight my special little one
May you awaken
to the light of the morning sun
Goodnight to starlight
Goodnight to the angelic moon
May peace be with you
May calm sweet slumber find you soon
At night we kneel
to say our prayers
And we find peace
from worldly cares
Now rest your head
and close your eyes
And dream of
starlit summer skies
Goodnight my child
Goodnight my special little friend
And while you're sleeping
Protecting angels heaven send

(by Marshall Jensen)

I feel a heavy weight when making big decisions. Entrusting my-self to make the right decision can be hard. "I'm paralyzed without you" is a phrase that got personal as I experienced facial paralysis when

leukemia spread to my brain and spinal fluid. A lot of heartbreak occurred for me when I suddenly couldn't move my face. It's a surreal experience to not be able to express yourself. "The magical effect that a smile has on others is well-known. Mankind has an innate inclination to love. A person who meets others with a smile drives away their anxiety and troubles and spreads tranquility and comfort. This is because smiling is a commendable characteristic, and the one who smiles is complemented."[27] I wanted to smile so big at every nurse and doctor who came into my room, but my face would not allow me to do so. Slowly, their faces changed to reflect my own. It didn't match my optimistic personality on the inside anymore. The harsh juxtaposition of this experience is difficult to express on paper, but when you lose your smile it dampens your spirit and the spirits around you. I've always counted on my big, white smile to cheer up those around me and lift the spirits of strugglers that cross my path. Losing my smile made me feel like losing a huge part of myself. Lifting others turned into me lifting the picture of my face and smiling on the end of popsicle sticks that my wife made me. I would hold them up in hopes of letting the staff and my family know I was still smiling on the inside even if my mouth muscles couldn't turn upward on their own for now. Never take the ability to smile for granted. Share a smile for me today.

If you find yourself at a crossroads in life that you never intended and your life takes you climbing up a cruel mountain that takes away prized treasures, how do you get through every day? I do it by looking at my beautiful, bubbly smiling boy who gives me joy and reminds me that I've made his happiness possible. His smile is my smile.

So many tender mercies are granted to me in times of sorrow. Memories come alive in stories and some treasures are laid up in heaven. I'll keep singing our son the lullaby with his angels protecting him. During my son's prayer tonight he says, "Please bless that Heavenly Father can always be with us and that daddy can still take care of us." My body may be weak for a long time. I pray those with capable bodies will be there for my son now while my body is not able. May we use our bodies to reach out and love others.

Holy writings of scripture often mention singing.

"Sing, O heavens; and be joyful, O earth; for the feet of those who are in the east shall be established; and break forth into singing, O mountains; for they shall be smitten no more; for the Lord hath comforted his people, and will have mercy upon his afflicted."

When we learn of resurrection my son points out that when we rise from the grave, we will feel like singing. He really likes verses that mention our immortal spirits may join the choirs above in singing the praises of a just God. Here are a few we read together:

"Break forth into joy, sing together, ye waste places; for the Lord hath comforted his people, he hath redeemed [you]."

"And he hath brought to pass the redemption of the world, whereby he that is found guiltless before him at the judgment day hath it given unto him to dwell in the presence of God in his kingdom, to sing ceaseless praises with the choirs above, unto the Father, and unto the Son, and unto the Holy Ghost, which are one God, in a state of happiness which hath no end. And then shall that which is written come to pass: Sing, O barren, thou that didst not bear; break forth into singing, and cry aloud, thou that didst not travail with child; for more are the children of the desolate than the children of the married wife, saith the Lord.

"Then shall their watchmen lift up their voice, and with the voice together shall they sing; for they shall see eye to eye. Then shall they break forth into joy--Sing together, ye waste places of Jerusalem; for the Father hath comforted his people, he hath redeemed Jerusalem."
-Isaiah 52: 8-10 Bible, KJV

Even when we are suffering loss, we can tell our hearts to beat again through song.

No matter how many times you have suffered a broken heart in any form: loss, depression, anxiety, mental illness; if you are reading this book at this moment . . . you have the desire to tell your heart to beat again. Keep re-jolting your beats and breathing until you have done what you are alive and meant to do. No matter your region, culture, religion, or era of this earth—you are meant to exist and thrive *here* and *now*.

My wife's grandmother died on the ranch she grew up on. Hundreds of her grandchildren came together and sang a special song for her called "Angels Among Us." In a back-to-the-future moment, they had sung this before at her fiftieth wedding anniversary celebration. Music is a gift that helps us convey feelings that words can't touch.

I am alive! I thank God every day for this. It is truly a blessing and a miracle. It really makes you think about what's important, and cherish every moment. I wrote another song about this while I was in the hospital in June. I was in one of those "meaning of life" moods. It's called "The Story."

Tell me the story . . . of how we came here and where it is we're going.
The sun shines down . . . on the truth of these words.
We're formed body and soul . . . born with nothing material and that's the way we'll go.
Tell me the story with words soft and slow and I will listen with my soul.
Before we arrived from the spiritual eternal sky, we stood among kings and nobles.
On our fate, we did decide.
Raised from the dust, endowed with a sacred trust in a world of fallen mortals we'll struggle as we must.
Won't you tell me your story with words soft and slow and I will listen with my soul. Speak words of justice and mercy, give peace in the hereafter. Read every word of the story, but leave room for another chapter.

(by Marshall Jensen)

Beat 4

BEATS OF LAUGHTER

MARSHALING HEARTBEATS REQUIRES LAUGHTER.
LAUGHTER AND LOVE ARE SWEET, SWEET MEDICINE.

Do you know what can be really funny? Chemotherapy. I remember my first day of chemotherapy thanking our neighbor, the president of the homeowners association, for his pep talk before my debut. He is a kind and selfless man, always willing to help with a smile. He visited me at home, sharing his experience with cancer and chemotherapy.

He warned me upfront about "the red stuff," a vesicant. A vesicant is a chemical agent that causes burns and the destruction of tissue both internally and externally.

With a warning more likely to be seen on radioactive waste, you can only imagine how excited I was to have this stuff injected into my body. Even the nurse had to wear an extra gown and gloves for safety.

Thanks to my neighbor, I knew I could live through it, so I went forward with the inoculation.

My nurse was so patient. She had to inject the vesicant really slowly by hand for fifteen minutes so that it didn't mess me up too badly.

After "the red stuff," I got a dose of Vincristine that prevents your cells from dividing. At my towering stature of 5 foot 6 inches, I'm sure many assumed my cells had stopped dividing a long time ago.

I also started steroids, and it seems my nightly dosage kept me up like an energy drink. My cute little wife could hardly keep up with me while I made laps around the nurse's station, jabbering on and making jokes. This did not continue as my treatment intensified, but hey, why not have a little fun while you can?

Truth be told, I felt pretty darn good in the beginning. No harsh side effects, no hair loss, just a lot of bed rest, pills, and pokes. My blood levels were steady so I didn't have to receive any blood transfusions or insulin shots. Chemo affects everyone differently, and in the beginning, I was one of the more fortunate.

Then I got to try Methotrexate. When I heard it was an appetite suppressant I was going to nick-name it the "Junk Food Drug." I changed my mind just slightly when the nurse came in with a syringe full of Mountain Dew. Methotrexate thus became "Chemo Dew." It reminds me of a drink my wife and I used to mix when we had a newborn: Mountain Dew and Sunny D on busy days when we needed a lot of energy.

The asparagus drug I mentioned previously is not a pill, it is actually chemotherapy. The full name, "E.coli-Asparaginase Cytarabine" is quite intimidating (E.coli, seriously?) so you can imagine why I was a little nervous. I showered and put on a pair of jeans rather than sweats because I didn't want to show this big bad asparagus drug any signs of weakness. The catch, this one is administered "intramuscularly." A shot, well, four shots actually, two in each thigh. "Luckily" they were able to have two different nurses come in and shoot me up at the same time, so I only had to get two sets of two shots simultaneously, instead of four successive pokes. My wife said the only other time she's seen me that nervous was the day I proposed to her!

Those tight jeans got me in an emo mood. One cool thing about being isolated on a cancer wing is that I have all the time with my guitar. Some of the nurses and neighbors seem to like it too—no complaints yet. I even had one nurse comment on how she can't believe that I can just sit there and jam and carry on a conversation at the same time. She says she has played piano for over twenty years, but has never been able to do that. For me, it's therapeutic.

There was a tragedy one night though. The bridge on my beloved Ovation ripped from the body of the guitar! It was perched nicely on the guitar stand and the sterile air must have filtered away at the tightly woven strings. The broken wood was enough to make the toughest nurse cry at the sight. I didn't notice until morning and was utterly devastated. I am next to certain it is due to the arid lack of humidity in these hospital rooms. I hooked her up to Pappa Willie and tried to resuscitate her back to health, but I think my cancer diagnosis was just too much; she needed a break from all the drama. Fact: sodium chloride doesn't fix a broken guitar bridge. Don't "fret" however; I have another guitar from home and I am not without. Plus Carlos, my other guitar, is happy to be getting some attention. My Ovation LX has bogarted the stage for years now. To prevent a future casualty I am down-tuning the strings at night and using a guitar humidifier. So there is no cause for lamentation or discord, my music lives on!

I'm thinking of starting a new genre, "Chemo Emo." Instead of dying your hair black, and wearing skinny jeans, you shave your head and wear sweatpants. Instead of shouting shrill obscenities about the girl that makes your blood boil, you hum peaceful melodies about the

treatment that is making your blood normal. And finally, you don't try to imitate The Cure, you find the cure and you embrace it!

Another thing I have learned to embrace is a new set of vocabulary. Cancer gives you the opportunity to learn a bunch of interesting words and acronyms. Here are a few that have joined my repertoire.

LP

Those of you old enough to know what a vinyl record is may be under the assumption that an "LP" is a "Long Playing Microgroove Disc"—and that's what I used to think; but up here on East 8—that's what the cool people call our wing—LP stands for "Lumbar Puncture."

There is a similarity: they both involve a needle. The difference is that one reads music off a disc and the other goes into your spine. The other name for an LP is "Spinal Tap," which again to avoid misinterpretation, is not just a cheesy 80's mockumentary about heavy metal bands that came out the year I was born in 1984, but a procedure to retrieve/inject fluid from/into your spinal column. Initially, the LP didn't show any signs of cancer in my spine. Later on, as you know, blasts were found in my spinal fluid. Somehow they blasted their way through the barrier.

Hemonc

This is a fun one. I had to keep from laughing at the first doctor that I saw with "HEMONC" on their name badge. To me, it sounds like something I would call my little brother to tease him. We had a secret word that would stop us from talking all night when we shared a room as kids, "honkshoe." No one could make a peep after any of my brothers said it. Hemonc actually stands for Hematology/Oncology.

Hematology is the study of blood diseases and oncology is the study of cancer. The Hemonc is the doctor that gave me my diagnosis. This brings me to my next term . . .

Diagnosis vs Prognosis

I've always understood pretty well what a diagnosis is. In fact, my friends at work know that one of my favorite maxims is "diagnose before you prescribe." This is my way of reminding myself that every situation is unique and that it can be foolish to jump to a solution before you've really done your homework.

The term I kept hearing that I wasn't familiar with was "prognosis." A prognosis is more than just knowing what's wrong with you; it's forecasting the outcome of the disease and your chances for recovery. Ironically, I was flipping channels the night before I was diagnosed and saw the preview for the drama movie *50/50* about a young man who is diagnosed with cancer and has a 50/50 chance of surviving. I remember thinking, "That looks pretty cool. I think I'd like to see that." Little did I know that I would get to star in the main role . . .

Now for some details about my diagnosis/prognosis: the type of leukemia I have is very rare, especially in adults. According to the Leukemia and Lymphoma Society it is most commonly found in children one to four years old (7.8 out of 100,000 or less than 1/100th of a percent). In adults between twenty-five and twenty-nine the number drops to 0.7 out of 100,000, which means that the chance of me developing this cancer was less than 1/1000th of a percent, and all this time I could have been working my odds in Vegas!

Although there is no concrete data on recovery rates, my handy pamphlet from the Leukemia and Lymphoma Society informs me that children between one and fifteen years of age had a 3 percent chance of surviving in 1964. From 1975 to 1977 the cure rate increased to 58 percent and the most recent study done between 1999 and 2006 showed an 89 percent recovery rate.

I would ask you to be mindful of a few things when considering my prognosis. First, contrary to how I often behave, I am not under

fifteen years of age and adults don't have as high of a recovery rate as children.

Second, I have participated in several clinical trials: stronger chemotherapy regimens by the Dana-Farber Cancer Institute, biotherapy by MD Anderson, and finally T-cell therapy at the Hospital University of Pennsylvania. The purpose of the studies are to test the safety and effectiveness of certain cancer treatments that are similar to those being used to cure children, to test the effectiveness of a biotherapy that goes after a certain marker on my cancer cells instead of all fast-growing cells like chemotherapy, and to use my own immune system to go after markers on the cancer cells.

Third, and most importantly, the Lord is in charge of this whole thing. It is His will and His plan. You don't have to worry about some guessing game at 60 percent or 70 percent, trust in the divine prognosis.

Lymphoblastic

Far from fantastic, my "lymphoblastic" blood cells reproduce rapidly and out of control. They don't work properly because they are mutated. Your bloodstream then gets inundated with dysfunctional scrap and your healthy blood cells diminish.

Think of it like a football team that falls victim to a crappy recruiter. In my case, the recruiter is a chromosome mutation known as hyperdiploidy. For the first little while everything seems to be fine, but as Recruiter Diploidy brings on more immature and dysfunctional players the team struggles. Pretty soon they can't even get a first down without tripping over their own linemen.

Denial

During my cancer crusade, I have become familiar with 3 phases of denial:

1. Denial is a river in Egypt. In this phase of denial, you deny you're in denial by making jokes to change the subject.
2. "I don't have cancer." This is outright denial. You'll come up with any excuse to dodge reality: this is all a dream, the doctors are wrong, cancer is for mature people, I feel fine, or this is a practical joke.
3. "Cancer's not *that* bad." This is more on the acceptance side. You've taken the pills, you've watched your blood counts closely monitored, and friends and visitors have come with well wishes. At this point your mindset is: Cancer—no big deal, everybody gets cancer if they live long enough; cancer-schmancer!

Reduced Microbial Diet

I'm on a reduced microbial diet. Sounds pretty serious, right? The only thing the nurse can tell me is to stay away from grapes. I ask another nurse and she elaborates a bit on how grapes can grow a certain bacteria that isn't always washed off because they are in clusters. Other than that the suggestions are to avoid fast food (of course) and anything that has been sitting out (naturally). So in a nutshell, they use eight syllables to say what they could in two—no grapes.

*****

GRAPES AND TANNING DON'T CURE CANCER, BUT GRANDMA'S HOMEGROWN PEACHES MIGHT

I would like to personally thank everyone who approached me and said, "Wow, you look awful. Are you feeling alright?" To be honest, at the time, I wanted to punch you in the mouth, but in the end, it was your cruel honesty that helped coax me into a doctor's office. Ask my Mom, this is no easy feat.

What does this have to do with tanning you may ask? Well, I was feeling pretty self-conscious about all the "you look really pale" comments, so I visited the tanning salon to try to fix the problem.

Twelve minutes in the super-ruva-tano-magic and slicked up with tanning lotion, and I still looked like the albino in that weird *Powder* movie that came out in the nineties. The lady at the salon said it could take a couple of days for the tan to sink in, but when I started peeling white off of white I knew the endeavor was a failure.

The bottom line is tanning doesn't cure anemia, or cancer for that matter. In fact, I'm pretty sure it causes it.

On the flip side, I sneaked down the hall, pulled out the jar of Grandma Joyce's homegrown peaches I'd been saving in the fridge, and tiptoed back to my hospital room for some quiet indulgence.

I didn't feel much better after twelve minutes of tanning, but I swear I felt more than back to normal after twelve minutes of Grandma's peaches.

Grandma Joyce by Daryl Hunt. 100 percent GRATEFUL for her canned peaches.

LUMBAR LAUGHTER

A few phrases doctors and nurses should be trained not to say:

1. "Hmmm . . . I've never seen anything like this before."
2. "Whoops."
3. "Wow, that's bad."

I had a triple header scheduled: a lumbar puncture aka a spinal tap, followed by some intravenous chemo treatment, and then a bone marrow biopsy to top things off. I did my best to eat a big breakfast before they whisked me off to "Angio."

Angio is short for Angiography—a medical imaging technology in which they use an x-ray-type machine to get a better view of my central nervous system during the spinal tap procedure. The first thing that I noticed about the room, other than that they keep it as cold as a refrigerator, was that they had some great music playing. I inquired as to the source of the tasteful playlist and was surprised to find that they rock Pandora in Angio.

As things turned out they hadn't prepared my chemo drugs in the lab yet so I had about twenty minutes to "chill." Don't worry, they brought me a warm blanket. Rather than sit and think about the giant needle that they were about to stick in my back, I decided to pretend that I was getting a spa treatment like acupuncture or something. I put my head back and relaxed to the smooth sounds of *James Taylor and Eric Clapton: The Unplugged Album* and really began to enjoy myself.

During this and other procedures, I don't really like to think about what's actually going on, so I try to make small talk with the doctors and nurses. As the physician assistant is poking and injecting, a song from Norah Jones comes on. I start chattering, "You know the thing

about Norah Jones; she is an amazing musician and songwriter—love her voice, but she is plain boring to watch . . . " Yada yada yada and before you know it we're on the last of three injections and what song comes on but Loggins and Messina's "Danny's Song." about love being more important than money.

My wife's father and uncles sang this song at our wedding reception and it always brings back good memories. AJ has been here at the hospital with me nearly every night and truly does bring tears of joy to my eyes each morning.

After a lumbar puncture—spinal tap, LP, whatever you want to call it—they require that you lay flat on your back for at least one hour. Apparently, if you don't, you're prone to get a nasty headache. So I'm in "recovery"—a nifty curtained room, and I'm staring up counting ceiling tiles when all a sudden my tailbone starts spazzing out. Not sharp pains, but electric tickling spasms. So the nurse comes in to examine my back and I am just giggling like a schoolgirl. She asks the standard questions:

"Any numbness or tingling?"

"Shortness of breath?"

"Pain in your chest?"

"Sharp shooting pain down either of your legs?"

No, no, no, no, I reply— just tickling spasms at the base of my spine! So she starts poking around and checking for swelling. As soon as she hits the spot I'm hooting and hollering and giggling unbearably. My wife is watching in complete surprise and the nurse says the magic words, "Hmmm . . . I've never seen anything like this before."

So what's the game plan? The nurse looks into it and says that the PA that did my LP is doing another procedure. She says that she'll have him come to check on me when he's finished. I go back to counting ceiling tiles and I figure out that if I hold completely still that the spasms will subside. The problem is (and those who know me know this) I can't hold still! Even when I try, the moment my foot twitches, or I get an itch and move my leg—zzzzzzzzz! Spasm, laugh, spasm, moan, spasm, ahhhhh, okay, okay, just hold still . . .

Well, this goes on for about twenty minutes before all the lower abdominal constriction leads to another problem . . . I gotta pee! It's not just casual, "Oh, I think I have to tinkle" either, we're talking about serious pain and discomfort. You should know that I received two units of platelets that morning, which is basically like drinking a two-liter.

This is where it gets really interesting—I can't sit upright, so the nurse tells me I have two options: try to use a handheld urinal while laying on my back, or have her insert a catheter. I'm not about to let her insert anything so . . .

It takes some serious and intense concentration while my wife holds the urinal, but I finally succeed. After this accomplishment, you might be tempted to think that my awkward back spasms stop, but they don't. I keep whooping and giggling and even AJ has to laugh because I am not a ticklish person.

The whole situation is pretty silly, albeit uncomfortable, and to make matters worse, it only takes about twenty minutes and my bladder is complaining again! After another gravity-defying urination, the PA finally shows up. He goes down the list of questions: numbness, tingling, sharp pains, yada yada yada . . . No, no, no—just laughing till I'm about to pee my pants. To which he replies, "Hmmm . . . I've never seen anything like this before."

After my mandatory hour of staring at the ceiling, they agree to let me go back to my room. The PA says he will check on me in an hour or two to see if the spasms persist. He says his best guess is that the needle hit a nerve and that is causing the discomfort. Funny thing

is that when I get back to my room and stand up, the spasms and giggling stop.

I have to consider myself lucky. If the doctors are worried about numbness and pain, and all I have to do is endure some tickle torture—I figure I got it pretty good.

BYOB—BRING YOUR OWN BONE MARROW

My cytogenetics test evaluates how the cancer corresponds to my chromosomes. I need to be clear here, this does not have to do with my "family tree" type of genetics. I didn't get my cancer from my parents, nor can I give it to my children. This test looks at the mutations in my chromosomes that triggered cancer. Initially, we believed that my cancer was due to extra copies in mutated versions of my ninth chromosome (hyperdiploidy).

However, the experts did an extensive analysis—my bone marrow wasn't very cooperative and found that my cancer is more complicated than we initially anticipated. My ninth chromosome is not the only one undergoing mutations. It turns out I have a rare variation of acute lymphoblastic leukemia. We find that my eleventh chromosome, and possibly others, are also mutating in a process called chromosomal translocation. This abnormality shows up in less than ten percent of people diagnosed with ALL and is most common in infants less than one-year-old. What can I say? I like to be exceptional!

In short, I'm a mutant, and yes, in a twisted way this has always been a secret dream of mine. It started when I used to play Teenage Mutant Ninja Turtles with my brother Conrad. Even though I liked Raphael more (he's cool but rude)—I was always stuck being Michelangelo (he's a party dude) because I was younger and smaller, and pretty much had to do what I was told. It was okay though because

Michelangelo had nunchucks which are way more entertaining than the little daggers that Raphael had to fight with.

Go ahead and turn on the "Teenage Mutant Ninja Turtles Theme Song" while reading this next part.

For clarification, this doesn't mean that my parents are cousins or anything like that. Though they are second cousins once removed. The lineage referenced is in regard to this type of cancer. As you may have already surmised, I have a less favorable prognosis than my initial diagnosis. In layman's terms, it's a worse kind of cancer. The reality, however, is that it is so rare that any data we look at is not statistically significant. For this reason, my wife has begun to call me a "scientific pioneer." I figure that's better than a couch potato.

I'm just waiting for my "mutations" to give me some kind of superpower. I've already got some numbness in my fingertips (a combo of chemo and guitar), so I am hoping for some wolverine claws or something like that.

I search the web for good-looking bald guys . . . Billy Corgan of the Smashing Pumpkins? Mr. Clean?

Now, as far as I know, neither of them has cancer. Their baldness is for other reasons, but I must say that they both sport it quite handsomely.

The former Pumpkins frontman said, "I didn't find Jesus. He's been there the whole time." I can relate to Billy hollering, "Despite all my rage I am still just a rat in a cage!"

SO FRESH AND SO CLEAN CLEAN

My wife and son catch Respiratory Syncytial Virus also known as RSV. Even though she feels miserable, AJ does a great job taking care of our son while I try to avoid the germs. I don't feel sick, but they test me at my clinical appointment and sure enough, I have it too.

What is RSV? For adults with normal immune systems, it's not much more than a cold. For infants, it can be more serious, and for bone marrow transplant patients it can be fatal. I have to go to the hospital right away when they call with my results.

My treatment lasts for five days. I inhale the drug Ribavirin in two-hour intervals at 6:00 a.m., 2:00 p.m., and 10:00 p.m. Before I inhale the Ribavirin I get to "puff the peace pipe," an apparatus called a nebulizer that I use to take Albuterol. This drug opens up my bronchioles so I don't have any coughing spasms from the Ribavirin.

Ribavirin works at an intracellular level. It disturbs the DNA of the virus and prevents it from multiplying. They aren't entirely sure how it works, they just know that it does. It has some dangerous side effects like chemo, so the nurses have to dress up like there has been a hazardous chemical spill when they administer it.

It also clings to my skin and clothes, so I have to go into a separate isolation room for the treatment. After two hours of breathing the funky stuff, I have to take a shower and change into fresh clothes. Only then can I go back to my room. That's three showers a day! I'm super clean! The epitome of Mr. Clean.

It's Halloween in Room 7007 on the East Coast. My wife is dressed as the tattooed Mormon and, of course, I am MR. CLEAN! Bald, shiny head, white, crisp shirt, a golden hoop my wife found downstairs in the hospital shop and she even uses her white eyeliner on my furrowed brows. I haven't lost those or my mustache to chemotherapy yet. We are pretty creative for yet another hospital holiday. Dressed as Mr. Clean, I "will clean your whole house and everyone will be singing" is a great persona. He knows how to make living fun—even the hard stuff like cleaning is a joy.

Every year I fine-tune my joy by writing myself a letter to reflect on and review the prior year. This is similar to James Clear's account in *Atomic Habits* where I ask myself several questions and then answer them the next year.[28] Some of my past questions include: Are you thankful? Are you charitable? Are you becoming the man you want to be? Are you still writing music? What has taken priority over eternity?[29]

Heart Jolt 4:

AT THE BEGINNING OF EVERY YEAR, SIT DOWN AND WRITE YOURSELF A LETTER INSTEAD OF MAKING RESOLUTIONS. DO NOT READ THIS LETTER UNTIL THE FIRST DAY OF JANUARY THE FOLLOWING YEAR. IT IS A GREAT EXERCISE TO HELP TAKE A PERSONAL INVENTORY AND BE HONEST WITH YOURSELF OF WHAT NEEDS IMPROVEMENT. DAYS BEFORE MY DIAGNOSIS I WROTE, "HAVE A POSITIVE ATTITUDE. BELIEVE IN YOURSELF AND THOSE AROUND YOU. FACE CHALLENGES WITH COURAGE." HOW FITTING THIS ADVICE WAS FOR WHAT I WAS ABOUT TO UNDERTAKE. I THEN TRANSCRIBED THE FOLLOWING QUOTATIONS IN MY LETTER:

"HE DOES NOT BELIEVE THAT DOES NOT LIVE ACCORDING TO HIS BELIEF." – THOMAS FULLER

BE PATIENT WITH YOURSELF AND AVOID PERFECTIONISM. PERFECTION WON'T BE ATTAINED IN THIS LIFE, BUT IN THE NEXT. DON'T BE UNREASONABLE, BUT DEMAND OF YOURSELF IMPROVEMENT. LET YOUR HIGHER POWER AND OTHERS HELP YOU AND THAT WILL MAKE ALL THE DIFFERENCE.

IF THIS ADVICE WAS GOOD ENOUGH FOR LAST YEAR, I'M SURE IT'S GOOD ENOUGH FOR THIS YEAR. DO THIS EVERY YEAR AND YOU WILL TRANSFORM YOURSELF INTO THE VERSION OF YOURSELF THAT IS PURER EVERY YEAR. EVEN WITHOUT THREE SHOWERS A DAY!

*****

I am running a fever, so I stop by the clinic. After some blood work, a chest x-ray, and this really fun procedure where they stick a suction tube up your nose, I am "nadiring." Nadir is an Arabic word that means "opposite." In astronomy, the nadir is the opposite of the zenith, and can also be used to describe the lowest point of a star or planet's orbit.

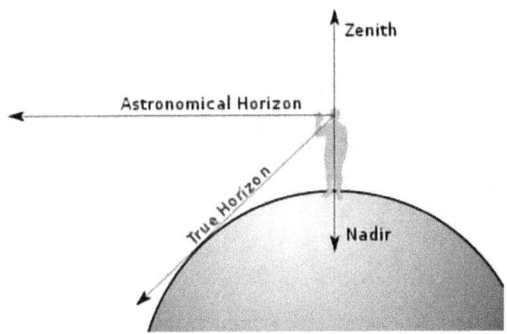

A cancer patient reaches their "nadir" when their blood counts hit rock bottom. Thus "nadiring" describes that your blood counts are spiraling, and spiraling they are. When I come in, my platelets are at a 10, which is super low when you're used to seeing counts in the 300 range. My neutrophils or my "fighter cells" that attack bacteria and infection are at zero. Finally, my overall count, or my hematocrit, has dropped from 33 percent down to 26 percent. If I drop below 24 percent they give me a blood transfusion. I am admitted and given a platelet transfusion right away.

It is a pretty lonely afternoon—my TV isn't working, my cell phone battery dies, and I have only brought one book. My nurse brings me a new packet the hospital has put together and I read through every pamphlet. Things get interesting when I look in the mirror in the

bathroom. My nose and forehead are red and puffy. As I wash my hands I notice the rash is running up my forearms and then I lift up my shirt and, yup, nasty itchy rash all across my torso too.

I page the nurses' station, "I'm getting a little rashy in here." My nurse brings in some IV Benadryl, and let me tell you that the liquid stuff hits your head quickly. As I'm starting to feel tired and a bit dizzy, the nurse gets up to leave and says, "Just let me know if you have trouble breathing." I hear myself say, "Okay."

Okay!? What? Not okay, how am I supposed to call you if I can't breathe! I spend the next sixty minutes forcing myself to stay awake so I don't fall asleep and stop breathing— I start to think that "paranoia" is a possible side effect of Benadryl. Needless to say, the rash clears up within an hour, and I feel much better when my beautiful wife arrives with a bag of things for me.

The nadiring continues. It may have been all the cheering and fist-pumping during a certain basketball game, but my hematocrit drops to 23.3. I received two blood transfusions and with each one— more hives. We're not sure why I'm not reacting well to the transfusions, but moving forward they will give me Benadryl prior to each one.

My nasal culture reveals I have type B influenza, thus the fevers and feeling awful for the past week. The trouble is you can't really beat the flu when you don't have any fighters or neutrophils. The good news is that they have specific antibiotics that I am now taking that will fight for me.

*****

It's Another Boy!

Well, not really . . . I just received an ultrasound picture of my heart. It looks a lot like the one we received when we first saw our little baby boy in an ultrasound picture. A cardiologist took an ultrasound picture in order to measure my heart's volume and pumping capacity. Did you know that your heart beats approximately 100,000 times in one day? That's 35 million times a year!

The ultrasound machine displays red or blue to indicate which direction your blood is flowing. This helps determine whether or not the heart's valves are functioning properly—I'm happy to report that mine are. However, the technician does tell me I am "lungy" because my lungs keep getting in the way, so I start holding my breath. It definitely helps keep my lungs off the screen, but I keep wondering if the lack of oxygen will hinder my heart's performance.

A respiratory exam shows that I'm great at "inspiring." It's not what you think, though; it just means that I can take in a lot of air. I'm also pretty good at "expiring," which means breathing out. For this exam, I get to sit in what can only be described as a glorified phone booth. It doesn't look like much, but this transparent confessional goes for forty thousand bucks! I don't know about you, but unless it can travel through time and take me on an excellent adventure, I think I'll go with the Corvette.

After some puff-puff-give in the respiratory machine to measure my lungs' capacities, comes a blood draw. My neutrophils are coming back—yes! I'm at 1.0 now when a normal is 1.8. A mucus sample is taken to see if I still have the flu. In the past, they've inserted a suction tube up my nose to get a sample. But today I have to try not to laugh when a guy comes in with a sample cup and asks, "You ever done Farmer Joe Blow?"

I almost rebut, "I believe the politically correct term is Snot Rocket." Instead, I kind of chuckle, plug one nostril and give it my best shot. I hand him the cup and ask, "Will that work?"

Excitedly, he responds, "Oh, ya, that's perfect!" Wow, I haven't seen anybody that enthusiastic about mucus since Egon scraped some samples from the New York Public Library in *Ghostbusters*.

***

The woman in the waiting room across from me thumbs through some beads on a rosary necklace. She makes the sign of the cross and then kisses a pendant that's hanging from her neck. She nervously rocks back and forth. I return to my reading.

"Marshall!" calls a slender, young man in navy blue scrubs with dark, wavy hair. The woman is kissing a card now that she holds in her hands and saying a silent prayer. The man leads me to a large room with tile floors and a caution sign on the door, "radioactive materials." The man pulls back a curtain and asks me my date of birth. He explains the procedure, the purpose is to make sure my left ventricle is healthy and working correctly. The left ventricle pumps blood from the heart to the rest of the body. First, he is going to inject me with a phosphorus solution. We then wait for twenty minutes to let it circulate through my bloodstream. After that, he will inject the radioactive solution that facilitates the imaging device. We wait another ten minutes and then I go to another room for my "photo shoot." My joke will be, "Does this radioactive solution make me look fat?"

The marathon was topped off with a spinal tap—yay! It went pretty well with no tickle fits, but my back is a little more sore than usual. After seven hours at the hospital, AJ and I can't wait to get home and see our boy who is really starting to get confident on his feet, chubby in the cheeks, and often sports Thomas the Train Engine PJs.

*****

FENTANYL FUN . . .

Allow me to go into detail for the next few chapters about my t-cell therapy and treatments. My timeline gets skewed as I go back to the past and into the future thinking of all the times I've spent in and out of hospitals in different cities. Leukemia blasts were taking over my body and inflaming the bones in my ribs, back, joints, and connecting tissue, making the pain overwhelming. The blasts caused pleurisy, irritating the lining of the lungs, so the lubricant that is usually between the lungs and body linings dries up. It hurts to breathe. Pain medications are administered around the clock and still, there is no break. It hurts so badly to stand and breathe because of the pressure it puts on bones and joints where the blasts are taking over. The leukemia is so packed in the marrow that they could not get any bone marrow when a biopsy was attempted, so I'm dominating the requirement of at least five percent blasts in my marrow for the Pennsylvania study. My spinal fluid is clean! Another requirement check for another study.

The PICC line that has pumped poison, blood, platelets, and medications through my chest for so many years is now in my arm. I beg them to put it in the left so I can still strum the guitar with my right arm, and they allow it and allow me to watch the whole surgery. Getting pumped full of blood and platelets is literally a gift of life every time as my own body won't survive without this—thank you blood and platelet donors.

I am super doped up on drugs and my wife records funny things I say. After the bone marrow biopsy, I guess I look at the cute little lab worker and say, "Have I ever told you that I just love your big, beautiful smile." She looks at me like a deer in headlights. Then I say, "My wife and I have been discussing eternity and I wonder what you think happens after we die?"

Imagine all these sentences slow and drawn out as the technician looks on, "Did he really just ask me this . . . ?" I immediately fell asleep after asking the loaded question. Our cute lab worker is stuck in the room organizing the various blood slides and cores to take to the lab for further examination. She explains her thoughts on reincarnation to my wife as I sleep. She feels that we will go somewhere, but is not sure where. And that if someone in this life is really nice to you even if you are rude over and over, they probably owed it to you from a previous life when you were nice to them in a similar way.

The nurse is gathering chemotherapy bags in the room later and suddenly I awake and say, "We can't leave our nurse, he's making us cheeseburgers."

The nurse gets a puzzled look on his face like, "Where did that come from?"

Later my wife tells me I was lying there half asleep telling her how I was used as a slide for all the children as they were getting off the airplane at the airport and many other absurd things.

*****

DOUBLE YOUR FUN . . .

The headache greets me promptly in the morning. After some maximum-strength headache medication, my oncology team is inspecting my lingering hives. Following a great deal of speculation, they scheduled me to meet with the dermatologist who put my mind at ease when he explained that it is not uncommon for hives to persist for several weeks.

To complicate matters I begin to have bouts of double vision. They increase in duration throughout the week and I feel like I am living in a double mint gum commercial. We meet with an ophthalmologist in the eye emergency department. After extensive examinations, hours in waiting rooms, and an MRI, surprise, surprise . . . they have no idea what is causing my ailment. Apparently, causes of double vision are almost as difficult to decipher as the cause of hives!

Things grow even more exciting at 3 a.m. when I awake in my hotel room with a headache feeling like I've been smacked in the back of the head with a two-by-four. I looked in the mirror and realized that I can't move the right side of my face. The fun part is that I get my first ride in an ambulance, although I must say it's probably more exciting in the driver's seat where you can see all the traffic move aside as you cruise through red lights.

I'm at the hospital squinting with one eye closed; otherwise I have two cheeseburgers. There are a couple of good things about double vision: one, you have twice as many friends come to visit you in the hospital, and two, when you open up your wallet you have double the cash! Medical experts still are unsure if it is leukemia or something else causing facial paralysis. Mostly because some of the movement came back after a blessing from above. Doctors say if it is leukemia, that won't happen.

*****

I've been in the city of brotherly love long enough to pick up some of the local accents. I thought I would share this tutorial with anyone who is interested in speaking the Philadelphian language. How to speak like a Philadelphian:

Replace the hard "a" vowel sound as in ant with "ee-a"

Examples:

Ya = Yee-A

Cat = Kyat

Pants = Pyants

Precede the soft "a" sound as in awesome or drop with a short "oo" sound. The "oo" and "ah" should only take up one syllable. Shape your mouth like you're going to say "oo" and then open up to the "ah" sound.

Examples:

Water = Woo-ah-der

Bought = Boo-aht

Audio = "oo-Ah-dio

The vowel sound in words that end in "or" such as "floor" should also be pronounced this way but only open up halfway to more of an "uh" sound.

Examples:

Door = Doo-uh

Fort = Foo-uht

Board = Boo-uhd

Finally, talk (t'oo'ahk) about your local sports (sp'oo'uhts) team with resentment, and then cheer for them like you can't (kyant) remember how many times they've let you down.

It's pure doctrine in our household that laughter is the best form of medicine! Watching *Seinfeldt*, *Big Bang Theory* and *JK Studios* are pretty much forms of worship for us these days.

I am a jokester on bad days. I turn to laughter when I've been isolated in my hospital room for weeks with no neutrophils. Chemotherapy does that to you.

Sometimes one of my battle weapons is goofiness. One morning, I woke up giggling because I have this silly idea. While my wife is sleeping on the plastic orange hospital cot, I slip on my sneakers and sneak into the hall. I have queued up "Eye of the Tiger" on my iPhone and I turn the volume all the way up. Just before I pass the nurse's station I hit play . . . Bada-bada-bada-bada-bada-bada-bada-bada—Dunt . . . dunt, dunt, dunt . . . dunt, dunt, dunt . . . dunt, dunt, dunnnnnn! As I'm sauntering by I start throwing air punches to the beat; dunt . . . dunt, dunt, dunt . . . I keep the music playing as I walk my laps for the morning, and I'm pretty sure everybody that gets a glimpse of my antics has a good laugh.

The shenanigans didn't stop there. The woman that cleans my hospital room is bilingual. I tell her I am going to play a song on my guitar for her. To be honest, I'm not sure what I am going to play, so I take the easy route–The Blues. I summoned what Spanish I can remember and sing:

No hablo espanol, Pero yo trato

No hablo espanol, Pero yo trato

Gracias por limpiar mi cuarto

It must have gone over pretty well because she has a huge grin on her face when she leaves.

Heart Jolt 5:

DOUBLE YOUR FUN PLANS TODAY! DO SOMETHING THAT MAKES YOU LAUGH AND GETS HAPPY ENDORPHINS GOING IN YOUR SYSTEM. WRITE THE JOYFUL MOMENT YOU INTENTION- ALLY PLAN INSIDE YOUR DIGITAL OR PAPER CALENDAR SO YOU ACTUALLY PRIORITIZE AND MAKE THE TIME FOR FUN AND LAUGHTER EVERY DAY.

With every beat of laughter, more of my heartbeats are turning into pure gold. I learn to laugh even when I can't move my face, and I turn my common, dusty heartbeats to beats of gold.

Beat 5

BEATS OF GOLD

MARSHALING HEARTBEATS REQUIRES TURNING DUST TO GOLD.
BE WILLING TO SIFT THROUGH ALL THE DUST TO GET TO THE GOLD. THIS IS THE ART OF ALCHEMY.

One cab driver named Fassil transports me to the hospital with a golden gift of no charge after hearing my story. Although 'facil' means easy in Spanish, and he certainly makes things easy for me today, I find out it means king in Ethiopia where he is from. He proves to be striving to be like the king of kings when he gives me his personal cell phone number and offers to give me a ride free of charge anytime I need one. What a golden guy worthy of a golden crown.

I take my customary shower for the day and decide to wear my *Newsies* cap. Rather than go with my customary New York accent

though, my work friends know that one well, I decide to try some Irish instead. There are many random reasons for this.

First, early in my hospital stay my Grandpa told me all about my Irish ancestor Stillman Pond. My son's middle name is Pond just like my Grandpa. Second, my brother sent me a Louis L'amour novel titled *The Iron Marshal* and it just so happens that the main character is an Irish immigrant who finds himself out west. Third, the woman across the hall with AML—acute myeloblastic leukemia (it's like my cancer but with red blood cells instead of white) has Irish ancestry and a sweet daughter who is an amazing bagpipe player and teacher.

So I'm quoting silly stuff from that movie *Far and Away* with Tom Cruise and Nicole Kidman, "Tell me yuh like me hat, Shannon. Why can't yuh tell me yuh like me hat?" The nurses laugh, but I have a hankering suspicion that they are just trying to be nice because it's their job to help people feel better.

I know I'm running out of material when I start quoting Irish Spring commercials and Lucky Charms slogans. It occurs to me that I don't know what a real Irish accent sounds like, and it is a good thing that no real Irishman is around to clean my clock trying to fake it— I've heard about the "fighting Irish."

I must have subconsciously known that it was my last night in the hospital because as the day drew to a close I had the urge to invite anyone who would listen to me come to my room for what will now be referred to as my farewell concert.

I dedicate this song to my neighbor with AML, the bagpipe player's mom because she was having a rough week. I wish you could meet this woman though, she is just a ball of fun with a smile so broad that it can hardly balance on her face.

Remember when I listened and was inspired by Enya's version of the song "How Can I Keep from Singing?" Ironically, Enya is also

Irish. Well, I had to write my own version, or should I say, "me own vareshun" and sang it to the nurses. Ask yourself, how can you keep your heart singing today?

As the luck o' the Irish would have it, every January 11th my wife celebrates her very own unofficial holiday of Day O' Wishes Come True. If you know how much it costs or what to do exactly to make it official, please let me know.

Some of my wife's wishes have come true:

1. She has a child. A handsome, healthy son with his mom's button nose, cute little toesies, and strong hands. He gets those hands from his dad's side, but neither of his parents has them. He has been talking more and more and we are enjoying this stage and he loves snow. She has a reason to adopt or be involved with in vitro fertilization with my sterile fertility status post-radiation. She even donated eggs to a wonderful family. Our hearts are hopeful and they succeed in having some beautiful children of their own—twins! A boy and a girl.

2. Finding a cure for cancer is our daily life. One beautiful spring morning, we trekked miles and miles through the dust to finally arrive at the top of a hill decorated with golden flags for cancer survivors. My name was written boldly on one of those golden flags and I even sang a few songs on my guitar for the survivors' event.

3. She has a wish of helping people internationally. It's coming true through her job at the Global Service Center by helping people in Brazil.

4. When my wife was twelve, she sewed a baby outfit catastrophically ending with two different lengths of arms. She threw her arms in the air and said she wasn't a crafter. I bought her a sewing machine and after all these years of labeling herself, she

has been working well with her hands, sewing a mohawk hat, cute ribbons, and curtains. She's also been making the most nutritious meals.

The sunrise can't be sold
Nor can a price be placed
Upon her beauty
Yet both do I behold
Each steals my breath
I'm rewarded still, their
Subtle mysteries reveal
A story heard
But left untold
Beauty cannot speak
Nor can sunlight proclaim
Its radiance
Yet both do shine upon me
Communicating to my soul
A warmth and love
That makes me whole
But how could one as I inspire
The fairest loving, glowing fire
My heart sings to wonder
As an ever curious choir

(by Marshall Jensen)

We allocate drops of awesome to a small box that sits in our family room reminding us of the amazing things people do for us and the amazing happenings throughout our days, even on the bad and "nothing special" days. My wish is that every year our family can look back at the drops of awesomeness and remember how awesome the world is if we concentrate on the daily droplets instead of labeling the rain negatively. The Qur'an warns against the use of [gold] outside the frame of charity and righteous transactions.[30] Marshalling, or leading your life experience, teaches you that you can see goodness in everything, "It isn't what you have or what you are doing that makes you happy or unhappy. It is what you think about."[31] There are so many good people in the world who teach us how much goodness there still is even when it looks bleak.

One of these drops of awesome happened in a private waiting room when I spoke with a woman while waiting for my chest X-ray. She asked if the Y on my ball cap stood for Yale. She was a Yale graduate who studied biology. I explained to her it stood for BYU where my wife AJ attended college and was also a biology graduate. AJ attended a few biology classes at Harvard University. She walked into the Arnold Arboretum of Harvard University and sat down. Soon she realized on a whim, the class was detailing human egg donation. She was captured and didn't realize at the time that she would later be more involved in egg donation than she ever imagined. After I spoke to the woman in the waiting room about our situation, she asked if I wouldn't mind if she gave me a donation. I told her I wouldn't and she rummaged through her purse and handed me a hundred-dollar bill. I was almost speechless. I managed to mumble, "Thank you very much! I didn't even get your name." She said, "It's not important" and left. What a golden girl.

*****

151

MY GOLDEN BIRTHDAY

Your golden birthday is the birthday when you turn the same age number-wise as your birth date. My wife tells a fantastic story about her twenty-third birthday—her golden birthday. She visited a church in Brazil that was completely made of gold. Her golden birthday was spent gazing at lavish golden walls, tapestries spun of gold, glitz, and glam. She was free to gaze at gold, in awe, and also a bit stunned that a church like that existed while the majority of the people she spent time with everyday lived in poverty. Well, it just so happens that my golden birthday, thirty on August 30th, is in a hospital. My walls are sterile, my dark red curtains match the color of blood, and my day will be simple and full of gratitude that I am here. I am caged, but I am alive while many of the friends I have made along this cancer journey are not here anymore. While many individuals dread their thirtieth revolution around the sun, I will be more than thrilled if I can live to the ripe young age of thirty! Allow me to explain . . .

Five weeks of chemo in my home state brought my cancer to a mere 6 percent! My blood counts were great, my weight was up, and my lungs sounded good—no more bronchitis. I tapered on and off of prednisone due to a bout of hives taking me to the emergency room. We waited for one week to ensure I was evading their return post-steroids. This meant I'd start chemo the second week of August, and receive my T-cell treatment the following week.

This put me right amidst a cytokine storm as I approached my thirtieth birthday. What's a cytokine storm? A cytokine storm, also known as hypercytokinemia, is a potentially fatal immune reaction consisting of a positive feedback loop between cytokines and immune cells. This immune reaction is not necessarily a bad thing, it basically means that my new "mighty mutant ninja T-cells incredibly hulked" on the "criminal leukemia" in my body. They were victorious in this epic battle of cellular superheroes and I got to celebrate my golden birthday! It was awesome. My brother flew in and surprised me, and my New York friend brought her ukulele friend with a golden singing voice. We had a jam session to end all jam sessions in the breakroom. The nurses on the floor told me it was the best day of work they'd had in twenty years. My wife even bought me a box drum to passionately beat along with the glorious jam session and told me how lucky she was to have me in her life.

This Golden Year
This year I'm gonna start from a new beginning
I found a life that'll be worth living
I found a dream that'll be worth chasing
And a love that'll be worth making

This year I'm gonna think about things a little different
Gonna make the word can't non-existent
I found a chance worth taking
And a love that'll be worth making

This year I'm gonna see from a new perspective
I found a voice that'll be effective
I found a song that'll be worth sharing
And a soul that'll be worth bearing

This year I'm gonna walk with my head held higher
I'll spread my love like a flame spreads fire

(by Marshall Jensen)

Heart Jolt 6:

MY RINGTONE IS STILL PLAYING, "THIS IS MY FIGHT SONG" BY RACHEL PLATTEN. THE LAST LYRICS OF THAT SONG RING INSIDE MY HEAD OFTEN, "I'VE STILL GOT A LOT OF FIGHT LEFT IN ME". FIND THAT CAUSE YOU ARE PASSIONATE ABOUT. IS IT CURING LEUKEMIA? IS IT SOMETHING ELSE? THERE ARE SO MANY BOXES LEFT THAT STILL NEED THE RIDDLE FIGURED OUT- WHAT BOX CAN YOU OPEN FOR SOMEONE ELSE? REMEMBER THE DREAM FROM BEAT ONE ABOUT OPENING UP OTHERS' BOXES? WRITE DOWN SOMETHING GOLDEN YOU CAN DO FOR SOMEONE ELSE THAT THEY CAN'T DO TODAY.

BUT IF NOT . . .

David Bednar came to our home and taught us, a young couple struggling through cancer treatments by asking the following two questions:

"Do you have the faith not to be healed? Or is your faith dependent on outcomes?"

I have pondered these teachings and questions frequently. If the Lord swooped in every time and saved you from disappointment, heartache, suffering, and sorrow your progress would be stifled. You would not learn. Maxwell says it is better "not to shrink than survive" and to not "become bitter from drinking the bitter cup."

I've come to the realization that faith is not about what you want and desire, it is about accepting what the Lord wants and that becoming your desire. But what about when you get asked to do something that really doesn't seem right for you? Do you question the Lord? Well you know Lord, I know you have a pretty good view from up there in heaven and everything, but I really think... or it'd be better if... One thing I've learned is that the "Lord is not concerned with our ability or inability, only our availability. If we prove our dependability, he will increase our capability" -Neal A. Maxwell. The ancient King Benjamin taught we must be, "submissive, meek, humble, patient, full of love [and] *willing to submit to all things which the Lord seeth fit to inflict upon [you]*."

Paul tells us, "I will glory in my infirmities . . . for my strength is made perfect in weakness . . . for when I am weak, then am I strong" -2 Corinthians 12. This scripture runs parallel with my cancer treatments. Not necessarily that I'm glorifying *in* my infirmities (I'm still working on that part), but that I physically have to be brought to a point of intense weakness in order to be made strong again.

This happens many times and on many levels throughout our lives. Great accomplishments are almost never the product of a single triumph, but of many acts of steady perseverance. The American icon and home run slugger Babe Ruth held the all-time home run record for fifty-two years with 714 home runs. The amazing number of home runs is what we remember about "The Sultan of Swat." What we don't often talk about is that he had 1330 strike-outs! That means that he would strike out nearly twice as many times as he'd hit a homer! "Every strike brings me closer to my next home run," said the Babe.

We often have to endure a great deal of failure, weakness, and disappointment in order to become strong and achieve great things. Every time my cancer comes back it just brings me closer to my next home run with an awesome team supporting me.

There's a simple song my mother taught me about this principle of perseverance. I put it to music the best I could remember and recorded it in my hospital room.

You're not judged by the number of times you fail
But by the number of times that you succeed
And the number of times that you succeed is in direct proportion
To the number of times you fail, so keep trying
Keep trying, keep trying, keep trying, keep trying
You will succeed if you keep trying
Keep trying, keep trying, keep trying, keep trying
You will succeed if you keep trying

I have a stuffed friend named Meshach because he is accompanying me in my "fiery furnace." In the third chapter of Daniel we learn about three Jewish leaders, Shadrach, Meshach, and Abed-Nego, who refused to worship a golden image as decreed by the King of Babylon. They were brought before the king by penalty of death in a fiery furnace if they would not forsake their God and worship his idol. This is how they responded:

"If it be so, our God whom we serve is able to deliver us from the burning fiery furnace, and he will deliver us out of thine hand, O king. But if not, be it known unto thee, O king, that we will not serve thy gods, nor worship the golden image which thou hast set up" -Daniel 3:17-18.

"But if not," are three powerful words that separate true faith from faith dependent on outcomes. If plans were made for these men in the spirit realm they would have been consumed by the furnace and died—they understood that and were willing to accept it.

The key to trials is how we respond. I know that the Lord is able to heal me from this awful cancer, but if not, be it known unto anyone who reads this that I will not lose my faith. I am grateful and indebted to Him for every breath. I know that because of Him I have been, and can continue to be, made clean and inherit eternal blessings with my family, the best comfort I can have at this time of uncertainty.

Every day is a chance to reinvent your life. Even if you don't choose to reinvent your whole life, sometimes that choice is made for you. Your dreams and plans can change in an instant. Your life's purpose can entirely revolve around one thing, then suddenly be knocked off that path of revolution. Our lives revolve around finding the cure for cancer. When we travel for treatments, my wife works from whatever location we are in. When things change, you may find yourself lost. Some changes in life cause you to try to find yourself and figure out who you are again. That's okay. When it doesn't work to jump to the why and get back to the old normal, a new life will emerge if you are patient. I say the old normal because if we allow life's experiences to

change us, our normal will not be the same as it was before. We will learn something and act instead of just going through the motions, which will cause us to have a new normal with the knowledge we've gained.

Victor Frankl said, "To live is to suffer; to survive is to find meaning in the suffering— if there is a purpose in life at all. There must be a purpose in suffering and dying- but no one can tell another what that purpose is."[32]

When you've been through a lot, it will take time for you to process it all. Find the good places, the safe spaces. Find the resources you need, and people to take care of and to take care of you. Others need your care. Everyone has a different road to emerge and reemerge. No one can decide that road for you. However, if you feel lost, there are guides like this book and being guided takes humility. You'll make it. You'll be happy. You are strong. Most of all, your attitude in the face of it all will matter. If you are looking for a fight, then fight the darkness. Be an example to the believers, light, and intelligences. Mentor others and know it's okay to be smart and productive. Be an example of what love can be. Honor those who came before you. Fight for cures, raise awareness, create events, attend concerts, and uphold honor. Be a prominent part of the tribes and families for others. Be there for them, just as others have been there for you. Pray for guidance. People who need the wisdom you have to offer will cross your path and you will continue to bless the world through your actions. My golden friendships stay in contact even while I am being herded through leukemia corrals. Life is hard and keeps being hard, but love and help come from these golden friends. After one particularly rough hospital stay, a group of our golden friends showed up at our door and a hilarious rendition of the song "Lean on Me" ensued with one of them wearing our three-year-old's green and orange striped dinosaur hat that was ten sizes too small. Some satiable moves toward the end were much appreciated by someone facing death every day. I played the guitar while we all sang along. The song "Lean on Me" is a staple in our household and in our friendships. My wife has sung it to her best friend through break-ups, college let-downs, car accidents, life changes, and hard moments.

Struggles are placed in your path so you can know who you are and what you are made of, what you are capable of, and how you will handle and can grow from these experiences. Experiences bite sometimes and the growth and the gold that can come from them are one of the reasons you are here. We don't know why specific trials arrive, but we know they strengthen our character if we handle them well. My bones being melted down to nothing with chemotherapy can be stronger over time. I am intentionally making each moment a moment of gold as I don't know when the last moment will be.

THANK YOU FOR LOVING ME ENOUGH TO CUT ME DOWN

I had the privilege of going to Doc MacGrogan's oyster bar for dinner with my friend during my first trip to Philadelphia. It was delicious. Not that we had oysters. I'm not supposed to have raw fish right now with my weak immune system.

I was waiting to have my T-cells extracted, and he was awaiting an infusion to help treat his multiple sclerosis. Initially, we were all staring at our smartphones, then somebody made a joke about it, and we began interacting like people used to before the invasion of social technology. I'm glad we did because it gave me the opportunity to meet a truly awesome individual. He grew up in Bible Belt country in Tennessee then moved to Jordan in the Middle East when he was thirteen.

We found out that our diseases are nearly opposite—his immune system has gotten out of control and attacks his nervous system; my bone marrow has gotten out of control and my immune system can't seem to do anything about it. We swapped hospital horror stories and found that despite the differences between our ailments we had undergone several of the same chemotherapies.

He has been dealt what some would consider a tough hand, but still manages to keep a smile on his face. He was a long-distance runner in high school, but at age twenty-four he was diagnosed with an aggressive form of multiple sclerosis. He is now confined to a wheelchair, has gone blind in his right eye, and is beginning to lose control over his arms and hands. Needless to say, he helps me be grateful for all that I have.

Over dinner, he asked me, "Do people ever put you on a pedestal, make what you're doing sound really great?" I laughed and told him, "I'm inspiring for expiring, but most of the time I'm just perspiring." We laughed and I told him in the spring I'd received an award from the Utah Cancer Network as the Survivor of the Year. I told him when I got home, I held up the plaque and joked with my wife, "All I have to do is wake up in the morning (i.e., be alive) and I get an award for it." Notwithstanding all this, he related the following to me, "If I had the choice to be cured of M.S. today or to go back to when I was twenty-four and never fall ill with M.S. I wouldn't go back. I've had too many amazing experiences happen as a result of this disease. I've learned so much. I wouldn't trade it."

I am inspired by his words. I told him I have never considered my cancer diagnosis in that way and that I would need some time to ponder it. As I contemplate this interesting proposition, two things come to mind:

J.R.R. Tolkien who conjured up some of the darker scenes in *The Lord of the Rings*! The hobbits and travelers who endured the horrendous circumstances of their journey and had visions of devils and death. I've never had the elements conspire against me, or the jaws of hell gape open after me, but if those terrifying scenarios can be for one's good, then I suppose I too can gain experience and learn something from my trials.

Second, is a story related by Hugh B. Brown that has come to be known as, "The Currant Bush." He writes,

"I was living in Canada. I had purchased a farm. It was run down. I went out one morning and saw a currant bush. It had grown up over six feet high. It was going all to wood. There were no blossoms and no currants. I was raised on a fruit farm in the U.S. before we went to Canada, and I knew what ought to happen to that currant bush. So I got some pruning shears and clipped them back until there was nothing left but stumps. It was just becoming daylight, and I thought I saw on top of each of these little stumps what appeared to be a tear, and I thought the currant bush was crying. I was kind of simpleminded (and I haven't entirely gotten over it), and I looked at it and smiled and said, "What are you crying about?" You know, I thought I heard that currant bush say this:

"How could you do this to me? I was making such wonderful growth. I was almost as big as the shade tree and the fruit tree that are inside the fence, and now you have cut me down. Every plant in the garden will look down on me because I didn't make what I should have made. How could you do this to me? I thought you were the gardener here."

"That's what I thought I heard the currant bush say, and I thought it so much that I answered. I said, "Look, little currant bush, I am the gardener here, and I know what I want you to be. I didn't intend for you to be a fruit tree or a shade tree. I want you to be a currant bush, and someday, little currant bush, when you are laden with fruit, you

are going to say, 'Thank you, Mr. Gardener, for loving me enough to cut me down. Thank you, Mr. Gardener.'"

We often think we know the plan for us only to be disappointed when things don't turn out how we expected. We may be tempted to complain, "How could you do this to me? I was making such wonderful growth." It can be difficult, or even painful, but sometimes the divine has to remind us that He is the gardener, He knows what we are to be, and if we could only see from His eternal perspective we too would say, "Thank you for loving me enough to cut me down."

Take your time to heal. Don't forget the wonderful and inspiring person you truly are and don't deny your gifts of intelligence, compassion, care, and optimism to a world so desperately in need of such things. Find happiness in being the wonderful person you truly are. Marshal in joy. Turn the heavy lead of life into heavy GOLD. Due to the immense pressure that is present in this part of the earth, as well as the extreme temperatures, a diamond gradually begins to form from rock. The entire process takes between one billion and three billion years.

"[He] will fight for you; you need only to be still" -Exodus 14:14.

I am a cloud gazer. I see animals, trees, and even God's eyelashes in the clouds above me. I tune out the outer world and allow my inner, intuitive mind to drift and dream. The art of being still and imagining a better, beautiful world floats further away. In childhood, it occurs often, so why not as adults? Forget the conditions, the lines we aren't supposed to color through, to play and color past the borders and boundaries through educating your hearts more instead of just your minds.

Real doing comes from stillness—not endless busyness. My wife tells of a moment she felt most exposed, raw, and visceral. She says, "The moment I birthed my son. I threw off all my clothes and screamed at my husband to throw—no, not lightly sprinkle, but throw ice straight in my face. It was a moment that strengthened my soul in a way words don't efficiently describe. When our baby boy was placed in my arms, I felt I was holding the whole world in my arms to care for efficiently; a primal moment that no technology or virtual connection will ever touch. A birthing music playlist that I had meticulously chosen based on tempo and lyrics added to the existentialism of the moment. In my own battered and bloody body, I looked at his blue, small body knowing I am a creator." Re-jolt your life back to red, vibrant moments before the red blood pales to blue. She sometimes does this through red rock therapy. She was born close to earth day and hiking re-jolts her heart. Find how to re-jolt your heart and do it often.

Apgar Score: a measure of the physical condition of a newborn infant. It is obtained by adding points for heart rate, respiratory effort, muscle tone, response to stimulation, and skin coloration; a score of ten represents the best possible condition.

They wouldn't allow me as a father to cut the umbilical cord, and our baby boy was quickly whisked away to the neonatal unit since his Apagar score was a two. The very moment he was born my son had his first experience of being a gentleman. His Apagar score rose to an eight after meconium was removed from his nose and throat. As quickly as they had whisked him away, our son gave up his neonatal bed for a baby girl who was born very prematurely and would be in the unit for a long time. His skin turned pink, and we quickly went from a moment of desperation to admiring his loads of hair, and his mother's nose and toes. Feeling his smooth skin and smelling his baby's breath was euphoric. My wife says, "For a moment in my life, my soul balanced like a bird in flight, soaring above the pain, and all the sweat, blood, and the tears up, up, above the clouds. I was so happy to be

looking down from a higher place. It didn't matter what happened next or before . . . all that mattered was that moment. I had created something that was more valuable to me than gold is to the alchemist that makes it."

"And what went wrong when other alchemists tried to make gold and were unable to do so?" "They were looking for only gold," his companion answered. "They were seeking the treasure of their Personal Legend, without wanting to actually live out the Personal Legend."[33] "To me, this communicates that to truly obtain what one seeks, one must become what is being sought. When we find inside what we seek outwardly, the "treasure" cannot be withheld; it is actually only realized.

The treasure is realizing that ALL I seek already exists inside of me. When I realize the treasure inside, it has been found."[34]

Alchemy: a medieval chemical science and speculative philosophy aiming to achieve the transmutation of base metals into gold, the discovery of a universal cure for the disease, and the discovery of a means of indefinitely prolonging life.

"Commodities such as gold and silver have a world market that transcends national borders, politics, religions, and race. A person may not like someone else's religion, but he'll accept his gold".[35]

During the gold rush, gold was sifted from river beds, and dirt and gravel washed away due to the heaviness of the metal. Leading with your heart is the same way, the heart emerges once all other heavy possibilities are considered and ruled out. Former American freestyle wrestler and coach Dan Gable talks about the real ingredients required inside a human being to win a gold medal. With greater introspection, we realize that it isn't just the gold medals won in a tournament that he is referring to—it's every achievement in life.

Be the alchemist of your life. Conquer your senses by remaining "undisturbed in all circumstances. See everything—dirt, stones, and gold—as the same."[36] One of the greatest ways to turn your life to gold is through joy. There was a month during my treatment when we flew without our son and didn't see him the entire month. Then my mom flew our son to us. I have never seen my wife so full of joy. Waiting in that airport, her expressions and mannerisms were as giddy as a kid on Christmas morning times ten! She was so anxious, she could barely sit still in anticipation of holding her son again.

Once reunited, we crammed in as many yummy breakfasts, fun at the zoo and exhibits, and garden walks at the hospital as we could. Even the mundane task of driving him around in a grocery store was suddenly so much fun after it had been taken from us for a while. The absence of our son's smile helped us regain joy in the smallest moments and tasks by just being together again.

Amongst swirling clouds, we share much joy in the little things together like watching the sun set and the sun rise. One of our favorite songs is "You Are My Sunshine." Our broken pieces are slowly put back together through each golden sunset and sunrise. The Japanese idea of kintsukuroi or kintsugi is to repair it with gold. It's the art of repairing pottery with gold lacquer and understanding that the piece is more beautiful for having been broken. There have been many times I have completely broken along this journey and somehow the glue and duct tape that holds me together for a while turns to gold and turns every moment I breathe again into a beautiful, cherished moment. You can be so grateful for every moment that life becomes more beautiful than it ever was before realizing that it could be over in an instant. Ordinary, even broken moments become miracles.

"Those who are alike in happiness and distress; who are established in the self; who look upon a clod, a stone, and a piece of gold as

of equal value; who remain the same amidst pleasant and unpleasant events; who are intelligent; who accept both blame and praise with equanimity; who remain the same in honor and dishonor; who treat both friend and foe alike; and who have abandoned all enterprises — they are said to have risen above the three guṇas."[37]

Precious metals have been pursued by humans for centuries, and there is a joy attained with precious gold. Still, there is a futility of material pursuits and their lifelong obsession by their pursuers. In order to be the alchemist of your heartbeats, you need to use the right numbers in your recipe for life.

I wait for that magical number 0.5 neutrophils, to appear so I can come home. I get so used to the hospital that it is hard to believe I am really getting out on some release days. I push a cart full of my soft toilet paper from home (the hospital stuff is crap), new medications and ointments for my ongoing side effects from chemotherapy, the foam cover I lay on the hospital bed, and goodies of things friends have brought me during this hospital stay out to the parking lot. My wife stops me on this particular day I bust out of the hospital in order to take a picture of release day. As I pose for my "photo op," a family is approaching the hospital and I realize that nobody can see my silly grin under this face mask. I turn to an unsuspecting man and jovially holler, "Why am I smiling under this thing? It's not like it's going to show up in the picture!" Obviously preoccupied with whatever brought him to the hospital in the first place, he chose to ignore the outburst and I received even stranger looks from the children. My mom and my wife have a pretty good laugh about it.

When I found out I'd have to wear a mask in public during the entire span of treatment, I started envisioning scenarios of being out and about and how people would react until I was okay with their reactions. I tried it out and found it actually pretty comical. When my numbers and counts are good, I don't have to wear my mask. When they are low, I wear the mask to protect myself from others' germs though some act as though they think I am protecting them from whatever it is I have. It's a battle for health and a battle for the right numbers.

FRET, FRET, FRET

WORRY, AGONIZE, GRIEVE

ON GUITAR- PRESS DOWN

Where Nothing Begins or Ends

He forgives all that was not perfect
He loves all who he never met
He sings with you in your car rides
He is of nature
He is of friends
He is of family
He exists where nothing begins or ends
He is the clarity in your daily meditation
He is with you when decisions must be made
He is with you in the high mountain
He holds you on winter nights
He fills the night with stars you can wish on
He walks with you barefoot on summer grass
He soothes your searching foot
He encourages you to keep dreaming

(by Landon Gallant)

Beat 6

BEATS OF NUMBERS

MARSHALING HEARTBEATS REQUIRES NUMBERS.

Repeating number patterns occur throughout my journey. I often pause and pay attention to their meanings.

A normal healthy person has a neutrophil count of 1.8. Today I clocked in at an impressive 0.1. The doctor congratulates me on a 100 percent improvement. The next day, I hit 0.2, and then the next I hit 0.3. That's when the doctor lets me know if I measure 0.5 I can go home. So the next day I score 0.4, and I am poised to go home the following morning. But, my levels hold and I am still at 0.4.

I'm not sure if it is the music, everyone's prayers, or the luck o' the Irish, but my blood draw the next morning I hit 0.5.

Glancing at the clock suddenly takes you back to a specific moment of celebration, success, grief, and death. Time traveling to the very minute, the very heartbeat that something wonderful or terrible

happened—your body notes, and your mind may never forget the exact date or time your heart skips a beat.

I met my wife on Friday, November 13. Her favorite number since she was a little girl is 111 because it was her dad's call number at work. This number has repeatedly shown up as a pattern in her father's life. She was the third girl of six children and despite her father thinking, *another girl* after already having two, she was daddy's little girl. She was constantly following him around and wanting to do all he did on the ranch.

My favorite number is 3. Coincidence that we met on 11/13? The perfect combination of our favorite numbers. Coincidences may be a way for divinity to remain anonymous.

***

Headstrong holds a gala every year in memory of their son Nick to raise funds for cancer patients and their families. My wife booked a room in the massive hotel adjacent to the event. When she arrives, the tall, dark concierge hands her the room key. She is exhausted after the long flight with our young son. When she looks down, her eyes catch the room number. Room 1113. How in the world? What are the odds?

Looking back, this day was perfected and presented in detail by one higher power who is more acquainted with physics equations and much wiser than I.[38] I've studied the Bhagavad Gita for years and discovered that "every element is composed with a mathematical purpose. Numerology plays a key role in interpreting sacred texts, as in the Arabic language each letter has a numerical equivalent, according to the Abjad system. One author uses this approach to explain Qur'anic passages, and sacred words and phrases, demonstrating meanings which lie hidden beneath the surface."[39]

My wife was born the day after Earth day and loves everything to do with the Earth. I found some studies for her from the Qur'an when it comes to percentages and calculations of water and earth. "The word "bahr" (water) is mentioned thirty-two times in the Qur'an and the word "barr / ard" (earth) is mentioned thirteen times in the Qur'an. Both words in Arabic mean "earth." If we add the number of both words "bahr" (water) and "barr" (earth), we get the number forty-five. ("Water" = 32 times + "earth" = 13 times = 45 times). The number of words "bahr" (water) divided by the total number of words "earth+water", multiplied by 100 percent gives: (32 / 45) x 100 = 71.111 percent. The total of words "barr" (earth) divided by the total number of words "earth+water", and multiplied by 100 percent gives: (13 / 45) x 100 = 28.888 percent. With this simple equation, [the author] reached the miracle result that has been present in the Quran for 1,431 years, but that has been recently discovered and contrasted by scientific data. The percentage of Water on our planet is = 71.111 percent. The percentage of Earth on our planet is = 28.8888 percent. These are just some examples that show the incredible and inexplicable Miracle of Numbers. We have to consider that there are many more in the Qur'an"[40] and many other holy writings.

Your brain has an innate need to make order out of chaos. If you pay attention, these coincidences happen more often than you may notice. According to coincidence researcher Bernard Beitman, synchronicities are "indicators of an invisible network that connects everyone and everything" and "humans transmit some unobserved energetic information, which other people then process or organize into emotion and behavior."[41]

Heart Jolt 7:

ACCORDING TO DISCOVER MAGAZINE[42], HERE ARE A FEW STRATEGIES TO TRY:

1. PAY ATTENTION. COINCIDENCES HAPPEN TO PEOPLE WHO ARE MINDFUL AND NOTICE THINGS. KEEP YOUR SENSES OPEN TO COINCIDENTAL OPPORTUNITIES WHEN YOU GO ABOUT DAILY ACTIVITIES.

2. DESPITE WHAT YOUR PARENTS TAUGHT YOU WHEN YOU WERE A CHILD, NOW THAT YOU ARE OLDER, TALK TO STRANGERS. ACCORDING TO WORK BY RISK RESEARCHER DAVID SPIEGELHALTER, COINCIDENCES OFTEN ARISE OUT OF TALKING TO SOMEONE YOU DON'T KNOW. IF YOU DON'T INTRODUCE YOURSELF TO YOUR NEIGHBOR, YOU CAN'T POSSIBLY KNOW IF YOU WERE BORN IN THE SAME HOSPITAL, ON THE SAME DAY, IN A CITY SEVERAL HUNDRED MILES AWAY FROM YOUR CURRENT HOME.

3. SEEK MEANING. WHETHER YOU SEE A STRING OF NUMBERS ON A LICENSE PLATE OR HEAR A SONG ON THE RADIO, ASK YOURSELF IF YOU CAN MAKE MEANING OUT OF THE EXPERIENCE.

4. WRITE IT DOWN. KEEP A LOG OF THE COINCIDENCES THAT OCCUR IN YOUR DAILY LIFE. THE MORE YOU NOTICE COINCIDENCES, THE MORE LIKELY THEY ARE TO HAPPEN TO YOU.

MAYBE YOU'LL NOTICE A NUMBER PATTERN THAT KEEPS POP-
PING UP EVERYWHERE YOU LOOK OVER SEVERAL HOURS
OR DAYS OR EVEN YEARS. LOOK FOR THE MESSAGE IN THE
NUMBER FOR YOU AND SEARCH FOR ITS TRUE MEANING.

"Numerology has its basis in the ancient world and tells us that each number carries its own vibration and symbolic significance. It can mark the stages of our soul's evolution as we move from one frequency to the next. Repeating number patterns in our lives may call us to focus on certain aspects of our lives and rise to approach them from the best within us. Once we've recognized that there is something we must look more deeply into, we also must trust that we will be guided to the people and places that hold the right answers for us. Numbers, as symbols, can carry personal meanings as well. We may have our own lucky number that has served us well throughout our lives and another that reminds us of certain events of significance. If these are the numbers that are appearing, it may be the right time to delve into the past for clues about how to handle a present situation. Whatever explanations you receive about the numbers that are appearing everywhere you look, the important thing is to trust your own guidance as to what they are telling you. Each culture attaches different meanings to the numbers, so a Chinese interpretation may be different from an interpretation of Kabbalah. It is up to us to use our intuition to see which is the best fit for us. If someone has an explanation that doesn't feel right, then this is not the answer for you but may be just a clue to keep you moving on the path. By paying attention to the numbers around us, we use them as tools to improve

our connection to the universe and our awareness of our choices in life."[43]

My wife is an Albert Einstein groupie if there is such a thing. She's admired his uniqueness since she was very young. Her favorite T-shirt is Einstein's face. She even wrote seven research papers about him during primary school. Her infatuation persisted even into a few college papers. Her college roommate gifted her a poster of Einstein's famous quotes that still sits in her office today over a decade later. She frequently dives into topics like energy and ideas like string theory. Our latest conversation revolved around physics and the "string theory, a theoretical framework in which the point-like particles of particle physics are replaced by one-dimensional objects called strings. It describes how strings propagate through space and interact with each other. On distance scales larger than the string scale, a string looks just like an ordinary particle, with its mass, charge, and other properties determined by the vibrational state of the string. In string theory, one of the many vibrational states of the string corresponds to the gravitation, a quantum mechanical particle that carries gravitational force." My wife said if we apply this theory to our beings, we could answer a plethora of deep questions. Why do we gravitate toward some people and are repelled by others? Why do we want to travel back in time or wish we could see into the future? We can discover answers to questions about black holes and nuclear forces. It's simple math and numbers and our family loves to talk about it. Luckily our son also loves math and numbers. He is memorizing as many numbers of pi as he possibly can.

Because of this love, we speak of our mathematical and numerical relationships often in our household. My wife was raised on a wild 2,000-acre ranch. The trees on the ranch have more patterns and repeating parts than a perfectly symmetrical office building in the city. I am a city boy with a few country summers stirred into my pot. Let us travel back to the idea of trees. Trees number their lives with the rings in their trunks. The oldest living organism on the earth is a tree with numerous rings. My wife saw the bristlecone pine tree as part of an honors course in college. She observed the repeating patterns in the trees' trunks. She was amazed by mother nature's designs and how she calculated that the very element we breathe in is the same element the trees breathe out. This oxygen is the same element that carries our blood through our veins and delivers what our cells need to live. Then it is brought back to the heart where it is reoxygenated in order to begin the process again. Notice, the blood is not reoxygenated in our brains, but in our hearts. What the trees breathe in, we breathe out. The patterns in the trees' trunks are not linear but circular in their nature. They portray each weather year with each layer. The natural phenomenon astounded her as she realized that each ring represents every storm and sunshine the tree experienced for that year of its life. Blood vessels and even our heart rates hold similar stories of recording each passing year and what our bodies went through and overcame. As our blood repeatedly flows and our hearts repeatedly jolt, these repetitions help us to grow stronger in life. The more we repeat an action, the more the frontal cortex in our minds stimulates "wakeful relaxation" and that is why the action becomes easier to do. Think about it, you can memorize lines of poetry or master habits if you repeat them over and over again. My son memorizes algorithm after algorithm in order to master solving any case of a Rubik's cube. At first, it was hard for his mind to memorize, but the more repetitions he did—his mind didn't even have to work anymore. His eyes can now look at the cube and his hands dive in with muscle memory. Now he loves solving Rubik's cubes with all his heart!

"You can see the beating heart of the earth. And gaze into its eye. Get close to nature's heart. Listen." John Muir reminds us that spend-

ing time outdoors is restorative because we can see these repetitions and patterns in nature: a simple sunrise and sunset, for example. It looks so easy from where we are on Earth, but the amount of energy expended in that simple sunrise and sunset is more than Einstein could capture. The joy in these harmonious patterns isn't always something we see, it is something we feel just as my son has reached a point where he can blindfold his eyes after looking at a Rubik's cube and feel the solution. As we look out in nature, it's not that everything is perfect, that every blade of grass is cut to the same length nor that every sea lion is slim and cloned copies of one another. When you look out at a tree, especially a bristlecone pine tree, they are not perfectly symmetrical and they don't all appear the same. They are twisted and worn down from years of being beaten by extreme climates. Uniqueness dominates nature, there's a perfection to the imperfection. Imagine if we all looked and acted perfect, how boring life would be. Removing the image of perfection in your heart can be done by focusing on what makes you strong instead of your weakness. A pine tree is the strongest when it is focusing on its roots instead of being strewn around by whatever wind comes along next. It firmly plants itself and doesn't allow the wind to uproot its deep roots.

***

Jill, with Conrad's heart beating inside her, does not get her nails painted very often. But when she does, she paints them with heartbeats and pulses so that every time she looks down at her hands she can be reminded of the constant beat, repetition, and pattern of the heart keeping her alive. Her nails are a symbol to ground her and remind her to experience every moment and paint herself more of these meaningful, heartfelt patterns in life. She is rooted in her beats with her eyes and more importantly feels them with her every heartbeat. She uses the visual reminder every time she glances down at her hands, to feel more with her heart and think less with her head. She thoroughly enjoys every moment since she knows firsthand the fragility and preciousness in the fractiles of life. She is reminding herself that her beats are limited. She is acutely aware that there is no cure for life and that one day the heartbeats will end.

Repeat and refine your practice of loving life with every heartbeat.

The beat of love is numerical and lyrical. When you see certain numbers and hear certain songs, they may remind you of others. Other numbers and songs remind me of how wonderful life is. My wife is a mathematical nerd, quizzical, left-brained, logical, driven-by-numbers kind of woman, and I am a musical, right-brained artist. Naturally, we got married on November 13th, the same day we met, one year later. I even proposed with an epithalamium I wrote and sang. I like to tell people "we got married the day we met" with no explanation. I once posted on my wife's social media account, "So if you're the brains and beauty in this relationship, does that make me the soundtrack?" I love you sweetheart, and here is the math to prove it:

Perfect totient number

In number theory, a perfect totient number is an integer that is equal to the sum of its iterated totients. That is, we apply the totient function to a number n, apply it again to the resulting totient, and so on, until the number 1 is reached, and add together the resulting sequence of numbers; if the sum equals n, then n is a perfect totient number. Or to put it algebraically,

$$n = \sum_{i=1}^{c+1} \varphi^i(n),$$

179

where

$$\varphi^i(n) = \begin{cases} \varphi(n) & \text{if } i = 1 \\ \varphi(\varphi^{i-1}(n)) & \text{otherwise} \end{cases}$$

is the iterated totient function and c is the integer such that

$$\varphi^c(n) = 2,$$

then n is a perfect totient number.

The first few perfect totient numbers are

3, 9, 15, 27, 39, 81, and 111

For example, start with 327. $\varphi(327) = 216$, $\varphi(216) = 72$, $\varphi(72) = 24$, $\varphi(24) = 8$, $\varphi(8) = 4$, $\varphi(4) = 2$, $\varphi(2) = 1$, and $216 + 72 + 24 + 8 + 4 + 2 + 1 = 327$.

MULTIPLES AND POWERS OF THREE

It can be observed that many perfect totient numbers are multiples of 3; in fact, 4375 is the smallest perfect totient number that is not divisible by 3. All powers of 3 are perfect totient numbers, as may be seen by induction using the fact that

$$\varphi(3^k) = \varphi(2 \times 3^k) = 2 \times 3^{k-1}.$$

We hold numerical celebrations in our home. Before ever battling leukemia, we kept up the tradition of celebrating everyone's "day." Their day is the date of the month they were born. We celebrate that person every month on their day. My son's day is the 11th, my wife's day is the 23rd, and mine is the 30th. Whatever it is, the person wants to do that day to celebrate, we do it. Life is too short to not include joy in every day. Instead of waiting to celebrate on our birthday every year, we celebrate at least three times a month. My thirtieth celebration even extended to the celebration of my life on November 30th. On "our day" every month we get to do something special we have been wanting, have our favorite treat, or whatever it is we choose for the day. These monthly celebrations are getting a bit difficult as I have been hospitalized for years, but they also are becoming something different to look forward to in the dreary hospital walls. No matter how small the celebration, it's wonderful to feel special every month.

After three days in the hospital, I am too out of it to celebrate due to septic shock. My dad takes a turn staying with me at the hospital. I had just finished a round of chemo and was waiting for counts to recover, and I was completely neutropenic. Neither my wife nor I sleep well when we are away from each other. My wife finishes watching the movie *Gravity* and my gravitational pulls want to play a game of Ticket to Ride with her. We play on our phones when we are apart to help the time in the hospital go faster.

We finish our game around 12:30 am. At 3:16 am I texted her that I woke up with joint pain and a fever. Amazingly, she texts right back that she hopes it is a neutropenic fever. Sometimes when you have no neutrophils, you get a fever. She asks me if my dad is asleep or if he knows. He does and I get chest X-rays and antibiotics. She falls back asleep. At 5:27 she woke up to ask if I was able to get back to sleep. I do not respond. Fifteen minutes later my mom opens her door, "Get up! We are going to the hospital. Dad called and they are taking Marshall to the ICU because his blood pressure dropped." My wife hops in the car and boldly states, "I hate cancer!"

She knows something is really, really wrong.

In the ICU, I am having an episode where my whole face and neck are bright red, my blood pressure is critically low, and I am writhing in

181

pain. It feels like a burst of pressure in my face and neck. They have already put me on two blood pressure medications and right away they have my wife sign consent forms for a central line, an arterial line, and a ventilator. They ask if I want to be resuscitated if I lose consciousness.

My parents rushed out to the family waiting room with my wife while they did the procedure. When they are finally able to come back in, I have a large cable with protruding lines out my neck. This placement makes it easier to access vital organs. Another "episode" has occurred with no relief from the pain medications.

They quickly pull the PICC line out of my arm in case that is the source of infection. The rest of the day and into the night my blood pressure is terribly low. My wife's body is so tense, her food tastes like cardboard. She later tells me she was completely numb for nearly a whole day while my numbers plummeted and rose like a roller coaster. She stares at screens with changing numbers that record my body's oxygen, pressures, and heartbeats until her feeling comes back. She watches the numbers with so much intensity that she may as well have been hired into the Air Force to watch flight screens.

I ask if my wife is in the room. She assures me she is, and she keeps rubbing my feet so I'll know of her presence. I request that she go over my advanced directive with my mother. They read through the document and end-of-life decisions through many tears. My wife studied and taught end-of-life decisions for bioethics in college, yet she admits to my mother that it is completely different talking through these issues when they are about her own husband. Her emotions are raw and play a much bigger part in making critical decisions than her logical mind expects. I choose her as my agent. Despite her education, that moment suddenly fills with pressure and overwhelm. She's known me for almost six years and three of them have been fighting cancer. Now she is my advocate. Aloud she states she doesn't want my family to blame her or hate her if they disagree on a chosen medical intervention. My mom assures her they will support and discuss critical decisions if needed.

The sun slowly dips below the horizon along with my dropping blood pressure. The night calms alongside my episodes. This reassures me that the cause of my infection is the PICC line taken from my arm. My mom and wife both attempt to sleep in my tiny ICU room sharing one pull-out chair. Two little heads keep popping up to look at the numbers on the monitors with every beep.

The sun slowly rises and thanks to medication, so does my blood pressure. The morning brings results of gram-negative rods growing in my blood cultures. For those science nerds, detailed speciation will later show the specific bacteria as enterobacter. These bacteria are pathogenic and cause opportunistic infections in immunocompromised and usually hospitalized patients. It's generally caused by some form of mechanical site and, in my case, from the PICC line in my arm. Specific antibiotics kill it most effectively.

They pump liters and liters of fluid through my system in order to keep me alive while my blood pressure is low. A lot of fluid gathers in my lungs. I work through the fluid with oxygen, Lasix, and a spirometer. The bacteria cause the blood from my heart to shoot through my body system extremely fast so the cells and vital organs do not receive the oxygen and nutrients they need. For two days my limbs feel cold and clammy. My body tries to compensate for this loss of blood flow by sending what it can to vital organs like my heart and brain, therefore my legs and arms don't receive much of this blood flow. As a result, my kidney and liver numbers are getting higher and higher. If my blood pressure would have stayed down for much longer, there would be irreversible damage to these vital organs. Thankfully, my numbers look better each day, but my liver levels are still high.

3:27

A lost cause, a broken dream
I awake when the light is green
What do all these numbers mean?
Confused by the beeps and everything
Memories I won't forget
ICU, I wish we had never met
Drowning though I'm not even wet
Losing when I didn't bet
I'm like a crumpled jacket in the Lost and Found
Trapped where there is no way out, crying without a sound
Storm clouds begin to rain
My heart is full of pain
Questions running through my brain
Some things numbers don't explain

(by Marshall Jensen)

I feel and look like I've been run over by a truck. The director of the ICU himself took the time early in the morning to tell my wife, "Your husband is going to be ok. He is turning around." He also expresses his hopes for me to do the T-cell therapy trial again. As badly as I don't ever want to be back in that ICU again it is very possible after I receive my re-engineered t-cells.

I write a song called "Ten Days" when my wife and I have to avoid each other completely during a week and a half of my treatment plan. We are ill simultaneously. Yet, this ordeal in the medical intensive care unit causes non-existent communication between us. When I finally do try to talk, it is very hard to understand me due to my paralyzed face and lack of oxygen. Here is a little play-off of the lyrics of that song my wife re-wrote regarding the ICU experience:

I went three days without you, and I nearly lost my mind.
I watched your every heartbeat even when you closed your eyes.
I went three days without my command. I went three days without my husband.
I went three days in a dark and lonesome ICU, and then you stabilized, and then you spoke.
And you survived.
I went three days without you and I plead with others to pray.
Your name was spoken aloud at least a thousand times a day.
I went three days without your humor, I went three days without my animator.

I went three days in a dark and lonesome ICU and now you're recovering and now you stand.
And you survived.

(by Marshall Jensen modified by AJ)

When I am finally more aware of my surroundings, I stand with the help of a walker. My wife goes to see our son whom she hasn't seen for three days while my mom stays with me. I didn't know she had been there all that time due to my unconscious body. In the past when I've been out of it during treatments I've asked her, "Where were you!?" To which she replied that she was there through the really rough moments, but I just didn't know it. I came to the realization at that moment that there are times we are in such sorrow, anger, feeling defeated and so low that we don't realize the angels surrounding us. She is with me always even when I am thrashing under a ventilator or knocked out in a medicated coma and don't know she is there. When I need her the most, my angel is there. When you need it the most, your angels will also surround you and buoy you up even if you don't see them or realize they are with you. They are carrying you.

I am being carried by prayers, packages, phone calls, texts, and all efforts to support and help bear this heavy load. While my wife and I were dating, we discussed what we want in our eternity and to create together. She wanted "sparkling silver sands" and I wanted "golden oceans." We even drew it out on a whiteboard with silver and gold dry-erase markers. Even if I hadn't pulled through those three days, we would still create our eternal beach and water undefeated from a life led by our hearts.

My wife gathers a few small materials and chemicals to create a tiny version of our silver sands and golden water that fit inside a corner of my room. A little creativity, a box of kid's kinetic sand, silver and gold dye, and water, and three days later, we create our little eternal beach right here on Earth from my hospital room.

My wife says one of my greatest character traits is my capacity to recognize and appropriately respond to other people who are experiencing challenges or adversities as I am in the middle of experiencing the forces pressing upon me. Through my sufferings, I feel I am empowered to see and understand the sufferings of other people amidst my own suffering. I can detect sad eyes in others because I myself have felt that sadness in my own sight. I empathize with the starvation around the world because I myself have almost starved to death. This trial has given me the ability to detect others' trials and reach out and extend compassion more fully. Yes, I have my own distress, but somehow I am enabled to look and reach outward even when the natural man inside me wants to turn inward. Anyhow, my wife says it amazes her and my capacity to make those around me feel special is genuine. She says often our visitors will tell her, "He made me feel like the most special person in the room. When I was the one who came in trying to lift him up, I left feeling uplifted." My wife loves it when I take her to dinner for her "day" even if it's in a restaurant at the hospital. I tell her she means the world and beyond to me over delicatessen oysters at the restaurant McCormick and Schmidt. I truly mean those words. I am a verbal processor and have "diarrhea of the mouth." My wife spends hours listening to me. I may have passed this talkative trait on to my son, so now she listens to him blabber all day long too.

I proposed marriage to my wife with a verse of a song,

"If I wrote you poetry and music, tried my best to sing.
If I lived my life to serve and please you, bought a diamond ring.
If I owned the world and all its riches, I'd gladly give it up. But it
wouldn't be enough.
No, it wouldn't be enough to say I love you because words could not express
what it's like to look into those lovely eyes and feel such tenderness.
It wouldn't be enough to hold you closely at the end of every day
and tell you that my day was long without you. I hope that you're ok.
It wouldn't be enough- Amanda baby, but I'd do it anyway".

(by Marshall Jensen)

That is the first time I put a girl's actual name in one of my songs. My wife says she'd pick a song written for her over a material gift any day of the week and twice on Sunday. I wrote a song, "AJ" two weeks after I met her. She loves my sappy lyrics. She appreciates the meaning and depth behind lyrics with purpose. I gave her the CD I produced in Minnesota that first November 13th we met and she stayed up until early in the morning listening to every single song. She even texted me her favorite song numbers which ended up being number 11 and 3 on my album, *The Plan*. All songs are available on Itunes and Spotify by searching Marshall Jensen.

Alphas and Omegas bordered our wedding announcements since the symbols for them look like "a's" and "m's." We flipped the omega symbol on the border to look like an m. The "beginnings" and the "ends." My wife prefers sunrises and I prefer sunsets. She thinks breakfast is the most important meal of the day while my tummy just isn't awake enough yet. Road tripping, she'd rather stay one more night and wake up early to drive home while I prefer driving home that night no matter how late it is.

Another verse says, "If I wrote you love notes every afternoon with lots of mushy stuff, no it wouldn't be enough." My wife's journals are full of love notes from me. She has boxes and books full of them too. I don't miss many opportunities to tell her how much I love her. There are many special poems written for her over our years together.

*****

THREE YEARS

When I doubt the power of miracles, I am re-shown in an instant the season changes, when I regain hope after long nights in the ICU, when I feel the love of family and friends, and when I am able to surprise others. These moments are miracles and they remake my life.

Three years ago, on January 4th, I was diagnosed with ALL and this cancer crusade began. I fought leukemia three times in those three years. My wife stares at me, wondering how I'm still alive after all this. Her greatest strength is her love of learning and in three years she's learned a lot—more than she could ever write. Here are three lessons she did write down:

"First, be grateful for the 'normal' days. Normal days are actually glorious days in your book of life now. A day when you read, clean, do laundry, and actually raise your own child is a glorious day. It's not one spent in a hospital room worrying about numbers, germs, medications, and how many breaths you may have left.

Second, often you aren't in charge except for your own charge—be it positive or negative. We wish we were all-powerful. I still desire and believe in doing all that I can—learning and trying all that I can. But I am not directing my path and that means trusting that what is meant to happen is happening. Eternity is not the same as your short time on Earth. Sometimes on Earth, you must release the driver's wheel in order to surrender, steering your life toward the direction you want to go. Let it go in the direction it's meant to go. Drive toward the people you're supposed to know. Allow someone else to drive especially if you hit some rocky and dangerous terrain along your way. Allow the master to drive in the tough spots. Share your keys with him in order to unlock a journey that is more magnificent than if you tried to navigate those rocky ridges alone. The dangerous cliffs also hold the most beauty. Miracles still happen often through other people. Often through you. You can be the reaching arms, the healing hands, and the love others need. If you were healed with one touch in one moment, what would you learn?

Third, bodies can be restored. Even from the dust, despair, and even death. Restorative powers aren't limited to what has been before. Our bodies can be added upon and enhanced in ways unimagined.

I went from having one set of genes to another, and yet another from overseas, to now a set of completely re-engineered, living cells in my body. Incredibly, there are three different sets of genes all working together to keep me alive at this very moment. When the chemotherapy gives me neuropathy in my hands and feet, taking away my ability to play the guitar, my wife looks up, "Why would *this* happen?" She can't fathom how my guitar skills, which have literally gotten us through some of the toughest days, could be taken. Music. Talent. Nothing could ever stop me from singing until something does.Remember when I mentioned that the cancer made its way to my brain and my face is completely paralyzed?. Leukemia has crossed the blood-brain barrier. I don't realize how much I like to smile until I can't. My face slumped into a blank stare. It's difficult because I want to tell a joke or make a face, lighten the mood, let the doctors know I appreciate them, and let my wife know I love her. But all anyone can see is a blank stare. My facial paralysis recovers quickly on the right side and is mostly just on the left side now.

What a strange ailment. First neuropathy in my fingers that hinder my guitar-playing abilities, then paralysis that inhibits my singing, speech, and mostly my smile. I still trust the Lord is in control and do my best to smile inside with these setbacks. The chemo is again injected into my veins to try to fix my smile and my wife brings me several

smiling pictures of myself with a plethora of other emoji emotions on sticks I can hold up when I can't show my laughter and smile.

I am watching how others see me now. I look into their eyes. Nurses, family, doctors, and many have a saddened look of pity in their eyes. Almost like they have given up or they are just sorry. Succumbed to fear, the look on most of my caregiver's faces after seeing me paralyzed was, "This guy is not going to make it." One doctor still has hope and I trust him and cling to it.

My wife's face also tells a story of hope! Best of all, in AJ's eyes, there is no sorrow or pity. I look into her eyes and all I see is love. She still loves me. She still believes in me. I don't believe in can'ts anymore. I'm still baffled that months later, the neuropathy in my hands goes away.

I do exercises with my face in the mirror. From the outside observer, it's probably pretty funny. My face hardly twitches here and there but I stand in front of the mirror straining a smile under sluggish cheeky muscles. This goes on for a couple of minutes and I'm pretty exhausted afterward. To anybody else, it probably looks like some grouchy, old man with bulldog cheeks has been glaring at himself. The right side of my face recovers and slowly every day there are tiny improvements on the left side. Restoration! We can all be recovered, renewed, and resurrected from dust and from loss.

There is a law that states for every action there is an opposite and equal reaction. I am sometimes compelled to move. During my fight, I move to Houston, then Philadelphia, and finally home to Utah. I have met incredible people along the way and have done incredibly hard things. Here's to the last three years of T-cell treatments, biotherapies, and prolonging lives.

*****

Four for Me, None for You . . .
Back to the Future Again

As you know, unfortunately, this leukemia business is not my first hospital rendezvous. Remember when I was twelve years old I injured my eye in that roller-blading accident and spent several weeks at Primary Children's Hospital? The injury led to a bacterial infection in my brain known as meningitis—this can be lethal or cause serious brain damage. My brothers still claim I received the latter. I was in a coma for a full week, I had a respirator and tubes coming out of my head to relieve the pressure—it was a pretty serious ordeal. At the time, my dad actually worked at the very hospital where I was a patient.

Miraculously I survived. During my stay I had several friends from my sixth-grade class come to wish me well. One very special visit was from my good friend, Brandon, and the scandalous part for a sixth grader anyway, was that he brought a girl with him. Her name was Brianne.

So these two came to visit, and I still remember I was a little embarrassed because I didn't have a shirt on. They had brought me a Twix, but not just any Twix, the King Size, that's four chocolatey crunchy cookies, not just two! Oh wow, I still love these things.

One day while fighting leukemia, I'm hanging out minding my own in my hospital room, when who comes in? Brandon and Brianne—I'm happy to share that they are married now.

I bet you can guess what they brought me—a King Size Twix bar. Yep, four for me, none for you!

*****

After all the treatments, my body is tired. Heartburn is my new enemy. It comes and goes and getting Tums in the hospital is harder

than it should be. My heart may burn, but it causes my soul to be well nourished through spiritual feeding mostly in reading form as I lie in hospital beds.

My "daily bread" is a little different these days. Sometimes it's as silly as finding the courage to swallow a grody pill on an upset stomach, and other times it's strength to go another day watching my adorable little boy on a webcam because he has a cold and isn't allowed to come to see his daddy until his runny nose is gone. I am beginning to wonder if runny noses in kids are eternal.

Life is a day-at-a-time journey. There is wisdom in asking for and recognizing a greater hand every day. Even with cancer, I have been amazed. Most of my blessings come to me and my family through ordinary people amidst their day-at-a-time journey, who out of the goodness of their hearts allow us to be part of it.

My disdain for pill-popping is still here and I know I'm not alone. I thought of starting the "Anti-Pill Coalition" (APC)—a nationwide movement to engineer a pill that doesn't stick to your tongue, float to the top of your mouth, or leave a vile and unrelenting taste. Then I remember the darn things are actually saving my life. I can honestly say that I have taken more pills in the last week than I have in the last several years combined.

As a cancer patient, you have the opportunity to try many new and experimental drugs and nobody gives you a hard time.

After stints in the hospital, neighbors help us wipe down every wall in our house in preparation for the immunosuppressed patient's arrival. When I first arrive home, I'm not sure I am in the right place. The joint is spotless! The bathroom smells of fresh paint, my room is a new glossy gray, and I feel like I am on one of those home makeover TV shows. Many thanks to everyone for serving our family. I feel bad that I don't even know who all of those who helped us are. Hopefully, this book reaches a few more of you so you know how much your kindness means to us; it lightens our burdens and helps us to focus on new adjustments.

THANKS AND OBRIGADA . . .

After my last time in Philadelphia, our neighborhood greets us like true warriors! Many welcome home signs, and big, yellow ribbons tied around all the trees and posts. We couldn't have imagined anything like it.

My story of beating leukemia this third time is going viral, and reporters from all over the world are calling. The headlines of how HIV was being used to fight cancer now amaze people. T-cell therapy has great potential to cure all types of cancers in the future. We hope the viral story of this retro-viral immunotherapy will help many cancer patients in the future around the world. Many international articles are written, and my wife even reaches out and thanks them in their own language. As a linguist, it is fun to see each story being unique, not just a direct translation to another language of the same story. We found some in German (Danke), Slovenian (Hvala), Polish (Dzieki), Rwandan (Ellokepa Sawhay), African (llokepa saawhe Kinyarwanda language), Southern China (Xiexie), Turkish (Tesekkurler), Slovac

(Vd'aka), Hungarian (Koszonet), Czech (Dekuji), Serbian (Xbana), Finnish (Kiitos), Vietnamese (Su' cam o'n), Portuguese (Obrigada), and English (Thanks). The story was in the *Huffington Post* and the *Medical Daily.* HIV is being used to cure cancer! I'm doing my part to find the cure.

One of my brothers took his whole family within two weeks of hearing about my cancer and kindly moved down from Washington state to help us take care of our son and offer support during treatment. Family members are rays of sunshine in our cloudy moments. My brother loaned his family to us while staying active on the Air Force base in another state. What a man! We are still in awe of their sacrifice. We pray every night for the families who sacrifice for us.

Battling death from the front lines for years brings a new perspective to spiritual rituals like baptism. I was even able to re-baptize that same brother this year. Through the atonement, there will be no scars. Cares for this world sometimes choke out eternal words and promises. I am tired this round. It doesn't stop me from trying to grasp any light I can find no matter how dark it is. Strength is found in light. Friends organizing events and fundraisers empower me to dispel and hush my fears and have some peace. When your life is not ideal, you have promises in the life to come.

While reading during one of my spiritual feasts lying in a hospital bed, I was contemplating how it will be to meet another brother of mine, Jesus. I was thinking how overwhelmed with emotion I was when my eldest brother made his surprise visit a couple of months ago. I imagine reuniting with Jesus to be like that in a way—hugging a brother you haven't seen in a long time. Only, even more overwhelming in that, not only did this brother die for you, but he also suffered your every affliction and paid the price for your sins. I assume I might sob on his shoulder, but I may not have the strength to stand.

Who is the architect of your story? Of your every heartbeat? How are you helping future generations? Future cancer patients' boxes will be opened even if mine is not.

In order to learn to be the architect of your heartbeats, your heart needs a purpose. Dig up the why under the why. Dig deep to find the why and soulful purposes in your heartbeat. There are many spiritual numbers that signify the end of one phase and the beginning of another. Look for the signs of spiritual changes. Being awake and aware of these will lead you into the next beats of your life with certainty that when things end, it's only a beginning, a commemoration for greater things.

Beat 7

BEATS OF SOUL

MARSHALING HEARTBEATS REQUIRES SOUL.
MY SOUL'S JOURNEY IS DIAMETRICALLY OPPOSED TO
THE COLLECTIVE RATAPLAN, AND IT IS BEGINNING TO
MARCH TO ITS OWN BEAT; THE BEAT OF MY HEART
INSTEAD OF THE BEAT OF MY HEAD -THE WAY MY
JOURNEY IS TO BE.

ROUND FOUR

I've got soul, and I am a soldier fighting my way through the dark tunnel three times now. I've been cured three times, but the leukemia is back for a fourth fight. This relapse is hitting me hard. Everyone including doctors and nurses thought we had found my final cure. Blood tests aren't even being run. Similar to other relapses, I know before checking in due to pain and night sweats. I put a big smile on my

face (my smile is nearly back on both sides) and we take a family photo shoot with Heal Courageously. If you or someone you know has seen the darker side of life and are struggling, there are foundations and others who can help you see some light again, just as the camera's flash from Heal Courageously does for us. I am so weak and on so many pain medications, I have to sleep between each photo spot. Enduring the pain, I use family pictures as an excuse for the hospital to let me out a little earlier than they probably planned. I'm taking plane rides from one hospital on the East Coast back to another hospital in the west in order to officially sign the protocol for the T-cell study. The road to avoiding people, heavy crowds, and family gatherings is long. Socializing online isn't as heartfelt.

These are some words that uplift us during this season:

"He giveth power to the faint, and to them that have no might he increaseth strength . . . They that wait upon the Lord shall renew their strength; they shall mount up with wings as eagles; they shall run, and not be weary, and they shall walk and not faint" -Isaiah 40:29-31.

Remission lasted merely five months this time. Being back in the saddle so quickly has brought stress, financial burden, and physical exhaustion to our side saddlebags. I am fighting every day for a plan and for a crack at this T-cell thing again. Usually, the study does not allow another try, but my case of accidental complete remission before T-cells were injected and no cytokine storm is unusual. I fly back to Philly and, yes, it's worth another shot! The FDA is regulating this trial and in order to try T-cell therapy again not in remission, the FDA has to be petitioned and a whole new protocol unique to me has to be written. We are trying to buy some time for all this to happen. It's a little tricky with aggressive, chemotherapy-resistant leukemia.

The plan is now high-dose chemo and blinatumomab to keep the disease at bay. It's hard on my liver and I have to stop treatment periodically to give my organs a break.

I'm happy to try the T-cell therapy again, but getting there is proving difficult. My body is tired from this long fight and is definitely more beat up and not as upbeat this fourth round. I distract myself with other happy things to avoid cancer taking over every moment.

Philadelphia phlebotomists collect T-cells for a second time. The way they will be administered is different this time: in three different doses, starting with a smaller dose and ending with a larger dose. Last year I had one small dose—one-tenth of the units they initially planned. Immunology still works. T-cell therapy works. Never give up, give until you feel it. My heavy burdens are lighter through others' ordinary gestures. Some roads get lonelier the longer you ride on them. Each relapse is a bit more lonely. People don't know what to say or do anymore. It's hard to relate to a difficult journey sometimes when you're trying to keep your own journey happy.

MY WHY

Although the chemo, radiation, and spinal taps have been grueling and unpleasant I have recently been guided by this bit of wisdom attributed to Neitze,

"He who has a why to live for, can bear almost any how."

Allow me to give you a glimpse of my WHY.

My WHY is my beautiful family—the tender and lively experiences that leave me surprised by joy amidst a backdrop of uncertainty.

One night, after putting my son down for bed I slouch down onto the couch to watch the evening news and wind down. As soon as I am nice and comfortable I hear a soft, little voice from the hallway, "Daddy?" Expecting his usual antics to delay bedtime, I ignore the quiet plea. Fifteen to twenty seconds later, still soft and tender, I hear

it again, "Daddy?" This time I relent, leaving my comfy perch to find out what excuse he has to stay awake.

In one of many moments where my child has become my teacher he humbles me with these words, "Daddy, I'm scared. Can you show me how to pray for help?" I put my hand on his shoulder and we walk back to his bedroom and kneel in prayer asking for comfort, peace, and protection. With tears in my eyes, I tuck my little guy back into bed and he sleeps soundly through the night. The words are in the way of what my heart wants to say. When the night is over, instead of being upset about the bedtime delay, I am glad for that extra time to look into my son's eyes and teach him to pray when he is afraid.

My dear caregiving wife. To be with her is to breathe and she is another of my angels. For every breath that this boy takes, a heartbeat follows for her sake. When she smiles it is like the sunshine hitting my cold skin. Natural, rural, wild surroundings are a form of escape for her from the city. She lies down in the long wheat on the ranch, holding my hand as we hide in the long grass on her family ranch. Eventually, many aspects of the careful country girl's life and the driven city mom mix together like the wheat and the tears mixed together that night. After one country visit, we are home with medical pamphlets from Be The Match, the national bone marrow registry where we found my donor. She sits down on our soft, gray lounge chair and reads for hours about caregivers, about leukemia, about medical trials since my medical treatments didn't cure me after three tries. I watch her read and take in how beautiful my wife really is. I am breathing her in and can't believe she is mine forever. She wears a modest, but elegant gray dress with a light yellow pullover. Her angled cheekbones and strong but feminine jaw make her the epitome of beauty and strength while she reads,

"Your experience as a caregiver can be just as intense as the person who received the transplant. Your lifestyle, values, priorities, and relationships may change too. You need your own support and plans for how to cope. It is natural to sometimes feel overwhelmed by responsibility, caring for your loved one and other family members, the house, finances, etc. It is not unusual for caregivers to ignore their own needs. If you become exhausted and overwhelmed, it can affect your ability to provide good care."[44]

Time tests us and wears down caregivers and patients alike. I had a sudden diagnosis, a roller coaster of treatments, and high then low chances of survival. After months of medical intensity, we step back, smell some roses, and prioritize. Check out my album cover of my EP *Sugarland Sessions* which captures the moment where my wife learns to smell the roses even during the intense rollercoaster of cancer life. It is normal to feel sadness, anger, grief, guilt, and loneliness. We all discover our own path to recovery. She's been focused on me for so long, and I've been focused on the fight. Do you ever lose yourself and have to find yourself ALL over again? I am a different person now. She is a different person now. Characteristics I've noticed she's gained include grace, humility, gratitude, perspective on life, cancer and biology knowledge, and strength—all gained from life pursuits being put on hold for months and years. Progression and learning are needs that we thought were on hold and later realized that progress and knowledge accrued during the journey and especially during the pain.

I am amidst a whole lot of pain with little break even with two pain patches and pain pills around the clock. I am meeting with the pulmonary specialist due to persistent pneumonia. I finish another round of blinatumomab and get a break from the biotherapy. I am hoping it will give me a break from pain for at least ten days until starting the biotherapy again.

Break From the World

I'm having some trouble being myself
I can't remember what that is anymore
Because I'm not happy with what I used to be
I fall asleep while drifting in a painful direction
Now I wake up in the middle of nowhere
And I'm tired
And I'm lost here
And I need a hand
But I hide that
I'm scared that
No one will understand
Finally I wake up and open my eyes
And I don't like what I see
I start thinking, the whole world has gone crazy
Or is the world just fine and something is wrong with me?
So I'm looking for a new world
Where I can just be free and not worry
About money or the bullshit on TV
I'm alone but not myself
I just want a break from the world
Away from the world
I decide to change my mind
I decide to use my heart to be ME

(by Marshall Jensen)

My wife sees my relentless pain. We are hoping relief will come at least for a while. This pain has been the hardest and longest yet, and my wife tells me daily she wishes she could take it away from me. I learned from reading the Bhagavad Gita that I am not the body. Nor am I the mind or intellect even though I am terrified to lose that. Nor am I the ego. I am a soul, and remembering this helps me to rise above pleasure or pain. The soul is neither born nor does it die. Sri Krishna said that the soul is never born nor dies at any time. Soul has not come into being, does not come into being, and will not come into being. The soul is unborn, eternal, ever-existing, and primeval. The soul is not slain when the body is slain. Everyone has been sent to this world with limited breath/life span—so utilize them in the best possible way. Do not waste them or dissipate the energies.

I am staying on the biotherapy and whether I'm in complete remission when the time comes or not, I am flying east yet again to try T-cells a second time. We may have to wait a while until some leukemia comes back to try another round of T-cell therapy. The best way to treat leukemia at this point would be to try a different marker on the cancer cells. This means the T-cells have to be re-engineered differently than before and I will be the first to try a new marker. I wish I could be omniscient for a minute or have a crystal ball to plan for the next step.

"Behold happy is the man whom God correcteth: therefore despise not thou the chastening of the Almighty. For he maketh sore and bindeth up those he woundeth, and his hands make whole." In Job 5, the Lord says he will deliver Job in six troubles. This is our fourth fight with cancer, so I figure we have a couple more rounds if we even want to compare to Job's troubles. I have found solace in Job's words.

My leukemia makes its way back into my brain fluid. This frightens me because I do not want a recurrence of the facial paralysis I suffered last summer. My smile is still a little "slouchy" on the left side but

is getting there. Luckily AJ is absolutely adorable no matter what, so she helps even things out.

I have spinal taps twice a week and yesterday's sample was not quite cancer free but is very, very close. Once we get a month of clean results I will be able to proceed with the T-cell treatment try number two.

The F.D.A. is likely to approve the new protocol for my treatment. As soon as it's approved I will fly east and sign the consent which begins the four-week process of reengineering my T-cells in the lab.

If the timing is just right I will get my four weeks of clean spinal taps during the same four weeks they are engineering my T-cells and not give leukemia any extra time to cause trouble. The odds of us pulling that off would be pretty incredible!

My leukemia is already causing some trouble. Last week we found another tumor growing in my right forearm. It hurts and you can actually see a large bulge developing on my inner tibia behind my wrist.

We blast this tumor with a little more power than my last one. Hopefully, it works too because that's my guitar-strumming wrist! The radiation leaves me nauseated and wiped out, but, hey, I "ran" a 5k with a bag of chemo on my waist. Not to brag or anything—if you want to know a real hero you should meet my friend. Not only is he a cancer survivor, but the chemo messed up his heart so bad he had to get a new heart. You'd think it'd be enough for him just to get up and eat a bowl of cereal in the morning but this guy decided to run Ironman triathlons! Seriously, he just finished one. They call him the Tin Man because he is a heart transplant recipient. He's inspiring me through some of the toughest times.

He asked if I would speak with him at a Leukemia and Lymphoma Society dinner. I obliged and found myself telling our cancer story to a room full of runners and fundraisers. I got to meet the president of the 76ers who invited me to a ball game. I may not be up for an Ironman competition anytime in the near future, but I do try to take my dog out for a bike ride when I have the energy. Recently, a song about fighting for greatness, what I'm really made of, and that all life is beautiful popped up on my playlist while walking the dog and gave me an extra ounce of inspiration to fight the battle. This battle is raging inside of me whether I want it there or not and I choose to make every day the greatest as if it were my last.

BACK TO THE FUTURE DAY

Conrad was an intelligent kid. I'm pretty sure he would have majored in the sciences if he stuck around long enough to go to college. He had a great love and compassion for animals and would often bring a new creature home to live with us. You name it: fish, frogs, birds, lizards, snakes, rabbits, even our dog Misty. Conrad always seemed to find a way to convince our parents to let us "keep it."

He also loved computers and computer games. I could have easily seen him going into the computer science field. He loved music and singing. He had begun teaching himself hymns on the piano, and even writing and playing his own songs on the guitar.

We used to trade basketball cards and we bargained and swindled until we had built up a pretty substantial collection. He loved being active—basketball and rollerblading were two of his favorite activities.

At times it was hard to be his younger brother because one day he'd be my best friend and the next weekend he was too cool to have anything to do with me. At the time it was devastating, but I understand it much better now.

In simple terms, Conrad was fun. He used to tend to our younger brother and sister. Aside from the heaping pots of macaroni and cheese and the learning activities he came up with, he also had a very serious rule, "HAVE FUN."

On October 21, 2015, Marty and Doc drove their flying car into the *Tonight Show*. This was the day in *Back to the Future* that they traveled to in order to set things straight from all their time travels. I am also contemplating what I would do if I could go back in time. You see, seventeen years ago tomorrow my brother Conrad succumbed to his demons and took his own life. He had a life full of meaning and purpose and yet the clouds were too dark, and the pain was too strong. He has now been away from us just as long as he was with us and it still hurts. I never did get to say goodbye to my dear brother. However, as with many things in life, this tragedy inspired me to write a song, "I Never Got to Say Goodbye."

I remember what it was like before you were gone
I can still remember the day things went wrong
Everyone knew but no one would tell me
Everyone knew but no one would tell me
I already knew but no one would tell me
I already knew about you, I already knew.
I knew you would jump that day,
The sky was dim with clouds
Once I heard you say that you didn't want to be around
I knew you would jump that day,
Fall into the ground
Once I heard you say that you didn't want to be around
I always tried to hide it, but not from myself
Everyone thought I denied it,

But I just did it my way
You always said it, but I don't believe you
I already knew about you, I already knew
When we talked and when we fought,
I never thought that you'd be gone
You made me mad and you made me cry
I never got to say goodbye
Goodbye, I never got to to say goodbye
Goodbye, Goodbye

(by Marshall Jensen)

Now I find myself fighting for the very thing that my brother was desperate to escape, mortality. I can't tell you everything that led up to Conrad's decision to jump from that overpass. If I could time travel, that is the first place I would go. I would tell him how much I care, that his life matters to many, and how much we love him. I would take his hand before he jumps and let him be at ease within my love.

Within Your Love

When I take your hand
I can see the world
The way it should be
And I become at ease within your love

Though a storm is o'er us
Look what lies before us
Worlds without end
Just around the bend

When I am doubting
Fearing what may come
I become at ease within your love

(by Marshall Jensen)

I don't currently own a nifty time-traveling DeLorean, but I can live every day as if it were my last. I can reach out and be kind. If you know someone who is truly struggling, don't wait. Let them know they are loved. Help them get help. Don't wait for someone else to do it—it may be too late.

One thing I've learned as I've struggled through cancer treatments is that there is so much good in the world. There are so many good people who want to and are driven to serve by the light that burns within them. If you really want to change things and change the world, you've got to do more than just believe and wait on the world to change. You've got to get out there and try to change it. Get out there and do the Heart Jolts found in every chapter so we have more people living with love! We can only love others deeply as we put these words into action. Are you avoiding who you are and what your mission is on this earth? One thing you are responsible for is to do the work to love yourself and love others. It's maddening that more people aren't doing this work to use their hearts as much as their heads. You are not responsible for how others are not using their heart, but you are responsible for your own heart. Go out and speak to their heart as we all try a little bit more each day to lead each other home to our hearts instead of getting stuck in our heads.

WE ARE HOME

We all want to come home, be taken care of, and be in a safe space. I've never had ruby slippers or a dog. Right now I have two dogs and a couple of adorable nieces living with me that must have some ruby slippers. All I can say is, "There's no place like home." When you return home, there's no closing the doors of my heart here. Just as Dorothy followed her yellow brick road that led to a fantasy that was really just herself, my path has brought me to myself. I found this magical stairway that I imagine stair by stair walking me away from my head and into my heart. It's like the song "Stairway to Heaven" that I love to jam to. Walking my hands down the chords walks my soul home on my guitar. All the things I've given during this journey down my stairway have been returned to me one hundred times over. Just as Dorothy clicked her sparkling shoes together to return home, I discovered that I have an innate ability to return to myself. I can find a new me every day just by changing my attitude, taking the time to breathe, and choosing to be loving and helpful instead of resentful and angry. If I work on myself first every day, I am less likely to betray myself. The heaviness of every day will be light and fun just like Conrad made every responsibility when babysitting his siblings.

Christ is another symbol I look to when remembering to make heavy things light. We received a beautiful portrait of Christ more accurately depicted of Jewish ancestry rather than the Scandinavian approach by many artists. Painted mostly on Sundays, it holds such a

significant place in our hearts and strengthens my resolve. When you aren't finding the ability within yourself, find an enabling power. The artist is my wife's uncle who is acquainted with his own griefs and sorrows and yet he gives constantly. We are all one. Moments of trial, loss, grief, depression, temptations, addictions, abuse, disease, or any physical or spiritual limitations—if we rely on each other to heal, help, and forgive, that is where we can all be one in our hearts. Like the root system of the trees that connect more than we know, our heartbeats can connect similarly to other souls throughout the world. The portrait shows a man who suffered so that we did not need to suffer as much. No matter the outcome of our trials, our hearts will beat stronger together.

*****

Goodbye again to our home, our son, friends and family, cars, and dogs. Hello again to the city of brotherly love, and T-cell try number two! We made it across the country again. There were many days that we weren't sure we would even make it this far so this is a step in the right direction and a feat that was not easy. I was back in the hospital for quite some time with severe pain. I was released only to be able to pack up and fly here after a weekend home. The severe pain is the result of leukemia growing out of control over many spots in my body—hip, knees, ankles, wrists, and back. We flew here with the help of wheelchairs and first-class flights. I felt so pampered reclining the seats and munching on delicatessen snacks. Our flights took all day and the plan was to meet with the doctor the next day to start preparing for T-cells. Our room view is gorgeous overlooking the Delaware River. As we are now used to, the plan changes . . .

I wake up in our hotel room and cannot move. I inform my wife that I can not get out of bed; we have to call an ambulance because I can not even lift my arms to get dressed. She doesn't like the idea. We've had our fair share of emergency room experiences and the one here previously was by far the worst . . . waiting in the ER for five hours writhing in pain then waiting another half day or so for a room to open in the hospital. That was our last experience in the city of brotherly love and not the best option. She listens to me beg for an ambulance in my state of anxiety and panic. I haven't slept much at all for days due to pain. AJ pep talks me into going in for my appointment two hours early. She tells me if I can just roll into a wheelchair she'll get me to my appointment where we would ask the doctor for admission today instead of tomorrow. She assures me that if I am not able to roll into the wheelchair that she will dial 911.

I do it. It hurts astronomically. With pain ravaging my entire body, she helps me dress and roll over into that wheelchair. We take a taxi to the hospital to find out that I am not ready for T-cell treatment due to the cancer being out of control. If I were to receive T-cells at this stage either the T-cells will wreak havoc or they would take a while to react (if they work) and cancer will need to be treated with steroids or chemo that will kill off the T-cells. So last year, there wasn't enough leukemia to create the desired reaction; this year there is too much. We need the sweet spot in order to try this treatment again. The plan is we wait for my blood counts to tank, then recover, then go on to the actual plan. As we've grown accustomed, that plan could definitely change. Ironically, I am coloring in an adult coloring book that distracts me from pain and the current page is the quote attributed to John Lennon, "Life is what happens when you are making other plans."

Clofarabine is a chemotherapy that's used to treat patients with refractory disease. I finish my third bag making me officially halfway

done. I'm no newbie to this, so I expect most side effects to come in about a week. My blood counts are definitely dropping, but they were super low prior to this due to cancer building up in my marrow. Blood transfusions and platelet transfusions or both are a daily occurrence. The pain does not let up at first, and I am nervous that the chemotherapy will do nothing to the disease. It does get better and I even walk a little without the use of a wheelchair. When I walk to the bathroom without my walker, my wife tells me how proud she is. She was even more proud when I make it halfway down the hall! I sometimes lose myself walking down the eternal hospital corridors. I stare at hospital walls that feel like prison walls. They feel that way because I am not free to do anything but fight this bloody cancer. I lose myself and all I used to enjoy outside of the hospital. We've canceled plans for nearly four years now. Instead, we are walking these hospital halls in these shoes. It lifts me to contemplate helping others search for a cure.

Our time these days is consumed with finding the cure for cancer, FaceTiming my little boy, and my wife works at coding while I make jingles for the credit repair company and send them my creative songs. Our hearts hurt missing our little boy this second T-cell trial try. We actually asked him this time if he preferred to stay back home where he could go to preschool or come with us and he chose home with grandma. They have a very special bond and we are beyond grateful to good mothers. We watch his Halloween program and his last soccer game via a screen. His preschool Halloween poems and songs melt our hearts. Battling across the country takes a toll on him, but we FaceTime him five times a day. We anticipate the day he flies here or we fly back home.

These past four years have taken a toll on my wife in the form of costochondritis. It's a condition where her heart literally hurts. Brought on by a lot of stress, she assures me it will go away when the stress lowers. As much as our hearts hurt missing our little boy, and as much as we'd love to give him a sibling, cancer often causes infertility. We tried two cycles of in vitro fertilization that failed before I relapsed this year. One cycle failed when we found out I relapsed. It is not helpful to compare burdens. We ALL have our struggles. Be they small, large, or somewhere in between. When we write all our problems on a piece of paper and throw them into a pile, we often find we want to grab our own right back after reading the struggles others face.

*****

SALT

So let's add some spice to our heartbeats. Here's a recipe for adding SALT to spice up your heartbeats:

SALT—Soul, Act, Love, Teach

Give a man a fish, feed him for a day, or teach a man to fish and feed him for a lifetime. You are all teachers more often than you realize.

I gaze over at the vibrant colors in a painting hanging in my library over another FaceTime call with my son and grandma. The painter, a young Brazilian boy, created a fisherman. I recall walking into the library, the lines in the fisherman's strong, muscular back greeting me. His muscles ripple through broad brush strokes as he works hard to gather his fish. He is not hanging back on the sidelines of fishing. He is jumping right into the water, right into the action, and working his muscles and mind in order to learn for himself, unlike the skinny gawkers on the side of the ocean judging his fishless net. If you're a spectator on the sideline of any sport are you reaping the health benefits of being in the game?

My wife cooks amazing fish. One Super Bowl Sunday, she asked my mom if we could make it a Souper Bowl Sunday by teaching her to make a few of her delicious soups. My mom gifted us an amazing family recipe book.

Heart Jolt 8:

I INVITE YOU ALL TO NOT JUST SIT AND EAT WHILE READING THIS BEAT, BUT TO CONTRIBUTE TO THE MEAL. THIS BEAT IS AN INVITATION TO PONDER AND WRITE DOWN SOME OF THE WAYS YOU WANT TO ADD YUMMY SPICES TO YOUR RECIPES OF LIFE FROM EACH BEAT OF THIS BOOK. AS THE SPICE GIRLS WOULD SAY, "SPICE UP YOUR LIFE!"

Think of the ingredient SALT and ALL it adds to the taste of life. Add even more spices to make life tastier, but for this beat remember to add: S, A, L, T.

S: SOUL—LIVE YOUR HEARTBEATS WITH SOUL . . .

Burton said, "It is only with the heart one can see rightly...

Sri Krishna said: "This individual soul is unbreakable and insoluble, and can be neither burned nor dried. He is everlasting, present everywhere, unchangeable, immovable, and eternally the same."[45] Sometimes what you see with your eyes navigating tons of carefully catered screens and web pages isn't good enough. Things of most importance are often invisible to the eye. What the world offers and thinks you need is often not healing or soulful. One way to look toward a better light source is by seeking an unrushed atmosphere. Too many of us rush. We rush right past the things that feed our souls trying to beat the clock in some unnecessary footrace. Instead rush to be an instrument in helping someone else, adapt your needs by being in the present moment. Now is the time to postpone later. Procrastinate later. Perform your duties without hesitance and without thinking of the outcome.[46] Be aware of others' needs and intentionally think of ways you can help. Each of you has very specific challenges. When talking to others, change your dynamic from 'I know how you feel' to listening to their specific circumstance in order to specifically help. Concentrate on what they are saying instead of what you want to say. Ask them what their needs are. Concentrating on their needs will help your needs feel lighter. Concentrating on people instead of a set idea can also help.

It's not about saying all you want to say if we are truly thinking of others. Personal experiences prepare you if you have quiet, still time every day. Sri Krishna said: "Some look on the soul as amazing, some describe him as amazing, and some hear of him as amazing, while others, even after hearing about him, cannot understand him at all."

Heart Jolt 9 by everyday health.

APPROACHING LIFE WITH AN OPEN HEART MEANS THAT WE HAVE OPENED THE DOOR TO GREATER CONSCIOUSNESS.

SPIRITUAL TEACHERS HAVE ALWAYS POINTED TO THE HEART AS THE SEAT OF CONSCIOUSNESS, AND RECENTLY WESTERN SCIENCE HAS FOUND EVIDENCE TO SUPPORT THIS REALIZATION. IT TURNS OUT THAT THE HEART HAS ITS OWN CENTRAL NERVOUS SYSTEM AND IS NOT SIMPLY UNDER THE RULE OF THE BRAIN AS FORMERLY BELIEVED. ANYONE WHO HAS TAKEN THE TIME TO EXPLORE THE HEART KNOWS THIS AND, MORE IMPORTANT, HAS REALIZED THAT THE HEART IS THE SOURCE OF OUR CONNECTION TO A CONSCIOUSNESS GREATER THAN THE EGO. APPROACHING LIFE WITH AN OPEN HEART MEANS THAT WE HAVE OPENED THE DOOR TO THIS GREATER CONSCIOUSNESS, TAKING UP RESIDENCE ALONGSIDE IT IN THE SEAT OF OUR SOUL. FORTUNATELY, AT THIS TIME THERE IS A LOT OF SUPPORT FOR THIS SHIFT ENERGETICALLY AS WELL AS PRACTICALLY. TO SOME DEGREE, APPROACHING LIFE WITH AN OPEN HEART IS AS SIMPLE AS SHIFTING YOUR ATTENTION ONTO YOUR HEART.

EVENTUALLY, YOU WILL BE ABLE TO DO THIS ANY TIME, ANY PLACE, BUT AT FIRST, IT MAY HELP TO TRY IT IN A QUIET PLACE WHERE YOU WON'T BE DISTURBED. SIMPLY SIT WITH YOUR EYES CLOSED AND DRAW YOUR BREATH INTO YOUR HEART. AS YOUR BREATH EXPANDS YOUR CHEST CAVITY, YOUR HEART EXPANDS AND OPENS. YOU MAY FEEL TENDERNESS OR SADNESS IN YOUR HEART, AND YOU MAY ALSO

FEEL RELIEF. ANY EMOTIONS THAT ARISE CAN BE EFFECTIVELY WITNESSED AND HEALED THROUGH THE MEDITATION PROCESS, WHICH BENEFITS BOTH YOUR PHYSICAL HEART AND YOUR ENERGETIC HEART. THE MORE YOU PRACTICE, THE MORE YOU WILL FIND YOUR HEART OPENING TO YOUR OWN PRESENCE AND TO ALL THE SITUATIONS YOUR LIFE BRINGS.

WHEN WE OPEN OUR HEARTS, THEY MAY FEEL TENDER AND VULNERABLE, WHICH SIMPLY MEANS THAT THEY NEED OUR LOVING ATTENTION AS WE CLEANSE AND HEAL THEM OF PAST HURTS AND BLOCKAGES. THIS PROCESS ASKS US TO PRACTICE SOME OF THE HEART'S GREATEST LESSONS--PATIENCE, COM-PASSION, AND UNCONDITIONAL LOVE. ON THE OTHER HAND, WE MAY TAKE UP RESIDENCE AS EFFORTLESSLY AS A BIRD RETURNS TO ITS NEST. EITHER WAY, APPROACHING LIFE WITH AN OPEN HEART SIMPLY MEANS RETURNING TO OUR TRUE HOME.[47]

Keep it simple and concentrate on needs. Simplicity inspires heart-felt questions.

When people ask how you are doing, how do you respond?

I respond intentionally.

I practiced answering "Living the dream" or "It's the best day EVER" even before the hardest cancer days.

Not only are people taken aback at this response, but I truly believe it despite what happens that day. Despite the poison flowing through my veins or radiation scarring my body, lungs, and heart—I truly have

the best days of my life amidst the worst days. I sit in the pouring rain and, at the same moment, the sun is blazing in the sky.

Do you want to have the best life ever? It's as simple as training your mind to tell your heart that you are living the best life! Whatever that life looks like or ends up being for you or however you want to train yourself to answer questions you are asked daily. Maybe you want a quiet and calm life? Then train yourself to answer when people ask how you are doing, "tranquil, so much peace" or "much stillness today," no matter what storms are raging around you. Find the eye of the storm by responding with intention.

You know you are in the eye of the storm when asked how you are doing or you ask how they are doing; you try to strengthen your emotional vocabulary or help them strengthen theirs. Avoid the "fines," the "goods," and the "oks." There may still be a storm raging around you even if you are calm. You can say, I'm being whipped around by whirlwinds. So many times when asked how we are doing, we use the same old "fines, goods, oks." If you learn to communicate with a more detailed explanation of how you truly are and encourage others to do the same then you will feel more understood and can be more understanding. Others will feel like they are being heard instead of just blowing off how they truly feel to the wind. That can create prevalent mental illnesses because 'how I feel doesn't *really* matter. They are just asking to be polite and I'll just answer quickly to be polite and we'll move on."

For you who are or have ever been married, remember how *everyone* would ask you, "How's married life" the first few months? Most people respond with a boring or predictable, "It's great!" or "It's going well." I would answer, "The sex is great" or "If I were any better I would be twins!" Sometimes inappropriately depending on who asked. I loved the shock factor, the laughter, and mostly the reaction from the unexpected answer instead of the mundane.

There are societal and mental stigmas and boundaries you draw on yourself in the culture you are raised in. These boundaries vary from culture to culture. One friend married at a very young age. She told me one day that one of my Latino friends was obviously hitting on her on a social media platform. But, by golly, she is a married woman! Knowing the loving character of my Latino friend well, he was brought up in a culture and raised to be very complimentary to women. He was not hitting on her at all, but merely saying and doing what he does to all women he knows. The thought going through my mind at that moment was not, "Oh, my word! I cannot believe he did that or said that," but rather, "Wow, more of us need to get out of the culture we were raised in and understand other cultures better." Have an open mind and an open heart to those who are different from yourself—to those who perhaps do not share your nationality, or religion, who do not look or act like you. Pause before judging others' actions wrongly.

Marshalling your heart requires being a friend. One of my favorite pastimes is reading religious books like the Quran and Bhagavad Gita. These special works are important to billions of people around the world. Learn to understand what is important to others. Especially those who are different from your culture and religious upbringing. I love visiting as many denominations, mosques, and congregations as I can. While I was recording music in Minnesota, I met one reverend while playing football with his son. He watched as I played my guitar once and declared me "a natural-born worship leader!" The next day he had me at the front of his congregation playing music and leading his whole congregation in praises to the Lord. Whatever you do, do it with your whole heart. Don't let differences build walls around you and those who are different from you. It's worth it to tear those walls down and enjoy the diversity, the oneness, the wholeness, and the spiritual awakening that occurs when more diversity is brought together

in one space. You are more like the people who live on the other side of your world than you are different from them. If you focus on differences instead of similarities, the world will give you boxes and say you can't get along because we are all so different. If you focus on similarities, those walls crash down and those boxes we put each other into are broken down to openness.

A brown parchment paper sits in my "memories and photos" box stored in the attic. It is addressed to my home, dated November 15, 2008, from Apostle Lewis, Minneapolis, Minnesota. It reads,

"Marshall, Thank you for sending a copy of your CD. We were truly blessed during your visit this past summer. I pray all is well with you and that the power of God continues to bless you. If you are ever in Minneapolis, please stop by and see us again. Stay strong in the word and in the power of his might! In them, Apostle & Prophetess Lewis."

Know the power of words. Use them to their best powers. Words create worlds.[48]

The power of a word "literally means that your words will essentially determine what you will try or what you fail to try, which ultimately shapes your expectations *and* your results moving forward. Each word you speak or write has a life of its own, a vibratory signature that creates waves in the same way that a note of music creates waves. And like musical notes, your words live in communities of other words and change in relation to the words that surround them. When you are conscious of the energy behind your words, you become capable of making beautiful music in the world. If you are unconscious of the power of words, you run the risk of creating a noisy disturbance. Words carry energy, and this gives language its power and its potential to heal or hurt. Most of us can remember a time that someone sent a word our way, and it stuck with us. It may have been the first time we received a truly accurate compliment or the time a friend or sibling called us a name, but either way, it stuck. This experience reminds us that what we say has weight and power and that being conscious means being aware of how we use words.

The more conscious we become, the more we deepen our relationship to the words we use so that we speak from a place of actually feeling what we are saying. We begin to recognize that words are not abstract, disconnected entities used only to convey meaning; they are powerful transmitters of feeling. For the next few days, you might want to practice noticing how the words you say and hear affect your body and your emotional state. Notice how the different communication styles of the people in your life make you feel. Also, watch closely to see how your own words come out and what effect they have on the people around you.

You may notice that when we speak without thinking or rush to get our ideas across, our words don't carry the same power as when we speak slowly and confidently, allowing those receiving our words time and space to take them in. When we carefully listen to others before we speak, our words have more integrity, and when we take time to center ourselves before speaking, we truly begin to harness the power of speech. Then our words can be intelligent messengers of healing and light, transmitting deep and positive feelings to those who receive them."[49]

It's better to speak five words that are understood and applied than ten thousand words that no one does anything with even if they do *sound* good. Quick and powerful words are "sharper than any two-edged sword" -1 Corinthians 14:9 piercing the soul, even the joints and marrow to provide a way to change thoughts and intents of hearts. Use your voice to fight every day for goodness. Language marks the coordinates of my life and fills my life[50] with meaningful things like the songs I write. Equipped with the right tools, you are more powerful

for good or bad change than if you owned the sharpest sword. To repeat, words create worlds. Words are energy. The power of the word has more effect on the mind than any blow from any sword.

Each word we speak has a life of its own, a vibratory signature that creates waves into the expanse of the universe.

When we speak or write, we use the vehicles of words to carry meaning, as well as energy, from ourselves to another person or group of people. We may be speaking to our baby, our boss, or an audience of 500 people. We may be writing a love letter, a work-related memo, or an entry in our own diary.

Some of us know this instinctively, while others come to this understanding slowly. Most of us, though, speak without thinking at least some of the time, blurting out our feelings and thoughts without much regard for the words we choose to express them. When we remind ourselves that our words have an impact on the world at the level of energy, we may find within ourselves the desire to be more aware of our use of language.

A fun way to increase our sensitivity to the power of words is to simply make a list of our favorite words and notice the energy they contain. We can write them down and post them where we can see them, or we can speak them aloud, feeling them reverberate in our bodies and in the air around us. This is like learning to consciously play an instrument that we have been playing unconsciously for most of our lives, and the effect can be startling and delightful. As we grow more comfortable and confident playing the instrument of language, we will begin to compose beautiful messages, creating positive energy every time we write or speak.[51]

We are all instruments, and instruments must listen to other instruments in order to sound well by themselves and while playing with others. Be an instrument to comfort and inspire. Or rile others up or to engage energy. Whatever instrument you choose to be, do it with all your heart. When using these instruments of the soul, the hearts of our children and those around us will beat with more love and your chosen message will penetrate stronger. Open the pathways into the heart. Your words deserve to be treasured, to be words that are giving life instead of taking it. Continually seeking wisdom and knowledge allows you to be present for more of life's minutes. Prepare through the use of great books that nourish not just feed. Everyone feels they don't know enough because no one does. Being relatable causes words to come alive. Your perspective is limited to the universe's perspective, but you have a wealth of universal words available to you and you ought to use them.

My young wife and her father were driving down a dusty road. She was intensely studying the picture of a cell in her biology book. She asked her dad about some interesting parts protruding out of the human cell. His analogy of the universe and planets revolving around a sun in comparison to the floating particles in our cells around the nucleus followed. Even the tiniest particle—the atom is relatable to the galaxy and the universe. Apparently, the small things truly are the big things according to biologists. Apply actions not just motions after reading and discussing great ideas. Ideas provide strength and a foundation of truth. Prophets, shamen, and wisdom seekers have special attention in our world for their words are as vital to success as are ancient texts. Relatable words strengthen our desire to do good in a troubled world. Use your words to bring peace to your children in tumultuous times.

Music is another magnificent teacher and way to bring soul to words. Let your words convey deep wisdom and sing with grace in your hearts -Colossians 3:16.

A: ACT—ACT WITHOUT BEING TOLD TO ACT . . .

I acted this way and that's how I changed my life . . .

Don't be the know-it-all in the room on every subject. Allow others to teach you. Assume responsibility for learning. Let others share, help, and gain confidence. Christ gave responsibilities to his apostles. He repeated the question three times, "Lovest thou me? Then answered, "Feed my sheep." The Savior invited an enquirer to act when he asked what he could do: "One thing thou lackest. Sell what thou hast and give to the poor. Thou shalt have treasure in heaven." Challenging yourself helps you notice the hand of God in your life. Inadequacy is merely a launch pad to aim high.

Have a desire to learn, study, understand, and live using your own efforts. Diligent learning prepares yourself and your kids for life challenges. If you are a parent, are you preparing your kids to seek learning by study or are you preparing to wait and be acted upon? Are you giving them the equivalent of fish to eat or consistently helping them to act, seek, and fish for themselves? That which is in the mind needs to be felt and owned in children's hearts, not just relying on parents. The feeling is the meat of the world that you are ready for after the milk of thinking.

Unity and patience are the step by step, line by line process. Day by day as you choose to act, your hearts will change to unity. Unity empowers more change and strengthens yourself and those around you. Ancient writings teach us if you are void of wisdom you despise your neighbor, but if you are an understanding person you hold peace. Weaknesses are challenges that inspire change. You will change the world to live in harmony through developing kind and peaceful attributes. You will be more gentle with your own and other's weaknesses. Learning and living are the building blocks to harmony. When you learn an instrument, you start with the basics and build from there until you can create beautiful and harmonious music with others who are also learning their instrument. Creating beautiful, harmonious lives happens through small steps. Some steps are steps of excursion, not just passive absorption.

L: LOVE—LOVE EACH HEARTBEAT AND LIFE . . .

CHARITY IS KEY IN THE POWER TO CHANGE YOUR HEART. ONE FEBRUARY DAY, AFTER A DECADE OF TRYING TO HAVE CHILDREN, THE EDWARDS (THE COUPLE THAT ALLOWED US TO STAY WITH THEM WHILE I WAS BEING TREATED IN TEXAS) WERE ABLE TO LISTEN TO THEIR TWINS' HEARTBEATS IN UTERO. "IT WAS THE MOST AMAZING AND EXHILARATING FEELING EVER. I HAVE THE BIGGEST SMILE ON MY FACE AND THIS OVERWHELMING FEELING OF GRATITUDE AND EXCITEMENT FOR THE FUTURE." IN 2015, TWINS JUBILEE AND JONATHAN WERE BORN TO JOHN AND SHERILYN EDWARDS WHO HAD TRIED FOR YEARS TO BE PARENTS. IT TOOK THREE WOMEN TO GET THESE SOULS TO THE EARTH. THEIR MOTHER, MY WIFE-THE EGG DONOR-, AND THE SURROGATE WHO CARRIED THEM FOR NINE MONTHS. THE DARK-EYED, DARK-SKINNED SURROGATE BIRTHED TWO BLONDE-HAIRED, BLUE-EYED BABIES. THIS EXPERIENCE CHANGED THE HEART OF EVERY PERSON INVOLVED AND CONTINUES TO DO SO TODAY. "WHEN THEY WERE BORN I REMEMBER THE LORD INFUSING MY HEART WITH THIS AMAZING FEELING OF LOVE. EVERY TIME I WAS CLOSE IN THEIR PHYSICAL PRESENCE I HAD THIS AMAZING RECIPROCAL

FEELING OF LOVE COMING FROM BOTH OF THEM. BABIES ARE JUST PURE LOVE IN PHYSICAL FORM. THIS LOVE I FELT FOR THEM MUST BE HOW MUCH THE LORD LOVES US ALL. THIS TREMENDOUS LOVE I FEEL FOR MY CHILDREN IS ALWAYS THERE NO MATTER HOW BADLY THEY MISBEHAVE. I CHERISH THEIR PRESENCE EVERY MINUTE WE ARE TOGETHER. THESE FEELINGS HAVE NEVER ABATED. EVER. SOMETIMES WHEN I SPEAK TO AJ ABOUT MY GRATITUDE MY VOICE CRACKS BECAUSE HAVING CHILDREN WAS ONE OF MY MOST DEEP-LY HELD DREAMS FOR MY LIFE. I REMAIN SO PROFOUNDLY GRATEFUL FOR WHAT HER GIFT HAS DONE FOR MY LIFE. IT WAS AMAZING. WE CRIED AND HUGGED."[52]

My wife says donating eggs was the best gift she has ever given in her life and that this experience of hearing the Edwards hear their twins' heartbeats for the first time reminds her of the importance of giving the best gifts she can to others throughout her life. Love is another of the best gifts.

If children or others are not responding to you, maybe you just can't teach them yet, but you can love them. If you love someone today, maybe you can teach that same person the day after you show your love toward them. Maybe there is a disruptive person in your life. Know and love them personally. Your love gives them power. Ask, "How can I help people resolve their problems? How can I help people and myself overcome their bad habits and vices?" Through many years of service, love, and helping others you are changed. The more people you see and are moved toward compassion to help, the more valuable your life feels.

One teacher started telling her students she loved them one by one as they left her classroom. At first it was awkward. Over time things changed, they grew to love her, and years later her students still remembered knowing each week that someone loved them.

Don't just speak or teach about love—*show* it. You need not remove yourselves from the crowds in attempts to feel better, entitled, or above others. We Are ALL One. Humanity needs your hands to lift up and heal, and you need to be lifted up and healed by others hands when you are in need. If you use your hands to lift and heal others, they will learn to do the same. Your hands equal love.

What good is life without love? As you show love to each person they become aware of their infinite worth. Seek to understand and reach out to individuals. Worry a little more about the location of others and what is going on in their heart and soul. Include them and listen even when they are different than you are or have differing opinions than yours. My wife read this passage from her dad with tears streaming down her face: "My sweet baby girl! A very fine line separates faith from fear. I don't pretend to understand it, but I think it has something to do with choosing to follow a compelling voice from deep within that whispers, 'Head up, move forward, smile through the pain and uncertainty, and trust in the one who descended below it all to usher you safely home.' Your opportunity becomes my opportunity to comprehend a little more clearly the depth of His perfect love. Look, listen, breathe, and know that He—and the rest of us—are very near. All my love, Daddy."

THERE IS NO FEAR IN LOVE

Even when 97 percent of my bone marrow is taken over by lymphoblast cancerous cells and chemotherapy destroys most of the bone marrow by design, there is no fear in love. After the destruction, any stride in the right direction is good news. I knew the fight was far from over in the beginning. The doctors kept reminding me of that during the first mile of my marathon.

I started reading the book of Job. It adds a spirit of love and peace that I have felt everyday through this process. If anybody overcame difficult trials he did. In the first chapter alone, Job's oxen are stolen, his sheep are burned, his camels are stolen, his servants are slaughtered, and tragically his ten children are killed. I was quite inspired by the way that Job handles this devastating news. The chapter concludes as follows:

"Then Job arose, and rent his mantle, and shaved his head, and fell down upon the ground, and worshiped, and said, Naked came I out of my mother's womb, and naked shall I return thither: the Lord gave, and the Lord hath taken away; blessed be the name of the Lord" -Job 1:20-21.

I love it! Job has a horrible trial and what does he do? He shaves his head and has a positive attitude. Well, you can guess who my new hero is, *and* his friends came to comfort him during his tribulation just like my friends.

AJ turns to me and asks, "Are you afraid of anything?" The question is suspended in the air between her little bench and my hospital bed. I take a moment to think about it, which is a rare exercise for me. Usually my mouth just starts yapping before I even know how I'm going to respond. I want everyone who reads this to know that I really thought deeply about this and I really meant it when I replied, "Honey, fear and love can't exist in the same sphere; and I have had so much love in this room that I couldn't be afraid if I wanted to."

There were so many who visited, called, texted, posted, emailed, cut your hair, shaved your head, fasted, prayed, served, cleaned, and showed compassion towards our family over the span of years.

During the years, I have felt surprised, tired, confused, sick, in pain, and even anxious—but never afraid. "There is no fear in love; but perfect love casteth out fear" -1 John 4:18.

T: TEACH—TEACH BY ASKING QUESTIONS . . .

Asking and answering is at the heart of all learning and teaching. The Master asks, "Whom say men that I am?" "Whom say ye that I am?" Some questions invite inspiration. Try to ask questions that will come alive. Sometimes just the right inflection or talking about feelings instead of making lists makes all the difference.

Where have you been? Where are you going? What is the best thing to do? If I was to ask you these questions pertaining to this book today you might answer: I am focusing on meat after milk. I will implement the ideas to teach people, not lessons and to concentrate on the needs of others. You've learned the meat, don't turn back to teaching the milky way without SALT. Remember what happened to Lot's wife in the bible when she turned back. She turned into salt.

We need not only talk, but we need to *listen*. Listen for new ideas. Listen with your heart and soul. Do not just lecture. Look outside the box, use analogies and stories like in sacred teachings not with a monotonous pattern. When taught with variety, learners tend to understand and retain more. Use object lessons, write a question down, have someone read an article or story, etc. One book I read had thirty-seven different methods to teach.

My wife's favorite class in college was International Health. The teacher used methods where the lessons still stick with her to this day. One day he divided the students into groups that represented different populations around the globe. Two were in the United States and fifteen were in Asia. He distributed jelly beans that represented the goods and consumption of each population in proportion to the goods and services we consume around the world. She was shocked at how many jelly beans the United States consumed in comparison to the population of the rest of the world. To this day, she actively tries

to apply this lesson by consuming less and minimizing the amount of stuff in her life. That stuff will just rot away when she's gone after all.

When AJ was teaching bioethics in college, she would pass out four marbles to each student who had to use the marbles through their participation before a free-for-all discussion. Some learners chose to remain quiet, but still had valuable and interesting perspectives. Some participated freely and loved to talk. She loved to do this in order to hear from the quieter learners who brought so much to a discussion.

One young man told his instructor there was no way he could learn Portuguese and he was giving up. The instructor sent him to a Japanese class. After one time in the Japanese class, the young man came to his instructor and said, "I am sure I can learn Portuguese."

Respond to those you teach with questions, even if it's just a question to restate lessons taught in their own words or require them to express what they understand.

Prepare questions from the best books and prioritize learning and study. Evaluate your teaching. My wife minored in international development. Non-governmental organizations from her university would often go into another country and decide what they thought was best for their community and do it. Sometimes they would build schools, bridges, businesses, or whatever they deemed would 'help' the population to be better in the area. Oftentimes, what they thought would help would end up harming instead. It is imperative that we evaluate the effects of what we are doing, building, and teaching constantly. Ask yourself the questions, "When did they seem most willing to participate? When did they understand how the teaching applied to their lives?" We become so caught up in the busyness of our lives. Step back and take a good look at what you're doing. You may find that you have immersed yourself in the thick of thin things. Too often we spend most of our time taking care of the things that do not really matter in the grand scheme of things, neglecting the most important.

Add some SALT to your life: 1. Live with Soul. 2. Act without being told to act. 3. Love each and every heart and life. 4. Teach by asking questions. As you set aside things that don't really matter, you will have time to add more SALT to your life. I hope these ingredients can be passed on from your children to their children so the recipe just keeps getting better and better through time until you are all salt of the earth people.

*****

One analogy that I contemplate as I stare longingly out the window of my hospital room is what I have come to call "Spiritual Leukemia." Cancer, of any kind, not just leukemia, is cells growing out of control. The location of those cells, and the nature of their malfunction determines what type of cancer you have. The point is that cell growth is not a bad thing—it's necessary for life— but when it gets overdone or distorted it can have devastating consequences.

Leukemia is a result of the unrestrained growth of cancerous blood cells. These cells are not functional and basically crowd out the good cells and prevent them from performing their proper functions. If untreated it is fatal. Likewise, there are many activities like work, hobbies, social media, etc. that can crowd out the aspects of our lives that revitalize our relationship with the divine. If untreated, these behaviors can be spiritually fatal. It is important to understand that these actions are not necessarily bad, but if overdone or distorted, they can have devastating consequences.

Unfortunately, there is no perfect cure for leukemia. There are many methodologies— chemotherapy, radiation, transplantation— but nothing that will guarantee the cancer will be defeated.

Luckily, unlike leukemia there is a cure for spiritual cancer: having faith that we can overcome even the most egregious habits and behaviors. One of my favorite things to think about came from a talk about Christ.

"Don't think you can't. We might think we can't really follow the divine because the standard of His life is so astonishingly high as to seem unreachable. We might think it is too hard, too high, too much, beyond our capacity, at least for now. Don't ever believe that. While the standard of the divine is the highest, don't ever think it is only reachable by a select few who are most able. In this singular instance life's experience misleads us. In life we learn that the highest achievements in any human endeavor are always the most difficult and, therefore, achievable only by a select few who are most able. The higher the standard, the fewer can reach it. But that is not the case because, unlike every other experience in this life, this is not a human endeavor. It is, rather, divine work. It is a greater work of glory . . . to bring to pass the immortality and eternal life of man. There is nothing else like it. Not anywhere. Not ever. No institution, plan, program, or system ever conceived by men has access to the redeeming and transforming power of Deity. His invitation to follow Him is the highest of all and is achievable by everyone, not because we are able, but because He is, and because He can make us able too."[53]

You are more than a body, you are a soul. You are everything eternal. As difficult as life has been lately, it has also been amazing. Genuine love and care is shown by so many, even the old missionary who came in with his name tag upside-down and quoted scripture to me. It caused me to contemplate the word, "remission." When my cancer is in complete remission, it feels good to say that out loud. To know that this terrible malady has been removed. It marshals me to question what spiritual maladies I may be laden with. How good would it feel to say that they were in complete remission? How wonderful to know that they can be! And you don't have to take any toxic drugs or inject yourself with rabbit antibodies either. It just takes a seed of faith. The side effects I might add are also more favorable as they often include loss of feelings of guilt, higher sense of self worth, and increased confidence. Who doesn't want that?

Trust in a higher power. My wife says she wants to pretend that we aren't still at the front lines of this leukemia fight. It gets weary, and at times we are downtrodden.

Without the strength and power of relying on eternal truths, I'd try to do all things by myself. My wife's eyes furrow with worry and fear. Her eyes are like the sky after a rainstorm, misty hues of sage and sea. Her deep eyes tell stories of an unknown rolling landscape. Strangely familiar, like a mysterious dream. Her chameleon eyes absorb the beauty of her surroundings and reflect them ten-fold. They are a mirror of a verdant mountain pond in spring, clear and rippling from its core to borders. Her eyes are trimmed in lashes like arching pines. Her lashes bend backwards revealing her glistening emerald surface, delicate like the wings of an exotic butterfly. Her stare reaches unknown depths, neptune from the sun. I'm immersed in them, descending a submarine forest caught in her gaze like swirling clouds in an unknown planet. Then I watch her humbly close her celadon eyes to retrieve to her knees and talk to a higher power about why and how she can help her husband and son all over again.

One tiny five-foot nothin' pioneer woman was told one day by her husband to leave him on the side of the trail to die. She screamed, "I will not be a widow!" And threw him in the handcart, which she carried for so long. My wife is like that woman. After all, she is five-foot nothin'! She pulls our little family along and prays that I will live through another day not wanting to be a widow.

She knows how to get in front of this handcart and this trial. "And should we die before our journey is through, Happy day! All is well. We then are free from toil and sorrow too; With the just we *shall dwell!*" I nearly hit kidney failure this week and my life was spared again. I'm swimming through some deep waters.

Drowning in years of pleading for the leukemia to stay in remission, my wife watches the intense pain get worse even while I am on a huge dose of methadone and a morphine pump. My wife says a prayer every morning for the pain to be taken from me. She still can't believe I bear it, and feels her pleadings with the Lord aren't helping the pain to subside. Prayers are answered. In a moment of my deepest weakness, my strong wife grabs her journal and writes down that in case she is not strong enough later, that no matter the outcome, prayers are answered. Just as pioneer stories and trials inspire us today, my wife inspires me. One purpose of prayer is for us to align our will with the Father, not for God to change His mind about what should happen in our lives.

OTHER PLANS

As AJ and I continue to search for a cure for my leukemia, those words I mentioned earlier from John Lennon continue to ring true, "Life is what happens to you while you're busy making other plans." Nearly four years have gone by and we're still fighting. As I sit down to eat breakfast in my little hospital room this morning I realize just how lucky I am.

I realize that if someone hadn't donated that bag of blood hanging above my head—I wouldn't be here. As a cancer patient I'm lucky to know how fragile each moment is. It keeps me humble that's for sure and grateful for that special gift to breathe—to be alive.

When placed in a position of suffering, one often wonders, "What is the purpose of this?" and "What am I supposed to learn from this experience?" If I've succeeded at anything at this point it is getting people to pray. Your prayers truly support miracles.

Not one, but three bacterial infections send me into septic shock—a state that has a mortality rate of nearly 50 percent. The culprits are enterobacter, klebsiella, and lactobacillus.

My trip to the ICU has me fighting off the first two bacteria with the right antibiotics. However, the third bacteria, which I'm told is pretty wimpy to someone who has a healthy immune system, is lingering. My doctors suspect that it is hiding out in the central line in my chest. To avoid future complications we insert two IV lines in my left arm and schedule to remove my central line and hopefully any infection that may be hiding there. The plan at this point is to pull the line and continue to allow my body to recover from the last round of chemotherapy. It could take a couple of weeks to reach this point, but I am getting neupogen shots each day to help speed up the process. Barring any other setbacks we will proceed with three days of preparatory chemotherapy and then introduce my re-engineered T-cells. Septic shock hits again four days later. The infection moves from the lungs to the heart. Will I succumb to the infection in my heart? Divinity sometimes has other plans than a cure. Is the cure returning to my true home?

CODA

A CONCLUDING EVENT, REMARK,

OR SECTION.

THE CONCLUDING PASSAGE

OF A PIECE OR MOVEMENT IN

MUSIC, TYPICALLY FORMING

AN ADDITION TO THE BASIC

STRUCTURE.

Coding

BREATHE. SOMETIMES I HAVE TO REMIND MYSELF TO BREATHE.

November comes with everyone posting and expressing their gratitude and thanks, but it is my most painful month on earth. The depth of my pain only I know. The specifics measured in numbers and screens don't even touch the weight of the real pain. My wife opens up the sublime program she uses to code for work. My soul is fierce, but my body is suffering severely. My wife turns to her computer and codes in the hospital room to avoid watching me in pain. More medication. *Code a new step for tabs*. More medication. *Code a new step for a barcode*. More medication and the morphine pump aren't enough. *Code a new step to retain the contents of a bottle*. I up the fentanyl patch again and try a new drug, methadone because I am running out of options. My body becomes more and more resistant to pain medication after four years of so much medication. My wife

doesn't show it, but she cries every time she leaves the room to breathe. Coding on a computer is her distraction from watching the pain—a way to sit in the same room with me and try not to let me see her worry and tears. She wants so badly to decode my pain. I am worn down to the skin and feel like a ragged doll.

Then I code. Not the kind of coding she is doing, but the true, blue, hospital, life-threatening kind. I am admitted to the ICU in my second round of septic shock after surviving my first septic shock code the prior year. My wife stops coding and remains right by my side hopeful that I can get my blood pressure back up. I bounce back relatively quickly from the episode. The doctors know what infections caused it and I am fighting them with antibiotics.

AJ Writes:

Five days after our sixth anniversary comes his third and final code. One evening, I am sitting in the hospital room with Marshall playing a game, and then he suddenly starts coughing up blood. I blink over and over as if the red stain on the kleenex will disappear the next time I open my eyes.

Angel in Your Eyes

To be with you is to breathe
That's why I'm dying when you leave
I struggle through our long goodbyes

There is an angel in your eyes
I can't ignore it
I pull you close and kiss your forehead
And it's killing me when I start to realize
I miss the angel in your eyes

You're gone again, I try your phone
No answer yet, I'm all alone
You're gone again, no answer yet
You're gone again I hold my breath.

Until I see you again and you smile like the sunshine
I'm breathing you in and it feels like the first time
I'll never forget how you said that you'd be mine
Forever, forever

(by Marshall Jensen)

Again, septic shock. There is something different this time than the other two times. As the room fills with attendants and doctors, they pump Marshall full of fluids to stabilize his blood pressure. Only this time, they hand me his wedding ring. "We don't want to have to cut it off later." Wait. A. Minute. He'd been pumped full of fluids to stabilize pressures twice before and they didn't take off his ring. A sense of urgency fills the space. The urgency to find the words we all want to say. I tell him that if the pain is too much to bear, to let go and our son will be ok if the fight is over. As soon as those words come out, I turn from him and yell a silent, internal scream. The words are a lie. I'd felt the urgency

to say those words before, but I wouldn't. This time it is different. It's like someone is punching me in the gut, forcing the words out of me.

I just want to be numb like the lyrics of Marshall's song "Numb." I find myself wishing away all his physical pain and all the emotional pain I can feel and want to rid myself of my ability to remember this November day. He can't breathe. I can't breathe. I have a moment of solitude where I focus on my breath. We had discussed end-of-life decisions several times before this day. He told me his two greatest fears are losing his mind and not being able to talk or sing. He is facing the decision to either lose brain cells by not being ventilated or lose his ability to talk and sing by being ventilated. It is the bravest decision I've ever seen a man make in my entire life. It also ends up being his last decision. The second and last coma of his life lasts for three days.

BACK TO THE FUTURE:

Awakened by the blinking, beeping, my eyes focus
Through the quiet darkness
Dreams settle slowly
Whispers of a fortnight's journey
Softly swish through my thoughts
And I remember the contest

The Contest by Marshall

I DREAMED A DREAM, THE DETAILS OF WHICH ARE NOW OBSCURE. WHAT I DO REMEMBER IS THIS. AT THE COMMENCEMENT OF THE DREAM, I WAS AMIDST A CONTEST. IN FRONT OF ME WAS SOMETHING VERY DESIRABLE. THE OTHER CONTESTANTS WERE STANDING IN A LINE WITH ME AND THEY ALSO HAD AN OBJECT OF GREAT DESIRE BEFORE THEM. THE OBJECT ITSELF WAS LOCKED SOMEHOW-NOT NECESSARILY BY A KEY BUT BY SOME PUZZLE OR RIDDLE. THE OBJECT AND THE PUZZLE SEEMED TO BE DIFFERENT FOR EACH PERSON. MORE DESIRABLE THAN THE PRIZE BEFORE ME WAS TO BE THE FIRST ONE TO CRACK THE CODE-THERE WAS GLORY IN IT. OVER A LOUDSPEAKER, A VOICE WAS URGING EVERYONE TO HURRY, HURRY AND BE THE FIRST-TO WIN THE RACE.

ALTHOUGH I DIDN'T KNOW WHAT BEING THE FIRST WOULD BRING ME, I REALLY WANTED TO WIN! IT SEEMED I USED ALL MY MENTAL CAPACITIES AND PHYSICAL SKILL TO SOLVE THE PUZZLE OR "OPEN THE BOX" BEFORE ME. MY EFFORTS WERE FRUITLESS AND I BEGAN TO DESPAIR.

SOON I NOTICED A COMMOTION. EPIPHANY, I LEFT MY STATION AND BEGAN TO OPEN UP BOXES FOR OTHERS WITH EASE. DOWN THE LINE, I WENT AND SOON OTHERS BEGAN TO DO THE SAME. THE VOICE ON THE LOUDSPEAKER WAS SHOUTING AS IF WE HAD BROKEN THE RULES AND WOULD BE DISQUALIFIED. IT DIDN'T MATTER THOUGH, THOSE WHO HAD BEEN SERVED WERE HAPPY AND THOSE WHO SERVED

Many patients and doctors alike are still trying to crack the code of the cure for leukemia. Marshall put so much physical, mental, and emotional energy into being cured. Only to now have left his station, but not without helping others to be cured of their leukemia. Three survivors I know personally benefited and lived post-treatments that had not been FDA-approved yet, but since Marshall left his station has been approved. Marshall helped them along his journey to find their cures and open their boxes. He went through a lot of trials that saved others who were fighting for their lives. He cracked others' codes in a very real way by helping blinatumomab and T-cell trials become FDA-approved. Even if T-cells didn't fight back his leukemia once and for ALL, it has helped several friends and doctors to know the right doses and procedures. To shake off the dust and turn some treatments into golden cures for others.

There are more decisions that follow. While ventilated, the doctors say they can do surgery to collect the infected lung fluid to pinpoint which antibiotic would be best to use for the specific infection. They tell me there's a 50/50 chance they could slip during surgery and penetrate my lung (remember when Marshall watched that movie *50/50* before even knowing his diagnosis)? The slip would be fatal in his state. That's the hardest decision I've ever had to make in my life. Marshall's mother and brother are asleep in the next room after a red-eye flight. Another brother is in the room and thankfully there to discuss the pros and cons with me. "What would Marshall say?" Of course, he would take any chance possible to save his life. That's what he's done the last four years. Sometimes the right thing strikes like lightning. I know the right thing is to try the surgery. I don't want him to leave. There is no other way. The rain is pouring down in sheets outside and the lightning is blinding the skies. My heart fills with the gray of the sky and beats harder with each sound of thunder. The sound is far from natural. It lacks the resplendent beauty that it carried in a distant thunder crash. I cry out in the presence of the crash. For every thunder crash, I shudder in pain. For every breath I take, my heart beats with love for Marshall. A horrible, beautiful, painful, joyful love.

"You're a raging warrior, have no fear," I whisper in his ear as he lies in a coma. There is no stop in him, only GO like the energizer bunny. The surgery is a go. It is successful. The storm calms a bit and I realize I have not rested nor slept in days. Marshall's bestie Teri and my father hop on wifi-less flights to Philadelphia. As they are flying, things grow dire. Many of Marshall's songs contain lyrics about breath and breathing. I don't notice I am holding my breath while he is struggling so much for his own breath in the final moments. "You left me breathless and waiting . . . I could not believe my eyes . . . oh as you were walking by" are the lyrics he was singing that first November thirteenth—that moment I first laid eyes on him as I was walking by while he sang and played his guitar.

My father gets to the hospital as fast as he can. Marshall is hooked up to all the life support he can be and is not making progress post-surgery. I look up at the clock at 3 pm and think to myself, "Marshall really loves the number 3. I wonder if he will die within the hour." At 3:56, the doctor records his last heartbeat. "He's not here," I say aloud. His soul's on a mission. His body may be at rest, fast asleep, but his soul rises up, wide-eyed and singing hallelujahs as it is released from the pain. I run out into the hall and the first person I can hug is our

friend Richard, a researcher on the T-cell therapy study. He kept us in the loop as the study went on and he looks like my idol, Albert Einstein. He lost his wife to ovarian cancer, so I trust him to know how the moment feels. My dad comes in right behind him. "He's gone," I say in unbelief. He let go the moment my dad's taxi arrived at the hospital.

The room is peaceful and serene except for the wailing of the family on a FaceTime phone call. His family on the call all get to say goodbye to Marshall. He is guarded tightly in his family circle and is now released. I hope it is healing for them, as many of them did not get to say goodbye before Conrad's death. I hold on to his feet wishing he would take me along. With no feet to make him fall, he's allowed to glide up, up to the sun and the Son. Just like our son's balloon, he let go. In one of the last moments father and son were together, our son didn't realize the balloon wouldn't come back when he released it, and he cried the sweetest tears. At his dad's funeral, he will not let his balloon go as he knows it won't come back. Marshall sends red heart balloons as signs sometimes. He came into this world empty-handed with his hand up in the air like he was shooting a basketball, and he left empty-handed with both hands up as if to block a shot. One of the most important teachings of the Qur'an is the survival of the soul after separation from the body, and that death is not the end of human life but is an appendage to another's life.

"Death is certain for one who has been born, and rebirth is inevitable for one who has died. Therefore, you should not lament over the inevitable."[54] Teri's plane arrives a couple of hours later. I won't allow the hospital worker to move his body until she arrives. I don't know what else to say when Teri lands and calls. "Marshall is dead. Please arrive quickly." That is exactly the wrong way to handle the moment. My mind isn't capable of knowing the best way to handle things, so

I numbly lean into the truth. Teri completely breaks down in the airport, and the flight attendants rush to console her.

Teri is Marshall's biggest life support. She walks into the room after he's been taken off life support. His life support is there, and his medical life support is gone. His spirit left the room as I will find out later, to visit our son, but when Teri walks in something moves on the wall. His body had been lying there for two hours and nothing had moved in that time. "He's here," I say, "go ahead and talk to him." I leave the room so Teri has space to say her goodbyes. I think of all the physical limits we give to ourselves and our bodies. There is another dimension besides what we see and know with our physical senses. "Every self will taste death. You will be paid your wages in full on the Day of Rising. Anyone who is distanced from the Fire and admitted to the Garden has triumphed. The life of this world is only the enjoyment of delusion."[55]

His last writings focus on being busy making plans to try yet another clinical trial. God has other plans. His journal entries include something he wouldn't share with me or his mom. "I feel that my time on earth my last year, the Lord is giving me a little extra time to be with them before he calls me to the other side." His death is calm, peaceful, and spiritual. "There is no way to be certain about these things for anyone. When it is your time, it is your time."[56] A soul will not delay at its time.

The last thing he writes in his journal is about a beautiful musical number a choir sang, "Oh, That I Were an Angel" and the words "We can do hard things." We can do hard things. We can do hard things. I repeat this over and over, and the truth resonates in my heart because of all the hard things that are ahead and behind. Marshall was born in a house where his mother did hard things every time she gave birth naturally to her six children. He was born on his due date right on time

with an arm bent in the exact shape that seemed like I was shooting a basketball. Fitting for someone who loved the sport of basketball his whole life. He died in Philadelphia, Pennsylvania, home of the '76ers. You better believe we got sweet tickets to a '76ers stadium game from the vice president of the sixers. It was a great game. Life is a great game.

He sees great things in the midst of trials. He faces the battle and ends strong.

He boldly enters grace and mercy. He comes before the golden throne.

He leads with his heart to battle and stands strong. Now he rejoices.

He didn't give up the race. Through four battles, he rose again.

He is not cast down for the Lord holds him in the palm of his hand. He is a refugee and his calamities have passed.

He mounts up with wings like eagles. He runs and he is not weary. He walks and he is not faint (see Isaiah 40:31); He is saved from ALL his troubles (see Psalms 4:6). "O soul that are at rest! Return to your Lord, well-pleased (with him), well-pleasing (Him), So enter among My servants, And enter into My garden."[57]

"When their specified time arrives, they cannot delay it for a single hour nor can they bring it forward."[58] Allah won't delay a soul when its time has come.[59] He is battling in another field in the world of spirits. His mortal life is shortened in order for his services to be given there. He is opening boxes for others there too- eternal boxes. He is released from the lines of the world.

Remember the Lines

A mother's tears drop on a fresh face
A sincere soul is born into the human race
In a house in Logan with God's grace
The baby's bright eyes remember every line on his mom's face

He remembers the lines
Lines that stay with him forever
Lines that made life mine
These are the lines he'll always remember

He can't see the lines on his mom's face and what they say
She's watching her boy deep in a coma after another whole day
Groups of people come together and they pray
He awakes and he remembers all the lines for the school play

He buys lemonade at the little girl's stand
He helps the Italian widow to stand
His white car drives along listening to band after band
The white car's paint is chipping
Where the lines once were it's missing
His lyrics are the lines we all can remember

(by AJ)

SCAN ME

AJ WRITES A LETTER

Dear Marshall,

I've heard it said that "life isn't fair" but I disagree. Life is beautiful, painful, joyful, and sorrowful, but life is a blessing. Death, it's death that's not fair. It's not fair that cancer took you from us. It's not fair that someone so young and active can be afflicted with this disease. You were at the prime of life, a law student planning a future with your sweetheart, a skilled guitarist, a loyal leader, a husband, a father, a brother, and a son.

I wish you were still here to be the best daddy to our son, the kindest husband, and a living example to all around you to lead—to Marshall your life more with your heart. I wish that I didn't have to write this story because maybe that would mean that you would be writing it. You were the expert at leading every heartbeat. I wish that cancer considered the circumstances of those it afflicts before it overtook them.

I don't know if we would have had more children, but I think we would have tried to give our son a sibling. You would be here by my side watching him play his soccer games. He's a good defender, a "scrapper"—and has to be at his size. His coach puts him in the game just to shut some players down on the other team. You might even say he is just as "relent-less" as you were.

I sit here on the same grassy hill you were one year ago and I am watching our son play soccer. My eyes fill with tears that gush, gush, gush down my cheeks while my mind says, "Marshall isn't here to watch his son play." At that very moment, a tiny ladybug lands on my hand and my heart remembers what happened one year ago. You were watching our son play soccer at the park near our home. A ladybug landed on your hand and you showed me and said, "AJ, I know we are supposed to go to Philly now—it's the right choice." Jill gave you a whole jar of ladybugs for luck during your treatments and lucky you are.

*I want to thank you for choosing me as your partner and for spending the rest of your life with me. I feel privileged that you chose me and taught me to live every heartbeat I get worthy of its time and get to raise your son who is so much like you. As you know, he's doing an amazing job in school, with friendships, and in music. Especially with math and Rubik's cubes. **He is solving others' boxes just as in your dream.** I don't know if you realized how many lives you would change, but your drive and vision have affected countless individuals and their families. The ripples of your influence continue to extend.*

*I wouldn't be surprised if you're teaching and inspiring others in the world of spirits. I've felt you near checking in on our family from time to time. Our son has had even more vivid experiences knowing your spirit is near. **Thank you for sending red hearts and ladybugs.** It's good to know we have a special guardian angel with a guitar :)*

With love,

Amanda

This majestic musician who was fiercely loyal, a soulful human with a heart and passion for life, admired for his service and kindness, my ballistic optimistic died from a heart infection. The infection moved quickly from his lungs to his heart. We are shocked and we are trying fiercely to re-jolt our hearts every day. We thought he would live forever and his body would continue to beat back leukemia that ravaged it. His music, his laughter, his smile, and his soul fed all those around him. We will meet again, Marshall. He really was just as clean and pure those last few years as he had dressed that last Halloween as Mr. Clean. Marshall reached his final destination probably a little late like the man in the story from the Mr. Clean part of this book. Maybe a year later than he was supposed to as he did not write a single journal entry that last year of his life. I have admired him since the day I met him. In the end, a sneaky infection moved from his lungs to his heart and his body succumbed to the infection after being in a coma for a few days.

The night before Marshall passed, I went from the ninth floor of the ICU to the fifth floor and found a large, open restroom where I could kneel and pray aloud. In my mind, my thoughts were all ready to say, "Please bless us with another miracle." To my surprise, when I opened my mouth the words in my heart, "Please bless us with one more day," came out instead. I am grateful for that moment and every moment I had with Marshall on earth. His soul inspires me to live better, to live as the instrument and purpose that the divine wants me to, and strive to secure myself to heaven as Marshall and many other souls have.

How could he have known two years ago we sang a duet "Secure Yourself to Heaven" containing lyrics that would describe his passing so well? In one blink, you were bleeding. The heavens started raining and thundering. You couldn't breathe and fell into that deep coma.

The pain had ravaged you down to skin and bones, but you made your hardest decision in that final moment like the true warrior you are. I should have known when I married such a good man that you were restless to sing with the choirs of angels. Now you are my angel. I dug a grave to bury your body, but your soul is flying high released from the circles who loved you. You are soaring high and watching over those circles with a power that only you have to lead with your heart. Marshall and I performed the song that matched those final moments at a benefit my family held for him, Miracles for Marshall.

The experience of being with him in those final moments was incredible. As he was passing on, I was holding on to his ankles in what seemed like my last-ditch effort to keep him on earth a little longer. I was wishing I could just hang on and he would just take me with him when his amazing spirit departed from his body. Sometimes still today I wish that last-ditch effort would have worked as I sort through my emotions. Yet I have to fasten up my earthly burdens for I have just begun. Marshall truly is the winner of this battle and is finally allowed to fly high like the eagles. As much as I wish I was soaring high with him, I have a beautiful little boy who is a mini-Marshall, and Marshall's smiling, optimistic spirit lives on through his son. I will continue to raise him with Marshall's help from the other side. "Sri Krishna said: Just as boyhood, youth, and old age are attributed to the soul and the embodied soul continuously passes through these cycles, similarly the embodied soul passes into another body at death. The wise man does not get deluded and bewildered with such a change."[60]

I had no idea or premonition that this would happen. I woke up thinking that day that he would be able to pull through this sepsis just as he did a few weeks ago and the time last year. Just as he has cheated death so many times before in his life. I was so wrapped up in the numbers on the ICU screens. It became apparent that even though those

fake aspiration numbers looked great, he was going home. His first day, he was born in a home, and on his last days he knew the way back to his true home. Sri Krishna said: "Know that to be imperishable and indestructible, by which all this is pervaded; for none can bring about the destruction of this indestructible substance, the imperishable soul."[61]

Even though I didn't have premonitions, others did.

Our son was at our home with my mother while he attended preschool. Our son told three different people at three different times, "My daddy is very sick. I think he is going to die tomorrow."

The doctors handed me his wedding ring as they took him up to the ICU. His hands were already too puffy to wear his ring. He still took the time to call and sing "Happy Birthday" to a friend. It is the last recording of his singing we have and we now use it on every birthday.

The charge nurse on the ICU floor that day was the very best nurse on the entire floor. Her name was Anna and she is the goddaughter of Headstrong's president.

The doctor stopped in and said to me, "He will tell us if he's ready to go." He was. He was ready to go to a better dimension, let go of bodily pain, and win his fight in his time and his way.

He chose his time to go. They kept him on vasopressors and oxygen and monitoring to try to keep him alive while my dad arrived from the airport. I was watching in the third hour, and he was getting worse and worse. His favorite number is three and the thought kept entering my mind, "he'll go before the third hour is over." He hung on and fought his way out, but sure enough at 3:56, he was pronounced dead. It was beautiful and peaceful as his brother placed his hands on his head and gave a blessing of release. We played a beautiful song that a friend had sent over a text message. We played a lot of his own music. I'm sure his soul's vibrations had risen to match the heavenly music that caused large jam sessions to happen in heaven at that hour! Conrad, Nick, and Marshall praising with all the Hallelujahs they can muster.

That last night in the ICU, as I looked up at the bedside monitors, a picture of Marshall in his hospital gown with his bald head and puffy steroid cheeks was on one side of my mind. It was faded with a big, black X over it. I felt like Marshall was trying to tell me something. On the right side of the screen, was a clear, radiant picture of Marshall young, strong, and bold with blonde hair and defined cheekbones wearing a tuxedo. The pictures only disappeared from my view after I understood his message. He was trying to tell me—after I tried so hard to focus on that fuzzy left picture because that is how he has looked for years of cancer treatments—that he had the desire to now, again be that man on the right. That he was never really worn down with cancer treatment and not happy looking like the guy on the left. That's how he wants to be remembered because that is who he is again. **He was trying to tell me to lead my life more with my heart than my head.**

Circle of Life

THE SAME NOVEMBER DAY MARSHALL WAS DYING, HEAD-STRONG'S VICE PRESIDENT'S WIFE WAS IN LABOR WITH THEIR FIRST BABY. AS I WAS WATCHING HIM SLOWLY TAKING HIS LAST BREATHS, MY MIND WAS ALSO CIRCLING AROUND TO ANOTH-ER HOSPITAL ACROSS THE CITY WHERE A BABY WAS SLOWLY TAKING HER FIRST BREATHS. I RECEIVED NEWS THAT THE BABY'S HEART RATE HAD ALARMINGLY RISEN INTO THE TWO-HUNDRED RANGE. I WATCHED MARSHALL'S HEART RATE CREEP INTO THE TWO HUNDREDS AT THE SAME TIME. MATCHING HEARTBEATS. BOTH MARSHALL AND BABY KARSYN'S HEART RATES WERE BEATING TWO HUNDRED PLUS BEATS A MINUTE AT THE SAME TIME. KARSYN WAS BORN WITHIN THE HOUR OF MARSHALL'S PASSING, JUST BEFORE 3 PM. I BELIEVE NICK WAS PRESENT FROM THE OTHER SIDE FOR THE BIRTH OF KARSYN AND THE DEATH OF MARSHALL. DIVINE DESIGN AND DIVINITY STILL HAP-PEN IN THE MIDST OF CHAOS AND EUPHORIA.

A couple of days later I am invited to meet baby Karsyn, Nick's niece, at home. On the car ride over, I see 327 blazing at me on two different license plates. Just as Marshall's number was 3, Nick's number was 27. The temperature is 27 degrees celsius. On the ride there I sit in the backseat next to Khloe, another of Nick's nieces. While sitting there quiet and somber, Khloe abruptly says, "I saw Marshall flying." *This girl has some burning beats of attitude.* "Excuse me, Khloe, what did you just say?" She repeats herself. "I saw Marshall flying. He was coloring shapes. He was using red and drawing a big, red heart." My mind is blown. "How old are you, Khloe?" I ask. "Three. I am three years old." Immediately the lyrics from the song Marshall sang to me "She's an Angel" on our wedding day fly into my mind.

She's always talking about how she wants to be an angel. And I can't figure out just what she means. She's already one and they miss her up in heaven. So I thank the Lord in every prayer for sending her to me because she's my angel. **She holds her fingers out in three to show you just how old she will be. She's barely learning how to speak, but you should hear her go.**

And you should have heard Khloe going on and on with her adorable three-year-old jabber about the angel Marshall flying around drawing red hearts in the air. Whenever I see a red heart, I know it is Marshall and my heart beats fill with gratitude for the words spoken from this babe's mouth during this car ride. ***My heart burns with beats of gratitude every time I see a red heart.***

I walk into the cozy home knowing my angel is on my right shoulder while I meet Headstrong vice president's first and newest baby angel Karsyn. I know Marshall and maybe even Nick are there because as I hold her, she keeps looking past me to the same place above my right shoulder. I guess we really do have angels looking over our shoulders and that moment proves it. Everyone in the room keeps commenting how amazing that baby Karsyn is keeping her eyes open for so long and that she hadn't done that since she was born. Karysn's dad Michael plays Marshall's song "Keep Trying," so I sing the words aloud to her. She remains very still for the whole song then starts fidgeting as soon as the song ends. ***Beats of song guide our heartbeats.***

In true Marshall fashion, his viewing is held on C. S. Lewis's birthday. The "Star Spangled Banner" plays at church the next day. I picture him standing and boldly singing. Our wedding song comes on in a restaurant and I remember him eating spicy food until he cried. My broken heart is lucky to have loved someone so much in this lifetime.

Even though we didn't use his journal as a place to write down our words as I thought we would after he was intubated during his final coma, the journal is now a space where we can converse and I can hear his words when I miss him. I talk to him as if he is here because he is here.

I whip out my phone when I feel Marshall near and take pictures. I see him in lights, streaks, and orbs. Every year, a picture of Marshall and me with a sad little turkey is placed at the Hospital University of Pennsylvania as cancer patients and their caregivers are served a Headstrong Thanksgiving meal in the hospital. I buy a couple of meals every year in Marshall's memory and I see the picture over FaceTime. **My heart beats in laughter because the picture is so silly.** It's the most meaningful moment every year; I cry meaningful, heartfelt tears after that phone call and I feel Marshall is near.

Prior to flying back home to tell our son his father had died, I lie in bed. I can feel Marshall near . . . much more present than when he had been lying next to me in a hospital bed focusing on fighting for his life. Again, I feel as if he is trying to tell me something just like he had been with the pictures of himself in my mind the night before he died. It's difficult for me to grasp what he is wanting to say or wanting me to do. It is hard to write these words because it is an experience from another dimension. Moments of eternal nature often do not translate well onto a finite page. An experience of light, electricity, particles—those are the only earthly words my logical, scientific brain knows to use to describe the experience. It's also a little frightening. I keep closing my eyes and reopening them to see if what I am seeing is really real or still there when I reopen my eyes. I keep thinking, am I crazy? Is it just a light from the window? I reopen my eyes again to see his face again and my discernment gets better as I concentrate on his face—his beautiful, not cancerous face. It takes me an embarrassingly long time to recognize. It isn't the "cancer head" he had for so long. It's his thin face and the huge smile that he had before paralysis. After a while, I can finally tell that all he wants is for me to smile. I force myself to smile three times in a row. ***This moment is a gift of gold that causes my heart to beat with thanks.*** I have been touched by an angel. I flip over so my back is facing the spot I saw his face, and I succinctly see the outline of a shadow. My heart feels plucked and strummed like the strings on his guitar. Little twinges of sensations start up in my heart. The vibrations are super subtle at first, and I wouldn't have noticed if I wasn't paying attention. I address it out loud and give it my voice and my words, the shadow moves to the light and I am not afraid anymore. The darkness inside of me is brought to light that night and I feel healed for a time.

Lie awake staring out my window
The solemn moon gives off her light
Every heartbeat softly pleading
I wish I may, I wish I might

Spend the night wondering what it feels like
To hold an angel by my side
And when I dream I swear I can feel you
But when I wake it's cold and lonely

Begging for your light
Come and save me from this mess

It's a cold and lonely existence
And I try to be worthy of your love
Of your touch, of your sweet endearments

I never wanted anything like this
I want it so much my body aches
But it's deeper than I can feel
And I swear I'll do whatever it takes
To feel your light
Is any soul complete
Without another soul to please
Please stop the racing of my heart

(by Marshall Jensen)

If I wasn't paying attention, would there still be another unhealed part of me for years or forever? See your shadow parts and bring them to the light so they can be healed. The human part of us wants to keep it dark and hidden, but as soon as you bring it to the light, you will notice a shift. Every time Marshall strummed his guitar strings it brought up the frequency of my heart and my soul. ***Three heart-beats of soul beat for me that soulful night.*** I feel his soulful arms around me sometimes if I am truly in the present. ***Just as the night I met Karsyn, the soul knew how to catch my logical brain with the numbers on the license plates and temperatures.***

*****

After the infection reached his heart, his body lay peacefully still and his suffering was over. I flew his body home and arrived in our hometown three days later to tell our four-year-old son. The flight was long and usually on long, late flights, passengers come off the plane exhausted and like zombies. Not on this flight. Everyone came off chatting and so sweet to one another though they began as strangers. "When they [the angels] came, they said: 'Peace'; he said: 'Peace also be to you; a group of strangers.'"[62] These were his kind of people and how he was his whole life—always chatting, sweet and friendly even to those he did not know.

That is how we marshall on. There was not a stranger in Marshall's life. Everybody was somebody to Marshall and that's how the flight felt. I heard, "So nice to meet you" over and over as we were disembarking. Marshall's voice was in my head as I was coming down the airport escalator to greet our now fatherless child. My sweet neighbor said the community wanted to come, but it was so late. It was not the physical people I saw, but the hundreds of spirits I felt there literally carrying my spirit through as I scooped my young son up into my arms knowing what I had to soon tell him that would change the rest of his life. I knew there were hundreds of spirits from another dimension filling that airplane runway. An army of spirits filled the emptiness. My son never stands still, but that day my mom said he stood still for twenty minutes waiting for me to come out of that airplane. I was really tired and it was so late for a four-year-old so I planned on telling him the next day. But on the way home, he was insisting to me, "Mom, Mom, MOM. How can I tell if I've seen a spirit?" I hadn't mentioned anything about the army of spirits in the airport or his dad dying yet. I told him that was a hard question, but because of the experience that had just filled my heart, I answered him with words the best I could. "It's kind of like light or electricity, the wind or like particles. You can't

really see it, but it's there. I don't know if any earthly words can really describe it. I think you have to use heavenly words or words from another dimension." I didn't really want to have this discussion, but he kept asking over and over.

When we arrived home, I could tell he would not let up about it and we were going to have the talk *that night*. My mom had been taking care of my son while we were in Philadelphia for a month. I wanted her to be there when I told him about his dad so he could have some familiarity and stability and so I could have some support. I had days to prepare and studied the best way to talk to a kid his age about the death of a close family member. I had researched that kids his age, from three to five, care mostly for themselves in that situation. First, I was not to use words like passing or sleeping which may cause the child to think they would come back eventually. I had to say his dad died in a way he would understand. Second, I knew I had to tell him he would be taken care of because otherwise, he would worry about that. With those two things in my back pocket and with him being so persistent about spirits, we sat down on our couch. Later, our son told me other spirits were around him preparing him. Three times before I flew home, he had talked to my mom about his dad dying. The night before Marshall died, they were having dinner at a neighbor's and he'd turned to her and said, "My dad is really sick. I think he's going to die tomorrow." He not only said these words to my neighbor, but to my father. My father remembers those words with an additional, "I'm really going to miss my buddy," before getting on the plane to Philadelphia. Marshall often called our son his buddy.

On the flight home, I felt Marshall near telling me to listen for the words, "I knew it," so I was listening intently for those words from minute one after we sat on that sinking couch. I could hear Marshall whisper, "Start with a joke, don't make this so heavy on him."

Here are a few more tips Marshall's soul gave me on how to talk to our son during the long flight across the country bringing his body home:

-Quietly (attitude)

-Tell him he holds daddy's heart even in heaven; spirits have been called to watch over and protect you (gratitude)

-Tell a joke; lighten the mood (laughter)

-Daddy will oversee your care personally; he will care for you from heaven. I have work I am doing on the other side (soul)

-Do something fun like Doc McStuffins reincarnation music (song)

-Even though the sentence of death passed upon me, this experience shall be for his good. He will be stronger for this trial and I will be carrying out the Lord's plan -D&C 122:7. (gold)

-My room in the missionary training center was 122. Kez was told about his dad's death at 12:22 am on 11/22 (numbers)

I started to wonder if souls in other dimensions can use electronics and electricity. People tell of experiences with TVs turning on by themselves after losing a loved one. My experience was with my phone over and over just after Marshall passed. Weird stuff would happen. It would just turn on—playing his music! I felt like the songs that were turning on kept letting me know that I was not alone and that Marshall was home. Similar words would constantly play on the radio. I feel like he spoke to me through hertz, vibrations, and light—communications of the soul. "Mommy, what is it like to see a spirit?" Well, son, it's like the wind, electricity—I don't know how to explain it except it's like the vibrations of a different world. I'd just had a few experiences like that so I intentionally grabbed my phone and pulled up the first kid's joke that popped up online. I couldn't believe I was about to start this serious conversation with a joke and I needed all

the help I could get from Marshall. The first joke was, "Why did the teacher use the window to write down her lesson?" My son thought about it for a moment and then said, "Because she ran out of paper?" "That's really thoughtful," I said. He chimed in, "I KNEW IT." The very words I was listening closely for. I replied, "The answer is . . . so the lesson would be very clear." The first joke that popped up was appropriate for the difficult discussion we were about to have. I really wanted him to understand clearly. Thanks a lot, Marshall. When I told this to my family later, they said it sounded like a Laffy-taffy joke. Marshall always had Laffy-taffy stashed in our cupboards and was constantly reading the jokes. He loved them, and it was just the kind of joke Marshall would tell. Just then Kez chimed in with his question again, "Mommy, how can I tell if a spirit has been around me?" Oh my goodness, this little boy is really stuck on this at the moment!

My mom was quietly listening and my carry-on bag from the long flight was sitting in front of me. I grabbed the mechanical pencil from the front pouch. "See this?" I directed his attention to the pencil as I started pushing the lead out from the encasement. "Your body is like this mechanical pencil, your spirit is like the lead. When you die, the spirit goes out of your body like this lead came out of a pencil. It goes somewhere else." "Oh, that's cool," he said. "Daddy's spirit came out of his body . . . .(ok I thought, I am making this too complicated) . . . "Your daddy died." The words fell out of my mouth quickly and clearly onto the gray couch where his daddy had held him so many times. They didn't seem adequate to tell his little boy what was lost.

"Ok." He replied simply. I thought he wouldn't quite understand because aunts and uncles who had already told cousins his age had not really understood that their uncle was gone. So I was sure he wouldn't quite grasp it because his dad spent so much time away from us at the hospital. I figured in a few months, he would come to me and ask—"Hey, Daddy really isn't coming home this time?" But I underestimated my four-year-old's comprehension. Instead, he said, "I really want to go see Daddy's body." Hold on, I thought to myself. In the days leading up to this, I had researched more information on what to do before you take a child that age to the mortuary and I thought, "I'm not ready for that lesson yet!" I told him, "Sorry, but the building that has daddy's body is closed right now." He kept saying over and over, "Mommy, I see a spirit. I see a spirit." I didn't know how to talk about this part. It wasn't in all the research I had done. But there was something about grieving children needing to color, so I handed him a paper and said, "Draw for me what you are seeing." He took the paper and drew himself at the end of our upstairs hallway. He drew his dad's spirit flying over his head with a red cape. He tells me what it is and that dad was flying through his head. He said he saw red and white lights surrounding his father.

He still remembers this very vivid experience to this day, years later. My mom was respectfully quiet. I'd given her a paper listing different things she could and couldn't say in the conversation that I had spent days researching. For example, don't say "Be strong" or "Don't cry." At the end of the conversation, she went to bed. She told him it was ok to cry if he was sad. I figured he got the idea as much as he could at that point, so we both lay down in bed. My son started wailing—bawling his little eyes out. It was such a rarity for my son. He is a happy-go-lucky soul with a jolly, light attitude towards most anything, just like his dad! When he started wailing I held him close and said, "What's wrong?" He said, "I'm really going to miss my daddy. I'm really going to miss my buddy. I'm not going to be able to play Chutes and Ladders with him. I'm not going to be able to . . ." and continued to list off many things. I just held him tightly as he cried himself to sleep that night, shocked that he understood it that well. I did not think he would figure that part out for weeks. He released buckets of emotion that night. I could hear Marshall's spirit saying, "Oh, I don't want to see him cry so much." I almost told him that, but I held it in and just let all the tears flow.

I was so pissed at Marshall for dying and didn't even want to feel his close spirit because I was so mad at him for making us all cry for years. This was a very sacred experience that I hesitate to share in this book. Yet at the same time, I now know there is a z component that we can't see. An entity in another dimension. Why couldn't an entity that exists in all of us, a soul, a divine, whatever you call it, go on existing after our body dies? We are SO much more than a 3D body, just as your heart is so much more than an organ pumping blood to all the cells of your body. You are a multi-dimensional being having an earthly experience. It may not end here when all the cultures, eras, religions, and times are finished. It is finished. Is it? Where is our divine home?

ON MY JOURNEY HOME

Each individual has inestimable worth and something unique to contribute to others

-Daddy David.

Sometimes on the 18th day of the month, I yearn for home. I miss the warmth of family and friends in the mountains surrounding the ranch. I am a cowgirl in a big city. I long for a home, the stability and contentment that I feel have eluded me like chasing a butterfly since Marshall's death. Home is not so much a place as I grow older; it is people, a tribe.

Did you know some monarch butterflies go 3,000 miles every year back home? Or even more compelling is the arctic tern that travel 60,000 miles a year back to Antarctica? Freezing temperatures do not appeal to me; I gravitate to warmth like a salamander to rock in the sunshine. If I could talk to these butterflies and terns, I'd ask them how in the world they know their way around the world without Siri. I can barely make it down the street without her, but more importantly, I would like to ask them how in the world they know where home is. I will never forget the winding, country roads leading back to the mountains of my childhood ranch. I helped my grandpa build these roads. I had no idea at the time how valuable it was for my grandfather to allow me to be a female engineer at such a young age. Not the kind of engineer that has an engineering degree and gets paid loads of money for all their intricate projects. The kind of engineer that is holding really expensive equipment in the middle of nowhere to be sure the road does not exceed a certain government-imposed gradient.

Dear grandpa always gave his grandkids Tootsie Rolls. My son calls him Grandpa Tootsie Roll. At that age, it was practical and useful; not something I realized would be such a neat contribution to others on their trips up the steep canyon. Word of warning: cellular navigation is mostly nonexistent on those canyon roads. These country roads will serve for years to come, past my grandfather's death and eventually past my own death, to bring people back home.

Marshall taught a faithful vision. There was a long and arduous journey back home to a white fruit. Is it really about the fruit or is it about the people who take the journey with us? The white fruit's delicious taste will last only for moments, yet the joy we get from sharing that fruit with others will last forever. Is it really about opening our own box or about the friendships and meaning we get from opening others' boxes in our lifetime? For the monarch butterfly, is it the place they are going to or the other butterflies they are traveling with? Emerson said, "Life is a journey, not a destination." Our most important acquaintance on our journey is light. When going down a dark road,

know the way toward your light. See and honor the light in others. If you find yourself on a path needing to reacquaint or recommit yourself to your light, then do it. Your desires will be created by what you put into your journey in the world. "The world we could have is so much richer than the world we've settled for, " Malcolm Gladwell writes. If you desire good health, what are you doing daily to achieve good health? Instead of telling the world, your children your priorities, show them. If you desire prosperity, which actions are you taking to point you toward achieving your goals? Are you being successful in the tiny moments?

One thing Marshall focused on was exaltation. He knew with exaltation, no matter what things go wrong in this life or what wrong turns are made into darkness, detours taken, or back roads you follow before realizing they lead to nowhere, you have a chance to figure out how it all works and map it out if you have forever. Oh, how grateful I am for the company other travelers give me on my detours and main roads instead of as a lone monarch butterfly fluttering aimlessly—'minha mariposa' as Marshall would endearingly call me. Being stretched and painfully morphed into a whole different being is also a necessary part of our journey if we ever want the wings to fly back home. How we do things is more important than getting through the to-dos. Bind yourself not to a pasture or an addiction, chain yourself not to the plow or work all the days of your life. Set yourself free to find your calling and you'll return home somehow.

When you see others along their journey home being morphed in their cocoon, shaped, and polished, the rough edges being smoothed like a rock in a river, you need not judge, compare, or feel less than others. Don't be distracted by the comings and goings of other travelers or you'll be run over or stop in your own path or even worse wander aimlessly following them instead of learning and doing what was intended for you to do on your journey mimicking what or where someone else has already journeyed. There is no time to procrastinate or tarry on our journey home. You don't know when that last heartbeat will happen.

Bad things and pain happen to good people so you learn about a higher existence, and higher purposes, and use timing and time to become all you can—to give you your own beautiful set of wings with their own unique and distinct set of markings unlike anyone else's. If you don't have scars you don't allow yourself to morph into a beautiful soul with wings. You won't learn those things or you will miss out on all that you are meant to become in your life if you are too distracted, too self-absorbed, or too busy flaunting your colors to reach out to others in the midst of their struggle to morph. You can get out of the dark and dreary parts of your journey home and find the light by focusing on the innate lights of others, and their strengths, and helping them overcome their dark and dreary moments. Discover and develop your own eternal gifts by asking and paying attention to what specific assignments you have. Like the specific assignments my grandpa would give me while building roads.

You have divine assignments specific to you. Divinity has more in mind for you than you have in mind for yourself. If you are reading this, ask yourself if you can make an important contribution to the world. You can! Stephen Hawking had physical limitations in mortality. Yet, look at what he was able to accomplish with his mind! Focus on your strengths and stop comparing your weaknesses to others' strengths. Write down today what you're grateful for and do not let life's distractions eclipse the light you have to shine on others along the journey back home. Don't let rocky, steep mountains stop you from carving out the roads you were meant to build on your journey home. "If I could move this mountain before me, then I would lose the faith

that He can do it for me." Marshall sang. Marshall's last words to his friends and family at the end of his epic journey were, "See you when we get Home." Fatefully, his brother Conrad's last words were, "I'll talk to you when you get home." How grateful I am that my grandfather had the patience and took the time to allow me to contribute to building the roads of life - the roads that lead the heart to home. We each have an inestimable worth and something unique to contribute.

DIVINE ASSIGNMENTS SPECIFIC FOR YOU

Marshall was given a homework assignment from me that first November we met. I had attempted to give this particular homework assignment to a couple of other boys I'd dated. The assignment was to come up with the music for the lyrics I had written. I knew the right boy for me would be able to complete it. He told me he had completed the assignment early in the evening of our third date and all night long I was begging him to play the song on his guitar. Mysteriously, he refused. Usually, he jumped on every chance to bust out his chops on the guitar. We arrived near a keyboard and that's when this talented guitarist played his rendition of my song, "Speck of Doubt," on the keys! Is there an instrument he can't play?

Speck of Doubt

Fate brings togetherness unexpectedly fast
A hunter's keen eyes find their ultimate prey
Wanting this initial feeling to forever last
The vision begins encircling her eyes so gray

During that dusky dance, avoiding the mere chance
With each step we're pushing love about
Searching those eyes for specks of doubt

Hand leads hand, time finds a longing embrace
The same breath being shared, is being taken for granted
Risky trusting, yet hope still lingers on that face
One resisting, one is waiting for a response to what's been said

Still avoiding the mere chance, still upholding all confidence
With each breath we're pushing love about
Searching those eyes for specks of doubt

So irreplaceable, amazement never ceases, a bit of heaven tasted
Impossibility only follows a loss of sense of wonder
Refuse to allow precious time and effort to be wasted
The envisioned happens for those who reconsider

Finally taking the mere chance
While upholding all confidence
Desiring ALL the love about
Not one single speck of doubt

(by AJ)

You better believe he earned himself some extra credit in the form of our first kiss! It was the fourth day of the month and his mom's birthday. That same day in 1956, four famous musicians recorded their own CD at Sun Record Studios in Memphis, Tennessee- Elvis Presley, Johnny Cash, Jerry Lee Lewis, and Carl Perkins all had an impromptu jam session. Impromptu jam sessions were Marshall's favorite thing in the world!

Marshall went above and beyond by *recording* the fresh song which he gave me at the end of the night. He'd recorded the track on a hot pink CD (if you are too young to know what a CD is, ask your parents or search for it on Google) and wrote me a long letter in a circular shape in black permanent marker on the top of that pink CD. For weeks I had been begging him to tell me his middle name. Finally, at the end of the long circular sentences he had written it:

"Amanda, thank you for the homework assignment. I was hoping I could earn a little extra credit, so I dropped by my friend Jeff's studio and threw down a few tracks =) Now you can listen whenever you want! I hope you enjoy it, and I want you to know that I think you are such a sweetheart. <3 Speck of Doubt Recorded December 1st, 2008. Lyrics By Amanda Joyce Hunt . . . Vocals and Instrumentation By Marshall Kenneth Jensen. Love, Marshall Kenneth Jensen".

He didn't say a thing about it but played it coy and subtle. When I noticed he revealed his middle name, I loved it! Kenneth. He was as handsome and as hot as all the Ken dolls I had played with as a little girl. It was a message of the heart. Let this be a reminder—don't postpone delivering the messages of your heart to others during your life. Don't hide how you feel or they will never know even after your dying breath.

How am I supposed to explain
The way that I feel when I don't even know
A kiss has never felt like this
It's more than tender lips
It's everything inside
Everything I try to hide

What am I supposed to do
I don't want to leave
I'm breaking over you

I can't escape your eyes
They stare into my soul
They see everything inside
Everything I try to hide

I'm wishing over a four-leaf clover
That this is not the end
I know you told me, but you can't hold me
When I'm so far away

Feeling, breathing, wanting, needing
Everything you are
Longing, missing, hoping, wishing
On a falling star

This is what I keep inside
This is what I try to hide

(by Marshall Jensen)

Reaching out in loving appreciation, either through letter, email, or text, a message reinforces the good in another person and reminds them your heartbeat's purpose is to love. It tells them you are thinking of them. My mom and dad wrote me two heartfelt letters that I cherish. I reread them to sweeten my bitter moments and to lighten my heavy decisions.

Heart Jolt 10:

WRITE A LETTER TO A SPOUSE, CHILD, GRANDPARENT, OR FRIEND. CONVEY FEELINGS OF APPRECIATION AND DESIRE TO BE TOGETHER. A LETTER CAN DISPEL LONELINESS AND REMIND A PERSON OF THEIR INESTIMABLE WORTH. LETTERS CAN EVEN BECOME A TREASURED KEEPSAKE AND PART OF A FAMILY HISTORY THAT IS KEPT AND PASSED DOWN. FOR A SON OR DAUGHTER GOING THROUGH A DIFFICULT TIME, A LETTER CAN GIVE ENCOURAGEMENT THAT IS READ AGAIN AND AGAIN.

DIVE INTO DIVINITY AND READ YOUR "LETTERS FROM GOD," WHETHER THAT BE SCRIPTURES, THE AL QURAN, THE BHAGAVAD GITA, A NEWSLETTER OF INSPIRATION IN YOUR EMAIL, OR WHATEVER DIVINITY LOOKS AND FEELS LIKE FOR YOU. AT MOMENTS OF DISCOURAGEMENT, READING DIVINE WORDS WILL PROVIDE THE LEVELED-UP ENCOURAGEMENT WE NEED. THINK ABOUT ONE WHO NEEDS ENCOURAGEMENT IN YOUR LIFE, MARK THIS PAGE, OR STOP AND WRITE THEM A LETTER RIGHT NOW. REREAD YOUR DIVINE LOVING LETTERS AS MENTIONED ABOVE AND KEEP A VERSE NEAR TO YOUR MIND THAT BRINGS YOU HOPE AND MEANING.

People sometimes are leery of talking about memories of people who have passed on. But I want to encourage you to remember them in every heartbeat, in every song, in every breath. Please let's talk about them. Use their names, and talk about the happy times, love and memories they left behind. Especially on the hard months and days. Relationships don't end with death; they go on forever, and sometimes they can even become magnified after someone has died. They remain with us.

A Dehlin and Prince podcast made it apparent that part of the struggle in our earthly lives is taking something infinite and converting it to something finite. How does history become theology? How can you put on a piece of finite paper an infinite experience? I struggle at this moment trying to write of a glorious experience I had when my husband died . . . it seems like trying to put it in some finite language will take away from its glory. I use Portuguese to teach others, and it seems that language would be more appropriate when writing about my infinite moments. "There must be something great in the mortal soul. For suffering, it seems, is infinite, and our capacity without limit," C. S. Lewis once wrote.

I am a science major and I use the analogy of DNA— two strands that supply physical life. They look perfect when drawn on paper. Yet, if you zoom in on either real DNA leg, you'll see fragments of garbage. Code that was once used and vital for life is now cut off, discarded, and strewn aside the leg. If that analogy is too technical, there's also the story of the Grinch. Whoville was trying so hard to be perfect and happy, they didn't realize all the garbage they were producing. The Grinch had a very different perspective up on his mountain filled with garbage they were throwing out. Until a child, Cyndi Lou-Who came and you know what she said? "I myself am having some yuletide doubts." "Hypocrites," said the Grinch. And he was right. No matter

how perfect an image appears on a page or a group looks, they come with tons of garbage they have had to sift through and throw aside to obtain a perfect appearance. The garbage is still there even if we have mastered the art of hiding it.

I repainted our bathroom with a friend whose life seemed perfect. As the paint slowly dried, she let me know her family wasn't perfect. Our family's fight and flaws being on display allowed people to feel comfortable telling me of their problems since ours were so apparent. It was refreshing to talk to someone who was honest about the suffering and desires they'd had for a long time but the things no one talks about to each other because they want their families to appear so perfect.

Each of you will have your garbage days—those days when the universe itself seems shattered and the shards of your world lie littered about you in pieces. You'll experience those broken times when it seems you can never be put together again . . . but the garbage man will come. Even in times of global pandemic and shutdown. Even if only conquered in death, in the darkness of your sorrow, no matter your desperation, your grief, and your doubts, light-filled days will come.

You can have that brilliant, restful day of perfect pictures on a page, Christmas, and a moment of light. Then it can be followed by days, months, or even years of darkness, gloominess, and doubt. For those experiencing life's gloom, maybe you feel you don't fit in or that you aren't strong enough. Hope for the sun. It comes without fail. And for those basking in the sun, where every day feels like Christmas—reach out and listen to the grinches in your life too. They are right too from their perspectives alone on the mountain of garbage they just climbed. Help, ask, stay, even take a gander from their view that's much different than yours for a while, refrain from judging, and allow each person's unique process.

In Marshall's case, his DNA had three copies of chromosome nine initially, then even more garbage and trans-locations later after treatment. This ultimately led to his physical death, though his spirit was thriving. Many caregivers and family would find him with a large box of donuts reading scriptures every minute he could get to them; in his room, our car, in hospital beds. He didn't allow his own imperfections or the imperfections of others, especially mine,to lead to his soul's death. Neal A. Maxwell describes one of the fundamental choices of mortality: "Within the swirling global events—events from which we are not totally immune—is humanity's real and continuing struggle: whether or not, amid the cares of the world, we will really choose to care for the life of the soul."

Be gentle to those whose worlds are changing and rearranging. In the case of the Grinch, he realizes Christmas can still come without packages, boxes, and all the garbage. He realizes he can choose happiness, light, and have a soul despite what organizations of people are doing.

Marshall Your Heart Jolts II:

-TO JOLT YOUR BEATS OF LAUGHTER: MAKE SOMEONE SMILE TO-DAY. MAKE THEM SMILE THREE TIMES. MAKE THREE PEOPLE SMILE.

-TO JOLT YOUR BEATS OF ATTITUDE: NOTICE HOW MANY TIMES THROUGHOUT THE DAY YOU THROW A PITY PARTY. WORK ON DISINVITING YOURSELF FROM ANY PITY PARTIES, ESPECIALLY THE ONES YOU HOLD FOR YOURSELF.

-TO JOLT YOUR BEATS OF GRATITUDE: IF YOUR WORLD IS GET-TING SMALL, SIMPLY MAKE IT BIGGER. THINK OF THREE CITIES YOU CAN VISIT. THINK OF THREE PEOPLE POST-TREATMENTS OR PROCEDURES THAT ARE STUCK IN HOSPITALS OR AT HOME AND GO VISIT THEM. BE GRATEFUL FOR WHAT YOU HAVE.

-TO JOLT YOUR BEATS OF GOLD: REMEMBER NOT TO THINK TOO HARD WHEN TALKING, REMEMBER TO FEEL.

- TO JOLT YOUR BEATS OF NUMBERS: PAY ATTENTION TO THE NUMBERS AROUND YOU. NOTICE YOUR PLANE SEAT NUMBER, THE YEARS OF YOUR CHILDREN'S LIVES, THE YEARS FRIENDS HAVE DONE A NONPROFIT AND SUPPORT.

-TO JOLT YOUR BEATS OF SOUL: BE ABOUT SOULFUL BUSI-NESS EVERY DAY. GIVE SOMEONE YOUR PERSONAL CELL PHONE NUMBER AND DO A FAVOR FOR THEM. BE ON CALL FOR THEM. TALK TO SOMEONE WHO MISSES A DECEASED LOVED ONE. DON'T FEEL GUILTY FOR THE DAYS YOU FORGET.

When all is said and done, Marshall is still in the ground. The same place kings, prophets, richest, poorest, the kindest and meanest, murderers, slaves, mothers, fathers, husbands, sons, and daughters will all end up at the end of our lives. We cannot take with us stuff we work our whole lives to obtain.

His guitar sits in solitude in our front living room. The strings that were once tightened and played continuously are still. Why did I run before I cried? Why did I hide from what I needed most? I burn for a soothing embrace yet remain in the soft glow of his guitar and solitude. The guitar is constantly reminding me to show life and more love—to show the people in my life more love and give what I can while I am alive to give. The longer I wait, the colder the guitar, myself, and my relationships become. I've been here before and I yearn to get out. I chose you, Marshall. I chose to be here and where is here without you? Marshall isn't here with me. There is only room for one in this sorrow. And you aren't here for me. This is my existence in solitude. I cover my sorrow and pick up the instrument to play the strings that Marshall's confident hands strummed. I stare beyond the shiny, wooden surface of the guitar. It feels so empty without you to strum it. This isn't my place. Tell me what I'm feeling when I don't know how to feel. Am I just part of existence or is it a part of me? You now lie beyond what I can see. I used to live in the world, but now I question the world. How am I suddenly older and how did time change its pace? I am alone and in a few more years, I will be gone.

When I think about life I realize that taking will make you miserable and sharing produces a light heart. A heavy heart produces gloom, darkness, despair, sadness, and weight. Rejolt your heart using the boxes found throughout the marshaled beats and make your heart light.

I ask my son who is in charge of his happiness. He responds with, "My dad" and "I haven't been happy in years since he died." I think

for a moment with a heavy heart. Then I say, "Think again. That is the last thing your father would want you to say." He knows it all too well. YOU are in charge of your own happiness.

Cherish the season of life you are in even when it is a season you are more alone than you've ever been. No outside force can change your attitude. I give you this book with a lighter heart than the night my son told me someone else was in charge of his happiness. This book holds some of the truest gems and golden heart rejolts from Marshall's life— deep lessons he learned while fighting pain and knowing his beats were numbered as all of yours are.

There is only a small period of time that we have to do all we've been sent to this earth to do. Marshall frequently lived life like the energizer bunny in fast-forward. He would try to smash so much in a day. I remember nights of having one game of Scrabble on one side of the table and a game of chess on the other side. While one person was taking their turn at one game, the other could be taking their turn on the other game. Allow life to be the most fun game you've ever played, the truest treasure you ever shared with someone else, and your happiest moments despite the pain and the uncertainty. One day you will be buried in the ground or burned to ashes. Do you want your soul to soar and say I did ALL that I could with that body of mine or to be wishing you did more with every heartbeat while you had them? Only YOU can decide—no one is in charge of your happiness but you.

A marshaled mission was fulfilled on the earth and even the intense pain and suffering that lasted four years couldn't rob a smile from a paralyzed face, a heart from being full of music, and a soul from an unshakable faith. Beats of attitude, gratitude, song, laughter, gold, numbers, and soul prevailed to the very end.

*****

END

AFTER THERE WAS SILENCE

Pulsing beats

Strike lightning from the sky

Beckoning the souls up

Darkening small enclosures

Sunbeams pilfer separation

Ice is the Exterior

Dark conceals

Grieving tears

Womxn withdraw and whisper

Silent stillness

Progression, commencement

Surrender, Float, Glide

Men gather and sing

Motionless harmony

Tense pain calms

Taming oscillations

Reducing their reasoning

I turn in disbelief, what is this screeching about?

Death, I sympathize. The prior was about loss.

Music answers nevermore, what does the quiet hush?

There are no words, she shuts her mouth

We'll continue singing even after there is silence.

The fatherless turns to his mother, what is this song about?

The light, she replies. The next is about the sunset.

He inquires again, what do the words say?

There are no words, she replies

Your father sang before he had words.

I will sing for him since he is silenced. I will smile for him since my smile is his.

(by AJ)

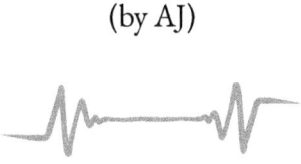

Acknowledgment from Hal Elrod:

The author, Amanda Jensen, has been through one of life's greatest challenges: losing a spouse due to cancer. Her husband, Marshall, was diagnosed with the same cancer that I was, and was treated at the same hospital. Sadly, he didn't survive. Thanks to AJ and this book, his legacy will.

SOME OF AMANDA'S
COACHING REVIEWS:

"Amanda is literally the best. I just finished her program. I lost my misconceptions about health and wellness. I gained new habits and actually reached my goals. Amanda taught me to make lasting shifts in my lifestyle and she taught me how to be more mindful of my choices. Most of all, I learned that health is a life-long process, and it helps to celebrate the wins along the way. Every time I meet with Amanda, I come away a better person. She truly encourages people to be their best and to become better through mindful daily, healthy choices" -Erik

"Amanda is wonderful to work with. Very good with encouragement and scheduling. Love working with her. This program has been pretty easy and I'm learning better habits." -Margaret

"I love working with Amanda, she is so friendly and helps me stick to my plan." -Betsy

"Amanda is a personable, attentive coach. Nearly halfway to my goal and confident to succeed. Feel better than I have for years."-Dave

"Amanda is a super awesome coach and I love speaking with her, she really encourages me to keep going."-Ashley

Amanda Joyce is a contributing author to Encouraging Widows, a compilation of widow stories and encouragement.

Author Bio

Amanda Joyce

AJ is a teacher, and a health and life coach who was raised on a ranch instilling in her the importance of nature and the outdoors.

A Light the Night award recipient, she raises funds for cancer research and patients. She was interviewed around the globe about revolutionary immunotherapy.

AJ is a certified ACE health and wellness educator at Profile where she helps transform lives through smart science. She also helps caregivers through her startup, Wildly Healthy, to find time for their well-being. She encourages resets for hearty and healthy wellness habits in her books.

Author's Note

Thank You for reading this book and allowing Marshall's legacy to have an impact on your heart. Many of the words here were written in Marshall's hand and I was his editor in life and in death. He asked me to compile his writings in a pamphlet before he died and I decided a pamphlet wouldn't suffice, so a book it is! Some quotes and sources have multiple origins and I have done my best to find where they came from.

Love this book? Don't forget to leave a review!

Every review matters, and it matters a *lot!*

Head over to Amazon or wherever you purchased this book to leave an honest review for me.

I thank you endlessly.

-Amanda Joyce

NOTES

ONE: Beats of Attitude

1 Einstein, Albert. *The World As I See It*. Translated from German by A. Harris. London. Published by the Bodley Head, 1935. Print.

2 Brault, Robert. *Big Goals vs. Lesser Goals*. January 1, 2021 by A Genius Paradigm. Retrieved at <geniusparadigm.com>.

3 Elrod, Hal. *Miracle Morning: The Not So Obvious Secret Guaranteed to Transform Your Life before 8 am*, 2012. Retrieved on Audible.

4 Chamine, Shirzaid. *Positive Intelligence: Why Only 20% of Teams and Individuals Achieve their True Potential and How You Can Achieve Yours*. GreenLeaf Book Press. 2012. Retrieved on PQ Application.

5 Santos, Dr. Laurie. Science of Well-Being course. Yale University. 2018. Retrieved at coursera.org.

6 Al Qu'ran 3:[159]. Translated by Muhammad Farooq-i-Azam Malik.

7 Clear, James. *Atomic Habits*. Page 26. New York: Avery, 2018. Print.

8 Frankl, Victor. *Man's Search for Meaning*. Page 66. Boston: Beacon Press, 1959. Print.

9 Cocca-Leffler, Maryann. *Rain Brings Frogs: A Little Book of Hope*. Harper Collins, 2011. Print.

TWO: Beats of Gratitude

10 Bhagavad Gita: As It Is. 4:22.Translated by A.C. Bhaktivedanta Swami Prabhupā-da. The Bhaktivedanta Book Trust International. Los Angeles, 1972. Print.

11 Al Qu'ran 31:[12]. Translated by Muhammad Farooq-i-Azam Malik.

12 Al Qu'ran 3:[145]. Translated by Muhammad Farooq-i-Azam Malik.

13 Tefzger, Karen. *Minimalism A to Z: Finding Joy, Contentment, and Purpose in Life with Mimimalism.* Self-published, Amazon Digital Services, 2019. Kindle

14 Chamine, Shirzaid. *Positive Intelligence: Why Only 20% of Teams and Individuals Achieve Their True Potential and How You Can Achieve Yours.* Green Leaf Book Press. 2012. Retrieved 11 Nov 2022 on PQ Application.

15 Green, John. *Looking for Alaska.* New York: Speak, Penquin Group, 2005.

16 Shetty, Jay. 2022, *Inner Power: Power Through Purification,* session 128. Workshop. Retrieved at <jayshettygenius.com>.

17 Holland, Jeffrey. "Lessons from Liberty Jail," BYU Devotional. September 7, 2008.

18 Clear, James. 3-2-1: "The value of a schedule, intellectual humility, and the benefits of a good relationship". Retrieved 29 Sep 2022 at jamesclear.com.

19 Panchamuka Exports. 2022. *Positive thinking in Bhagavad Gita.* Articles on Hinduism. Accessed 11 July 2022. <https://www.indiadivine.org/positive-thinking-in-bhagavad-gita/>.

THREE: Beats of Song

20 Fetell Lee, Ingrid. Joyful: The Surprising Power of Ordinary Things to Create Extraordinary Happiness. New York: Little, Brown Spark, 2018. Retrieved on Audible.

21 Palmer, Luke. Ideas of time. Accessed 30 Aug 2022 with permission of the author on Facebook.

22 Al Qu'ran 31:[6]. Translated by Muhammad Farooq-i-Azam Malik.

23 Zachariah, Preeti. "Music is My Window to Life: T.M. Krishna", Mint, HT Digital Streams. Accessed 31 Oct 2015 at <https://www.livemint.com/Leisure/RTyU-wSSKjY1Xjtv692ElJP/Music-is-my-window-to-life-TM-Krishna.html>.

24 Lorde, Audre. *Uses of the Erotic: The Erotic As Power.* New York: Out & Out Books, 1978. Print.

25 Fetell Lee, Ingrid. "The Aesthetics of Joy," Designed by Gander and Development by Hyphen. Peachy. Accessed 13 Nov 2022 at <https://aestheticsofjoy.com>.

26 Uchtdorf, Dieter. "You Can Do It Now!", *Ensign.* November 2013.

27 Ahmed, Ismael. "Smile it's Sunnah," Siasat Daily. Accessed 31 March 2022 at <https://www.siasat.com/smile-its-sunnah-2118174>.

FOUR: Beats of Laughter

28 Clear, James. *Atomic Habits.* Page 245-46. New York: Avery, 2018. Print.

29 For some of the original copies of Marshall's letters, see amandajoyce.com.

FIVE: Beats of Gold

30 Al Qu'ran 9:[34]. Translated by Muhammad Farooq-i-Azam Malik

31 Carnegie, Dale. *How to Win Friends and Influence People.* New York: Holiday House, 1964.

32 Allport, Gordon. *Man's Search for Meaning* by Victor Frankl. Preface. Boston: Beacon Press, 1959.

33 Coelho, Paulo. *The Alchemist.* New York: HarperCollins, 1993. Print

34 Palmer, Luke. Ideas of treasure. Accessed 30 Aug 2022 with permission of the author on Facebook.

35 Kiyosaki, Robert. BrainyQuote. Retrieved 7 Nov 2022, from <https://www.brainyquote.com/quotes/robert_kiyosaki_627063>.

36 Bhagavad Gita: As It Is. 6:8.Translated by A.C. Bhaktivedanta Swami Prabhupāda. The Bhaktivedanta Book Trust International. Los Angeles, 1972. Print.

37 Bhagavad Gita: As It Is. 14:24-25.Translated by A.C. Bhaktivedanta Swami Prabhupāda. The Bhaktivedanta Book Trust International. Los Angeles, 1972. Print.

SIX: Beats of Numbers

38 Al Qu'ran 11:[1]. Translated by Muhammad Farooq-i-Azam Malik.

39 Islamyciencia, "The Miracle of Numbers in the Qu'ran". Funci 2018 Retrieved 31 March 2021at <https://funci.org/the-miracle-of-numbers-in-the-quran/?lang=en>

40 Islamyciencia, "The Miracle of Numbers in the Qu'ran". Funci 2018 Retrieved 31 March 2021at <https://funci.org/the-miracle-of-numbers-in-the-quran/?lang=en>

41 Paturel, Amy. "The Science Behind Coincidence: what's really going on when we encounter uncanny connections?", 2019. Discover. Retrieved 2 Feb 2022 at <https://www.discovermagazine.com/mind/the-science-behind-coincidence>.

42 Paturel, Amy. "The Science Behind Coincidence: what's really going on when we encounter uncanny connections?", 2019. Discover. Retrieved 2 Feb 2022 at https://www.discovermagazine.com/mind/the-science-behind-coincidence.

43 Taylor M., Daily Om Numerology (2021) E-mail to Amanda Joyce, 30 June 2021.

SEVEN: Beats of Soul

44 Living Now: Special Issue for Caregivers: 2017 National Marrow Donor Program Issued: 11668; Retrieved June 2017 at <bethematch.org>.

45 Bhagavad Gita: As It Is. 2:24.Translated by A.C. Bhaktivedanta Swami Prabhupāda. The Bhaktivedanta Book Trust International. Los Angeles, 1972. Print.

46 Panchamuka Exports. 2022. *Positive thinking in Bhagavad Gita.* Articles on Hinduism. Accessed 3 March 2022. <https://www.indiadivine.org/positive-thinking-in-bhagavad-gita/>.

47 Taylor, M. (2022) E-mail to Amanda Joyce, 4 August.

48 Mason, John. *Never Give Up: You're Stronger Than You Think*. Grand Rapids, Michigan: Revell, 2017, Page 46.

49 Taylor, M. (2021) E-mail to Amanda Joyce, 30 June.

50 Peter L. Burger and Thomas Luckmann. *The Social Construction of Reality: A Treatise in the Sociology of Knowledge*. New York: Random House, Inc, 1966, Page 22.

51 Taylor, M. (2022) E-mail to Amanda Joyce, 30 June.

52 Direct quote from Edwards, John and Sherilyn.

53 Corbridge, Lawrence "The Way," *Ensign*, December 2014.

CODA:

54 Bhagavad Gita: As It Is. 2:1.Translated by A.C. Bhaktivedanta Swami Prabhupā-da. The Bhaktivedanta Book Trust International. Los Angeles, 1972. Print.

55 Al Qu'ran 3:[185]. Translated by Muhammad Farooq-i-Azam Malik.

56 Jensen, Marshall personal journal entry, 16 Nov 2014.

57 Al Qu'ran 89:[27-30]. Translated by Muhammad Farooq-i-Azam Malik.

58 Al Qu'ran 16:[61]. Translated by Muhammad Farooq-i-Azam Malik.

59 Al Qu'ran 63:[10-11]. Translated by Muhammad Farooq-i-Azam Malik.

60 Bhagavad Gita: As It Is. 2:13.Translated by A.C. Bhaktivedanta Swami Prabhupā-da. The Bhaktivedanta Book Trust International. Los Angeles, 1972. Print.

61 Bhagavad Gita: As It Is. 2:17.Translated by A.C. Bhaktivedanta Swami Prabhupā-da. The Bhaktivedanta Book Trust International. Los Angeles, 1972. Print.

62 Al Qu'ran 51:[25]. Verse 5. Translated by Muhammad Farooq-i-Azam Malik.

Next Steps

Discover more of what strengthens your heart muscle by checking out **amandajoyce.com** for further heart-centered learning. Fill out the joy journal and strengthen the way we are all leading our world. Let's lead more with our hearts, with kindness over the need to be right and powerful.